The World of

W. Edwards

DEMING

The World of

W. Edwards
DEMING

Second Edition

Cecelia S. Kilian

SPC Press, Inc.
Knoxville, Tennessee

To order more copies of this book,
or for a complete listing of SPC Press publications,
write to
SPC Press, Inc.
5908 Toole Drive, Suite C • Knoxville, TN 37919
1 (800) 545-8602

ISBN 0–945320–29–9

2 3 4 5 6 7 8 9

To Jack, John, and David

Table of Contents

W. Edwards Deming

(Photo by Helaine Messer)

W. Edwards Deming

W. Edwards Deming has been for over 46 years a consultant, with practice worldwide. His clients include railways, telephone companies, carriers of motor freight, manufacturing companies, consumer research, census methods, hospitals, legal firms, government agencies, and research organizations in universities and in industry. All the inter-city motor freight in the United States and Canada, for example, is studied by statistical procedures prescribed and monitored by him. He is best known for his work in Japan, which commenced in 1950 and created a revolution in quality and economic production.

He was invited in 1946 to India to assist in design of samples for the Census there, and then to Japan. He was invited in 1950 by the Japanese to return to Japan to teach methods for achievement of quality. He taught there the theory of a system, cooperation between components, and the destructive force of competition. The whole world knows the results of his teaching. Japan soon became an economic power.

The Deming Prize was instituted in Japan in 1951 in honour of Dr. Deming's teaching. The Emperor of Japan awarded to Dr. Deming in 1960 the Second Order Medal of the Sacred Treasure. The President of the U.S., 28 years later, awarded to Dr. Deming the National Medal of Technology.

He was elected Honourary President of the British Deming Association. Many other independent study groups have been organized to study his teaching both in the U.S. and other nations.

He is a member of the International Statistical Institute, an academy, and of other professional and scientific societies.

He was elected in 1986 into the National Academy of Engineering, and into the Science and Technology Hall of Fame in Dayton. In 1988, he received the award Distinguished Career in Science from the National Academy of Sciences.

He received his doctorate in mathematical physics from Yale University in 1928. A number of universities have awarded to him the degrees

LL.D. and Sc.D., *honoris causa*: the University of Wyoming, Rivier College, the University of Maryland, Ohio State University, Clarkson College of Technology, Miami University, George Washington University, the University of Colorado, Fordham University, the University of Alabama, Oregon State University, the American University, the University of South Carolina, Yale University, and Muhlenberg College. Yale also awarded to him the Wilbur Lucius Cross Medal and the Doctor of Laws, *honoris causa*. Rivier College awarded to him the Madeleine of Jesus Award.

He is the author of several books and 170 papers. His most recent books include OUT OF THE CRISIS (Center for Advanced Engineering Study, Massachusetts Institute of Technology, 1986) and THE NEW ECONOMICS FOR INDUSTRY, EDUCATION, GOVERNMENT (same publisher, 1993). Since 1946 he has been Professor of Statistics at the Graduate School of Business Administration of New York University. He has also been, from 1985, Distinguished Lecturer in Management at Columbia University. He has lectured in many universities in this country and abroad. His 4-day seminars have reached 20,000 people per year for over ten years.

Dr. Deming is a perennial student of the theory of music and has written two Masses and several canticles and anthems.

About the Author

No person has been privileged to have as close and as long lasting a professional association with Dr. Deming as Cecelia S. Kilian. For the past 38 years, she has acted as his consultant, secretary, confidant, and his girl Friday, both in Washington, and on many of his important professional trips within the United States and abroad. She is eminently qualified to write about the world of this legend of our time, in regard to the man, and his contribution to our world.

Ceil graduated from Scranton (Pa.) College and has attended The George Washington University. She enjoyed a secretarial career on Capitol Hill, where she was on the staff of the late Senator Styles Bridges (R-N.H.), when he was President pro tem of the United States Senate. She is past President of the former Executive chapter of the Professional Secretaries International, and has taught shorthand and typing at Holy Trinity High School in Georgetown. Her husband Jack is a retired administrator with Headquarters Marine Corps. Two sons, John and David, reside in the Washington area.

Foreword

It gives me great satisfaction to learn from my secretary, Cecelia S. Kilian, known to me and to the hundreds of people throughout the world as Ceil, that she wished to write about the thirty-eight years that have elapsed since she first started to work for me in 1954. She worked Saturdays, sometimes Sundays, and several evenings during the week. We often laugh about her so-called part-time status at the start. She was soon busy all day every day. She does the work of three people. She takes pride and joy in her work. She takes care of the office while I am away, which is most of the time. Calls on my telephone are transferred to her home when she is not in my office, to make sure that she works night and day. I am aware every hour how fortunate I am. I have not guided her in any way on this book, but I am delighted that she saw fit to write it.

W. Edwards Deming

Washington
1 June 1992

Chapter One
My Teaching in Japan 1950

Written by Dr. Deming, aided by his Diary

<u>Wednesday 14 June 1950</u>. On board at 12:28. It is a C-54, No. 554g. A bucket-seat job, very uncomfortable, as the space is mostly filled with cargo, just like the aeroplane that carried me from Tokyo to Honolulu 3 years ago. Well, anyway, there is a seat for everyone. The flight clerk announced his name, Corporal Jakus, and the flight to Johnston Island will take 4 hours and 4 minutes. He was a jolly fat Irishman. Keep your seat belts fastened and don't smoke until we have gained cruising altitude. It was hot and sticky. After 25 minutes we took off at 1:08.

I wondered why the navigator came back to peek out of the port-holes. Had we lost a wing or a fin? After a while came the announcement—we are going back to Hickam Field. We'd lost something. Down at 1:30. The pilot said he was sorry: didn't know what was the trouble,

1

but the thing just didn't have any power, and there was a terrific wind up front, and they all thought something had dropped off during take-off. He didn't know how long we'd be delayed.

At 3 o'clock I decided it was time for another lunch. Custard pie, milk, more Japanese soup and crackers, a beautiful salad of pineapple and other fruit. As I feared, I was about two-thirds finished when the call came for all passengers on Flight 241-14, Plane 554g, assemble at Gate 1. I hastily finished eating. Off at 3:30.

It is a jolly crowd on board—about 23 men and 1 girl. The men are nearly all officers and all must have high priorities to be on board at all. On the way down one of them suggested that the reason for return was that flight clerk had forgotten to kiss his girl.

Arrived Tokyo Friday 16 June 1950 at 2027 h Tokyo time. The aeroplane was a C54, bucket-seat job, operated by the U.S. Air Force.

Distances in English Miles

I had been in Japan January, February, and March of 1947 to work with Dr. K. Saito in preparation for the Census of Japan 1951; also with Japanese statisticians and American authorities on agriculture, housing, and fisheries. My wish was to learn about the Japanese. I spent my time with people that were studying Japanese culture, some even studying the language. I went to Kabuki plays and to at least one Noh play. I remember that Virginia and I sat on the floor in a box for the Noh play, there being at that time no Noh theater left standing. I worked with Japanese statisticians whenever possible.

The trip to Japan was one leg in a trip around the world. I had been invited by the great Professor P.C. Mahalanobis, who established the Indian Statistical Institute in Calcutta, to spend November and December 1946 in India. Thence I moved onward on 1 January 1947 toward Japan. The trip from Calcutta to Iwakuni is a storybook in itself, but not for now. One must remember that in those days there were no commercial flights. I had a packet of travel orders signed by the General of the Armies, including General Montgomery, valid on aeroplanes of the U.S. Air Force and the Royal Air Force.

There were canvas seats, blankets, sleep on the floor any time, plenty of room, or ride up front with the crew, earphones attached.

Saturday 17 June 1950. Matt Rose and Virginia came for me at my hotel (The Dai Iti, No. 1) in a jeep and took me to my office. I borrowed 2000 yen from Matt, and he sent a boy to the main telegraph office with my one-word message to Lola, "Arrived," and his 2000 yen to pay for the telegram. The boy came back with 980 yen change.

Much business has been saved for me. Talked with many people. I am to lecture next week at Tokyo University every afternoon at 2:30. A dozen other sets of lectures have been arranged, all the way down to the Island Kyushu. Some are only single lectures.

My office is a corner room on the first floor, easy to reach by the stair or lift. It overlooks the moat and wall around the Imperial grounds. This building is the Empire House, and is occupied mostly by the British, and it flies the British flag. Matt warned me against the restaurant on the ground floor—the cooking, he said, is English and is pretty bad. But he said I should not fail to visit the Australian PX on the fourth floor. Yes, they would be glad to take occupation dollars.

A Japanese woman serves coffee almost continuously, forenoon and afternoon. The cost will be trifling. Also, Matt says, we have a coffee room downstairs, supported by small contributions: go in any time.

To the Union Club for dinner with Virginia and Bill. We all had New York cuts. I had garlic toast with it, French fries, and fried sweet potatoes, and a marshmallow sundae. Bill paid, above my protests. I've done pretty well today. Then we went for a long ride in Virginia's car. Arrived at the hotel at 11:45. A dance was being held on the roof, but I didn't see anyone whom I knew, so I went to bed.

There is good bus service to my office, but the simplest way, especially at off hours, will be to take the train, as I did when I left my office last evening. The Shimbashi Station is near my hotel, and the Tokyo Station is near my office; one station (Yurakucho) between. The ride requires but 4 minutes, including the stop, and is free to Allied people. Trains are frequent, one every minute on the local line and about every 3 minutes on the Tokaido (express) line. There are trains on 18 tracks, platforms between tracks.

Sunday 18 June 1950. Now I found that I was wrong about the train being free. It was brought to my notice by the conductor in the Allied Section who came up to me, said something, and smiled; and I did the same. Enquiry revealed that we are now supposed to pay. I had certainly been riding free yesterday and today, but when I discovered that we are supposed to pay, I purchased a ticket good for 30 days, unlimited number of rides, 200 yen or only about 55 cents. I was amused to observe that the ticket is subject to confiscation if used beyond the date of expiration. In return for paying, we now have plush seats in the Allied Section.

Lying in bed this morning I wondered how long it would be before an earthquake would come. Then the bed began to rock, and it lasted a full minute. It was just about right—enough, but not too much.

To my office after lunch. To the PX at 4 where I purchased my allowance of rationed articles: 2 cartons cigarettes (special this week; usually only 1 is permitted), 3 bars Cashmere Bouquet, 4 bars Hershey almond. Unrationed: Ivory soap flakes, 3 cans toddy, 2 one-pound boxes candy, can tomato juice, jar cheese, box of Ritz, bottle of ink, 4 coat hangers, 2 small cans milk. I brought Nescafe from home. Foolish; there was plenty in the PX. Cigarettes were only 80 cents per carton. I had purchased two cartons (the limit) at Guam Friday. With the 3 cartons that I brought from home I now have 7 cartons. Not bad for a nonsmoker. The cigarettes and candy and excess soap are for tips. I can really treat the Japanese liberally.

Thursday 22 June 1950. Over 600 attended my lecture today. Dr. Saito translated. We arrived 12:55. Today's lecture was to begin at 1 o'clock. Late or not, they insisted that I go in for tea in Dean Arisawa's office. Then tea again, after the lecture, with fruit, beewa and cherries; also, sweet bean cakes today. The president and editor of the publishing company that is printing the Japanese edition of my 1943 *Statistical Adjustment of Data* came to tea before the lecture, and they had with them a page proof of the book. Many men came to meet me at the tea after the lecture, and to invite me to meet with various groups. I have agreed to meet with the Japanese Standards Association Tuesday evening, and the Japanese Statistical Association on 6 and 7 July. Professor Yamashita is going to show me his new tabulating machine next Thursday. We are to meet at my hotel at 2 o'clock. His machinery is near my hotel.

Dinner alone in the Club restaurant in the basement—a New York cut, with French fried potatoes, 65 cents; strawberry parfait, 25 cents.

The weather is hot and wringing wet. I really get steamed up giving my lectures, 2 hours. The hot tea before and after helps to bring on a temperature.

Tokyo is very noisy. Everywhere there are loudspeakers, screeching scratching music, with an occasional advertisement.

Saturday 24 June 1950. The people look better than they did three years ago. They looked hopeful then, and happy; but now they look really happy and their clothes are better, and they are eating much better.

The shops are now bursting with food, textiles, house furnishings, fountain pens, different from 1947. But prices are high. The average Japanese family must spend half its income for food.

Monday 10 July 1950. My lectures commenced today at 8 o'clock. Mr. Koyanagi and Mr. Kano were here at 7:40, as they had told me they would be. I was in the dining room of my hotel trying to get some service, and I paid no attention to the loud speaker calling my name. When I finished, I came to my room and collected the books and papers that I should need for my teaching. I don't like the idea of beginning at 8 o'clock. Too much of a crush in the dining room, and everywhere too much traffic.

The lectures are being held at the Japan Medical Association in Ochanomizu. We arrived a little late. The auditorium was full—230. Over 600 men had applied, and the limit was finally over-strained to 230. Professor Masuyama and assistants will teach the statistical control of quality in the afternoon. I shall teach during the forenoons the theory of a system, and cooperation. Mr. Kano is a wonderful interpreter.

Art Sharron and several Japanese picked me up at 11:50 at my lecture. We had told officials in the Ministry of Agriculture and Forestry that we wished to observe some field work on the monthly Farm Economic Survey. There were two cars, Art's and a Buick from the Ministry, which Art said they take out only for a VIP. Art had brought sandwiches and coffee for him and me: the Japanese had their rice. We visited three farmers; talked to them about the survey and many other things. The interviewer who does the work was with us. Their farms were very interesting. The farmers all served tea to us on the porch (I don't know the Japanese name for the standard porch on a farm). The second farmer ran a little store: served us pop and tea both in his store.

Then to a branch office of the cho. Tea there, with American wafers, sweet soda water, bananas.

Then to a Japanese restaurant, as a guest of the Ministry of Agriculture and Forestry. Beautiful waitresses. Ono poured sake for me and we had lots of fun. Art was afraid I'd be sick, drinking beer and sake at one time, and eating raw Japanese vegetables besides. It was American cooking: beef, potatoes, bread and butter, with knives and forks.

Arrived at the hotel at 9 o'clock. Art and I decided to look in at one of the numerous night clubs near by. Very interesting. We were shown to a table. Mariko and Hideko soon sat down by us, to entertain us. We danced with them, drank beer; cost 1100 yen or $3. Pretty expensive but worth it—once. Japanese night life has no counterpart.

<u>Tuesday 11 July 1950</u>. Same thing till noon. My lectures are going well, and the students are excellent. Then Mr. Koyanagi took Mr. Kano and me to the Bamboo Leaf, upstairs, not far from the Dai Iti Hotel. I think I could find it.

1. Wonderful bean curd soup.
2. Bean curd and shoyu.
3. An egg custard.
4. Tempura and fish fried in butter.
5. Rice, of course. Sake and a sake girl. Much fun.

Drs. Saito and Midzuno were waiting in my office at 2:30 to take me to the Institute of Statistical Mathematics. I had ordered an Army sedan, and they directed the driver. A long ride. I met the workers at the Institute. It was in two buildings, perhaps a mile apart. The girls use the abacus for adding and subtracting, a computing machine for multiplying. I saw no modern machines. Then we had a long conference, about 30 people present. Dinner was served to us in the big building. Wonderful food—soup, shrimp, roast beef, tsukiyaki (chicken cooked in a certain way), fruit (biwa and peaches). It was pretty hot and I was grateful for the fan that Dr. Saito loaned to me.

After dinner we talked for a while longer in the conference room, then walked to the railway station. Drs. Midzuno and Saito wanted to take me to Asakusa. They don't know that I've been there (7 July). We boarded a train, then changed to another, and at Shibuya we changed to the subway—my first ride on the subway here. It is very clean and orderly; otherwise like New York. Through Shimbashi and on to Asakusa, where we arrived about 9:20. We walked around a while, looking at the myriads of shops and nightclubs, then took a taxi to my hotel. The men took trains or the subway from Shimbashi to their homes. They did not know that I had already been to Asakusa. I was very tired, with another heavy day tomorrow, and I was glad to be left alone, finally.

Wednesday 12 July 1950. Up at 7 o'clock. I've given up trying to get breakfast in the dining room at 7:30. Mr. Koyanagi and Dr. Nishibori were here at 7:40. Mr. Koyanagi is a lovable character: I haven't a thing against him except for starting my lectures at 8 o'clock. The lectures are going well. The taxi that he ordered to come to the Japanese Medical Association at 11:45 to take us to lunch did not show up, and at my insistence he finally went along with the idea of taking the train from Ochanomizu, only a short distance away. Off at Tokyo Central Station and we walked to the Hamagaha Restaurant.

1. Bean curd and egg in fish soup (camagotofu).
2. Raw fish and shoyu. The bowl with the fish had in it herbs for flavor—wasade (horse radish), chiso, myoga.
3. Tsukiyaki, cooked on the table—meat, onions, konnyaku, and midsuba. The waitress in silk and obie cooked it.

Each of us was given a lacquered bowl with an egg in it. Beat up the egg with chopsticks, dip the Tsukiyaki in it as you eat it. I could do well without the egg.

Always at a Japanese restaurant the waitress brings a wet towel for your face and hands before and after lunch, and in between if needed. A wonderful idea.

Thursday 13 July 1950. Same start. I must admit that the 4 hour lecture 8 to 12 is tough, but probably harder on the students, all 230 of them. I give them an intermission of about 20 minutes at about 9:30. I've never had better students. I'd describe them as the top 5% of all the classes that I ever taught. The lecture room is terribly hot; just like a laundry. I am grateful for the electric fan that Mr. Koyanagi placed there to blow on me.

Mr. Koyanagi took me again to lunch at a Japanese restaurant. The main course was fresh eel, a specialty of this restaurant, and it was certainly good, but there were four courses preceding it and I had not saved much space. Sake and sake girls. I have been taking pictures of the waitresses and Mr. Koyanagi in these Japanese restaurants, and I hope that they turn out well. I am always seated nearest to the takanoma or shrine, as the guest of honor. Also, I am expected to lead off in the eating.

I now have calling cards, English on one side, and Japanese on the other. They were furnished by the Japanese government, through Bill MacPhee.

In the afternoon—about 2 o'clock—I made a hasty trip to the main PX, took a Japanese taxi, 100 yen or about 28 cents. I marvel at the ability of the Japanese to run these taxis on solid fuel, anything combustible. A common sight is to see one stalled and the driver working on the rear end of it, where the furnace is.

When I was here in 1947, American MPs were training Japanese policemen how to direct traffic at intersections. They would blow their whistles together, and go through the same motions. Now one sees only the Japanese policemen, and they do an excellent job.

Talk with Top Management

At 5 o'clock came Mr. Ichiro Ishikawa's dinner for the 21 presidents of Japan's leading industries. I talked to them an hour. There was a lot of wealth represented in that room, and a lot of power. I think they were impressed, because before the evening was over they asked me to meet with them again, and they talked about having a conference in the mountains around Hakone. The dinner was superb, American style, with knives and forks. I thought the food would never stop coming. Fortunately, the Japanese do not bring on heavy desserts. We had lobster, fish, chicken, and steak, besides all the other things that go with a dinner. The meeting and dinner were held at the Industry Club, not far from my office in the Empire House.

It was on Mt. Hakone, I may add, that I taught them the theory of a system, cooperation, move toward a single supplier for any one item, with an enduring fruitful relationship.

(Dr. S. Moriguti told me in November 1991 that when I talked to this group I was talking with 80% of the capital of Japan. Top management listened and learned.)

I told them that Japanese industry could produce the best quality in the world. If they would follow my teachings, manufacturers the world over in five years will be screaming for protection. (Actually, the Japanese beat my prediction: it took only four years.) The men there were afraid that they had blasted themselves forever by making shoddy goods, cheap but worth the price. I insisted that they could dispel this reputation in a hurry with goods of quality.

Years afterward some of the men told me that I was the only man in Japan in 1950 that believed that Japan could become known for top quality and be doing well in five years. They wished to believe me, but they dared not.

The system, I explained, would cover all Japan, not just one group of companies. This movement must be a prairie fire; all Japanese on fire. Everybody will win.

Work with your vendor to improve his incoming quality. Establish a long-term relationship with him for continual improvement, ever better and better quality, with lower and lower costs. Both you and he will win.

I invited Dr. Osawa and Mr. Suematsu to dinner next Monday night. Art Sharron says why not take them to a Chinese restaurant that he knows of. The Japanese would like it very much for a change. He (Art) will come too, with his wife, and will invite Mr. and Mrs. Hayami, and Shuko, a friend of theirs, and he will call and engage the private room upstairs. He is sure that Dr. Ozawa's and Mr. Suematsu's wives would be delighted to come, but that women do not come unless invited. So I asked Miss Toyoko Tomioka who works for Dr. Saito to call them and invite the wives. This was 2 days ago. Yesterday this note was on my desk:

> Dr. Suematsu called that his wife would not come to your hotel because his child is illness and child will not get rid over that illness by the 17th, and Dr. Ozawa has no wife, then, they shall go to your hotel without wives.
>
> T. Tomioka

<u>Friday 14 July 1950</u>. Morning as usual. I'll be glad when these lectures are finished. I hope the students don't get as tired as I do, and I hope that they have better luck getting something to eat so early in the morning. In the evening I can eat at the Club, the Marunouchi Hotel, and any number of Army snack bars, which are not bad. But in the morning ...

Mr. Koyanagi took Dr. Saito, Mr. Kano, and me to lunch at the Yoshino-sushi, a sushiya. Sushi = sour rice; ya = shop. Three little rooms upstairs, not really rooms but partitioned with movable lacquered screens. This is where the men of lower incomes who can afford a restaurant lunch might eat.

1. Beer and peanuts.
2. Sembei (shembay), small crisp rice biscuits, baked, flavored with shoyu.
3. Sushi—rice in pressed cakes, 13 pieces in a round lacquered flat bowl, each piece wrapped in a fish of some kind, or in seaweed. Stalks of young pickled ginger.
4. Tea. All very delightful and interesting.

That poor Chinese tailor with my pants which I gave him to mend last Friday! He has been here innumerable times, the boys at the desk say. He was here at 6:30 this morning. I could have crowned him, and yet I don't blame him: he had tried every other hour. 200 yen, but it was a beautiful job. I gave him a bar of soap and a Hershey bar for his extra trouble. This day Hershey bars went back on ration, I discovered later.

This night I gave a dinner party here at the Dai Iti Hotel for 11 Japanese statisticians. I nearly went nuts. After going to the PX Thursday and having everything in order, the waiters served my tomato juice and olives and hors d'oeuvres of sardines and cheese on Ritz to another party in the other private dining room. The mess sergeant sure bawled them out (the waiters) but it wasn't their fault entirely.

Some Additions

These lectures, I might add, put JUSE on its feet. Though I did not know it at the time, the people in attendance at this course paid 15,000 yen each. JUSE now had money in the bank. It had been merely a group of men devoted to the reconstruction of Japan, with no funds and with no idea about what to do.

How did JUSE start? As I understand it, Mr. Koyanagi had formed a group during the War to help Japan in its war effort. After the War, Mr. Koyanagi held the group together, the aim being now the reconstruction of Japan. The men told me that when they met they merely talked, ate, and drank sake, with no substance to their aim.

> I asked Dr. Nishiboro one time how could it be that they sat around and ate and drank sake when food was so scarce in Japan?
>
> His answer was simple. He worked in the Lamp Department of the Toshiba Company. Electric lights were scarce. He would fill his pockets with lamps, ride his bicycle out in the country, come back minus the light bulbs but with rice and sake, and they ate and drank.
>
> I must not forget to mention that Dr. Nishibori, listening to some American explain how the statistical control of quality had helped to produce top quality of American weapons, remarked, "Yes, I know about that. Six fire bombs fell on my house during the War and they were all duds."

Chapter Two
If Japan Can ... Why Can't We?

W. Edwards Deming is a man with a purpose. "So much to do, and so little time," he once commented to a colleague. Several people have asked him why he continues to follow a schedule that would intimidate most people half his age. Only a week prior to his 91st birthday, he traveled to Toronto, San Francisco, Detroit, Rochester, and ended the week working all day Saturday in his office in Washington. In Dr. Deming we find a man who is professionally acclaimed, financially secure, who loves to spend time with his family, and yet, who spends five to seven days per week traveling, teaching, consulting, and giving 4-day seminars to hundreds of enthusiastic students! Why does he spend his time and energy this way? His answers are characteristic of the man: "I love my work. It's fun for me. I wish American management to keep learning and growing and I wish to keep learning and sharing with them."

Prior to 1980, Dr. Deming lived a paradox. In Japan he was revered as the man who brought Japanese industry back to life. He not only helped their industrial leaders revive the burned remains of their industry, but he taught them the theory which they have used to become an economic power. The result has been an unparalleled story of economic growth and prosperity. In the U.S. however, he remained largely unknown.

During the post World War II period, U.S. industry enjoyed great success. As one of the only nations that survived the war with its industrial capacity still intact, anything produced could be sold and sold quick. While the rest of the world had to rebuild their factories, U.S. industry had an easy life. While Japan was learning new theory and incorporating it into new industrial practices, U.S. manufacturers were riding high on a wave of success, secure in the false assumption that they were doing everything right. But their success was brought forth, not by excellence of product and service, but by their temporarily exclusive ability to produce anything at all and sell it.

By 1980, economic indicators confirmed the perception that U.S. industries were stagnating. The United States per capita GNP had fallen from first to seventh place in the world. American productivity also appeared to be on the decline. Clearly, the U.S. industrial giant was doing something wrong. A bewildered nation watched in dismay as its economic leadership was effectively challenged.

The NBC White Paper, *If Japan Can ... Why Can't We?* brought some clarity to the problems faced by U.S. industries. It also introduced Dr. Deming. The following is a summary of the program which brought him into national prominence.[1]

If Japan Can ... Why Can't We?

In June of 1980, an NBC News White Paper put this question to television viewers across the country. Americans were not unfamiliar with the question, for Japanese dominance of consumer goods markets in the

---

[1]Summary of the NBC White Paper, *If Japan Can ... Why Can't We?* written by Clare Crawford-Mason and adapted, with her permission, for this section of the book.

U.S. was already a well known phenomenon. From electronic products to automobiles to advanced robotics, Japan was erasing its old image as a maker of junk and earning a new reputation as the producer of many of the world's highest quality products. At the same time, an increasing number of U.S. manufacturers were losing the loyalty of customers who were fed up with faulty, defective products and shoddy workmanship. What was going on? New insight was given to those who tuned in to NBC's 90-minute documentary on the evening of June 24th.

Throughout history, one of man's quests has been for higher productivity; that is, producing more for less. In agriculture for example, the development of new tools and techniques for growing and harvesting food has resulted, over the centuries, in ever-increasing yields with less manpower. But the aim of the documentary was not simply to communicate the benefits of high productivity, which were fairly obvious. The challenge was to explain the factors that accounted for a nation's ability to continually increase its quality, productivity, and competitive position, and the consequences of the failure to do so.

In the 1970s, Americans had found two easy targets to blame for their economic woes: inflation and high energy costs. But these problems were shared by Japan, Germany, and other nations whose productivity levels continued to grow. Former U.S. Assistant Secretary of Commerce Jerry Jasinowski and Dean Herbert Striner of the Kogod Business School at American University offered some other reasons for the decline of U.S. competitiveness:

> "We continue to consume far beyond our means, both publicly and privately. ... The ratio of Research and Development (spending) ... to our gross national product has been dropping. ... We've lived on the short term ... rather than thinking about long term investment. ... We do very little in the way of retraining to upgrade (workers') skills."

Other people interviewed pointed to the adversarial relationship between government and industry that prohibited businesses from making the most efficient use of their resources. Bureaucratic regulations were cited as a major drain on companies' funds, wasting money that could have been spent on research and development, plant modernization, and acquisition of new technologies. Inversely, industry leaders were blamed for working counter-productively in their attempts to evade or stall new government regulations, rather than concentrating on ways to prepare their companies to meet the new specifications. Moreover, the combative nature of relations between management and labor unions made it difficult for companies to institute any of the changes necessary to respond to competitive challenges.

In contrast, the program illustrates how in Japan, government and industry have worked cooperatively to advance common national interests. For example, when the Japanese government decided, as a matter of national policy, to shift resources from ship-building to construction of oil rigs, Mitsubishi's Hiroshima shipyard cut its work force by 1700 and redistributed the labor to an oil drilling construction project and other Mitsubishi operations, without a single layoff. By this guarantee of job security, Japanese companies enjoy absolute loyalty from their workers.

In a country which is virtually without natural resources, Japanese leaders recognized early on that their most important resource was the people. In response to this awareness, shared decision-making has permitted Japanese workers a larger role in the management of the factories and production lines. QC Circles have allowed employees to study their work processes and suggest improvements to the system. The acquisition of advanced machinery and robotics at many Japanese manufacturing plants has taken place with the participation and support of line workers. Advanced equipment has allowed employees to be moved to more mentally stimulating jobs, while the machines were left with the more tedious jobs.

The story of Japan's success, the transformation of its economy from post-war shambles to one of the most productive in the world, had never been explained as completely as the NBC White Paper did in 1980. The program was watched by fourteen million American households when it was first aired (not a huge television audience, although good for a documentary on economics). It then went on to become NBC's most requested program of all time, with thousands of requests for videotapes and transcripts in the years since. One reason this program has generated so much continued interest is because of the powerful, relevant message of one man who was featured in the documentary: Dr. W. Edwards Deming.

Dr. Deming is the American to whom many Japanese give credit for their remarkable turnaround; the man for whom Japan's highest industrial award for quality productivity was named. Ironically, W. Edwards Deming was not well known in his own country before the NBC program. Indeed, many viewers were surprised to learn that the success of the Japanese had less to do with a cultural affinity for quality than with methods of quality production taught to them by an American statistician!

Dr. Deming's invitation to Japan in 1950 by the Union of Japanese Scientists and Engineers (JUSE) gave him the opportunity to teach leaders of Japanese industry about the use of statistical analysis to improve productivity. "What I saw was a magnificent work force, unsurpassed management and the best statistical ability in the world," Deming said of the Japanese, "and it seemed to me that those three forces could be put together; and I put them together, so that Japanese quality, instead of being shoddy, became known as the standard within a few years. In less than four years, manufacturers all over the world were screaming for protection."

Deming warned that it was not possible to simply copy Japanese successes. American management had to understand its own responsibility for systems that resulted in poor or high quality, and that personal involvement at the highest level of management was necessary to effect changes.

Having dispelled the myth that America's quality and productivity problems were somehow the fault of workers, the documentary offered a look at an American company that had already made the commitment to implement a quality program, with the help of Dr. Deming. The Nashua Corporation, manufacturer of coated paper products and computer memory disks, provided an illustrative example of how statistical tools are used to analyze processes and reveal whether they are under control. It was shown that once that determination is made, it is easier to predict future performance and costs and it is easier to identify waste and eliminate it. With constant monitoring of the system, management can implement changes in all phases of production, marketing, and distribution, under the goad of Continual Improvement.

"Dr. Deming is the father of the third wave of the industrial revolution," said William E. Conway, then Nashua's chief executive officer, "and anyone who doesn't join that revolution, I think, over time is going to be in serious trouble." Judging from the number of companies that have sought Dr. Deming's help since the broadcast of the documentary, the message was heard far and wide. From the university classroom to corporate board rooms, to manufacturing personnel, to seminars around the world, Dr. Deming continues to teach his methods of quality production to eager audiences. It has become a matter of survival.

The growing demand for material and information on Dr. Deming's teachings led Clare Crawford-Mason, producer of the NBC White Paper, to launch a series of management training videotapes called "The Deming Library.[2]" Narrated by Lloyd Dobyns, the tapes help communicate Dr. Deming's philosophy through conversations with him, excerpts from his seminars, and interviews with individuals trying to implement Deming's methods in their own companies. The team that produced "If Japan Can ... Why Can't We?" also completed, in 1991, a three-hour documentary series on quality as the basis of competitiveness in the global marketplace. The program funded by IBM, is called "Quality ... Or Else!" and was broadcast on PBS stations during October, 1991.

At least three major results came from this NBC White Paper. First, the audience realized that U.S. industry could do something to improve quality and productivity: the "easy excuses" of inflation and energy costs were, by themselves, no longer valid. Then, American industrialists who watched the program not only grasped more fully the enormity of the problems that they were facing, but they also realized that answers to their dilemma were available. Perhaps most importantly, W. Edwards Deming was introduced to the audience as the man with effective answers. It was an introduction that would change his life irrevocably.

---

[2]*The Deming Library*, Films Inc., Chicago.

Chapter Three
Recollections of Japan in 1950

Introduction

Dr. Deming has put together his early recollections in Japan with the history of The Union of Japanese Scientists and Engineers (JUSE). This record is a valuable piece of history, illustrating the economic situation of Japan after the war. It also answers the often asked questions of how and why Dr. Deming began his work with Japanese industrial leaders.

In this chapter also, he provides us with a summary of what he taught the Japanese during those early years. Students of Dr. Deming will recognize much of what was taught. For while he has certainly expanded and clarified his ideas, they are not essentially different today—only more all-encompassing.

At the end of the chapter, Kenichi Koyanagi eloquently describes how the Japanese came to admire and respect Dr. Deming.

Some Early History of JUSE

In March 1950 I was invited to come again to Japan, this time to teach methods for achievement of quality (see Mr. Koyanagi's letter). A windfall from that visit was to put JUSE on its feet.

JUSE, The Union of Japanese Scientists and Engineers, up to the time of my visit to Japan in 1950, had been a group of men, held together by Kenichi Koyanagi. The group had been formed, nameless, by Mr. Koyanagi during the War to help Japan in its War effort. The aim of the group, after the War, was the reconstruction of Japan. The aim was clear, but the men had no plan. Dr. Nishibori often remarked to me that the men only sat around, drank sake and ate rice, talked: an aim without a method.

The group received some precarious financial support from the government. They had office space in the Osaka Shosen Building, long ago demolished, not far from Tokyo Central Station. Mr. Koyanagi provided for me, out of his space, an adequate office with two helpers: Toyoko (a girl) and Seinoske, a young man just graduated from Tokyo University. He could calculate a standard deviation.

Mr. Koyanagi had written to me: "There is no good secretary in Japan. I have therefore engaged for you two. One is girl, the other is boy."

Toyoko could use a typewriter. Japanese paper, and carbon paper especially, were of very low grade. I had brought with me a few sheets of American carbon paper and a sheet or two of German carbon paper. Toyoko used them over and over. After 20 uses, they were still better than a new sheet of Japanese carbon paper.

Attendance at my 8-day course in June 1950 in the auditorium of the Medical Association brought in money. The cost was 15,000 yen per person; attendance was 235, mostly engineers. My services were free, paid for by the U.S. Occupation Forces. Attendance at Osaka a few weeks later was 150, at Nagoya 125, at Hakata 85. JUSE was on its feet financially; a going concern.

A return visit six months later, and another six months after, with further return visits, swelled the working capital of JUSE. It was now established. Mr. Koyanagi had assumed the title of Managing Director. He had also persuaded Mr. Ichiro Ishikawa to be President. Mr. Ishikawa was wealthy, or had been. He was highly respected, influential, and the President of the great Kaidanren, the Federated Economic Societies of Japan, actually the association of the top management of Japan. He was a highly respected citizen and a great worker for all of Japan.

Japan in 1947

I had been in Japan in January and February 1947, working with the Economic and Scientific Staff of General MacArthur's Headquarters. I made it an aim in 1947 to get acquainted with Japanese statisticians. I attended meetings and gave a number of talks. I met some statisticians privately. Dr. K. Saito (not yet Ph.D.) was in the Japanese Census, well versed in statistical theory. I spent much time with him. I visited the management of factories and shops and stores. I owe much to Margaret Stone of the Economic and Scientific Staff for making good arrangements for me, and for traveling with me. She knew her way around. Miss Virginia Eyre (later Mrs. Bill Krossner) took me to Noh drama and to Kabuki. She was studying Japanese flower arrangement, and tried to teach me about it.

The Japanese were well aware before 1950 that they must export manufactured goods to bring in food and equipment. Industry had been blasted to smithereens. Twisted steel and smokestacks were grim reminders of industry. Small and large pieces of land where there had been factories were now planted in vegetables and rice. Japanese manufacturers were nevertheless turning out product, most of it for the American Army fighting in the Korean War. I had seen much of Japanese industry in 1947.

I remember that Dr. Hiroshi Sugiyama came up to Tokyo in 1947 to talk to me, wondering what he could do for his country. He had received his doctorate in mathematics from the University of Kyoto under the great Professor Schimizu. "What could he do for Japan?" That was his question. No one had at that time any remote vision of what was in store for Japan in the future: that Japanese industry, demolished, would in time rise to super stature. I explained to him, as I did to other statisticians, what we were doing in Japan in surveys of housing, agriculture, fishing, industry, unemployment. (Yes, there was unemployment in Japan in 1947.) I told him about Dr. Shewhart, the Bell Laboratories, my work with Captain Leslie Simon at the Aberdeen Proving Ground, and about the Census, about Dr. Morris H. Hansen, and others.

Japanese statisticians were in low spirits, well educated, but not active in a productive way. I told them that they were one of Japan's most important assets. No one at that time had any vision of how important they would become.

I was made the first foreign Honorary Member of the Japanese Statistical Society at a meeting in the Village of Kunitaki, in Tokyo-to.

Invitation from JUSE

The invitation came from JUSE in March 1950 to come again to Japan, this time to teach methods for achievement of quality (see Mr. Koyanagi's letter further on). I arranged my work to go in June 1950. Mr. Iciro Ishikawa (deceased 1965) was by this time President of JUSE, and Mr. Kenichi Koyanagi was Managing Director.

June 1950 came. I was teaching 230 engineers in Ochanomizu, in the auditorium of the Japan Medical Society, an 8-day course, 8 to 5 and often later. The heat was intense: I was dripping wet by 0830 hours. I later taught 150 engineers in Osaka, 125 in Nagoya, 85 or so in Hakata.

My interpreter was Mr. H. Kano (Ikky): perfect. His father had been President of the Yokahama Species Bank, and Ikky had lived in New York, London, Paris. He learned English and French before he learned Japanese. He could not go to Hakata, so Dr. Saito translated for me there.

The Involvement of Top Management

My duty became clear. Top management, through Mr. Ishikawa, had invited me, and I must explain to them their obligations, responsibilities, and methods for improvement of quality. Quality begins at the top. It seemed to me that quality of product and of service can be no better than the intent of top management. The only way Japan could experience success would be for the top management to be committed to the course of action.

Mr. Ishikawa and I had three sessions. At the end of the third session, he sent telegrams to the top 21 men in Japan, to invite them to the Industry Club on a certain Tuesday night. The meeting went off well. That was the birth of the New Japan, if a date can be put on it.

More conferences with top management took place that hot summer, and in subsequent visits: January 1951, June 1951, June 1952, and onward, 27 or 28 trips in all, I believe. Every man of top management was present at every conference. Japan and Quality were of serious concern to them and to everybody. They were eager to learn and eager to change to the new philosophy. They accepted my teaching and put it into action.

I continued the teaching of engineers. Groups of engineers went out to samples of households in January 1951 to study the market for sewing machines, bicycles, pharmaceuticals, by use of methods of sampling and inference that I had taught them.

Encouragement to Japanese in 1950

I assured management and engineers in Japan that they could produce best quality. I assured them that they would rapidly develop a reputation for excellent quality, even though Japanese products in the past were noted for shoddy quality—cheap, but worth the price.

Some Japanese products will capture markets the world over in five years, I predicted. Actually, the Japanese beat my prediction. They accomplished it in four years. In fact, when I was in London in July 1951, the London Express came out with headlines:

And Now Come Japanese Nylons
And They Are Of Good Quality

A number of men in top management told me in later years that I was in 1950 the only man in Japan who believed my prediction. They hoped that it might come true, but did not understand how it could, though they would try.

A Summary of Teachings
to Top Management and to Engineers in Japan

1. The customer is the most important part of the production-line. Without him, there is no production-line. This principle seemed to be a new thought in Japan. The flow diagram shown here was in the black-board at every conference with top management, and every day in the teaching of engineers.

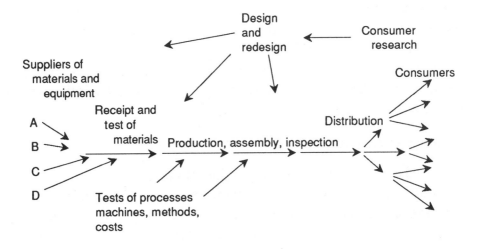

Figure 3.1
Production Viewed As a System.

    Improvement of quality envelops the entire production line, from incoming materials to the consumer, and redesign of product and service for the future. This chart was first used in August 1950 at a conference with top management at the Hotel de Yama on Mount Hakone in Japan. In a service organization, the sources A, B, C, etc., could be sources of data, or work from preceding operations, such as charges (as in department stores), calculation of charges, deposits, withdrawals, inventories in and out, transcriptions, shipping orders, and the like.

2. Quality is determined by the management. Outgoing quality can not be better than the intentions and specifications of the management.

3. The consumer is most important. What will help him in the future? The customer can not tell you what he might need and buy in the future. This responsibility lies with the management of the producer: Japanese manufacturers. My advice was to strive for long-term relationships with your customers.

4. Your supplier is your partner. Make him your partner. Work together on continual improvement of quality of incoming materials, and reduction of variation. To this end, develop a long-term relationship with a supplier in a spirit of mutual trust and cooperation. Supplier and customer will both win.

> I observed in 1947 and in 1950 the wretched quality of incoming materials—off gauge, off sized, wrong material, non-uniformity, highly variable. No wonder: Japanese industry was demolished. It would be necessary to work with suppliers to improve the quality of incoming materials.
>
> Note that I used supplier in the singular. It might be good, I explained, where feasible, to choose and work with a single supplier for any one material. The aim was better quality, and of course, reduction of variation.

5. Chain reaction from improvement of processes:

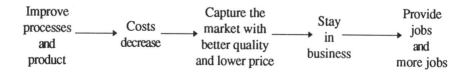

Figure 3.2
Chain Reaction From Improvement of Processes

THE SHEWHART CYCLE
FOR LEARNING AND IMPROVEMENT

THE P D S A CYCLE

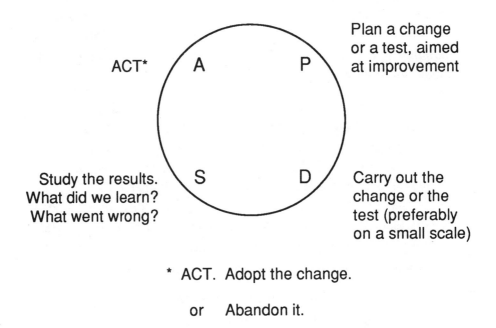

ACT* A   P   Plan a change
or a test, aimed
at improvement

Study the results.   S   D   Carry out the
What did we learn?   change or the
What went wrong?   test (preferably
on a small scale)

* ACT. Adopt the change.

or Abandon it.

or Run through the cycle again
possibly under different
environmental conditions.

Figure 3.3
The PDSA Cycle

6. Need for trust and cooperation between companies. Anything new learned in one company must be taught to all other companies, competitors and everybody. This must be a blaze that envelops the whole country. Fires here and there will not do it. Those were my words. Little did I understand at that time that cooperation is a Japanese way of life; that they could not live on that island without cooperation.[1]

7. Development of trust and respect.

I sought to understand the problem of the Japanese, and to move forward from their understanding about quality and the management of quality. I associated with them as much as possible, as in 1947, and with Americans that were doing the same. Noh plays helped us to understand Japanese culture.

Development of trust and respect must have played an important part in Japanese ascendence in quality, as one might infer from page 8 of the pamphlet, *The Deming Prize*, by Kenichi Koyanagi, 1960.[2]

> Special mention must be made of the fact that the Deming Prize was instituted with gratitude to Dr. Deming's friendship as well as in commemoration of his contributions to Japanese industry. When Dr. Deming gave his 8-day course in 1950, Japan was in the fifth year of Allied occupation. Administrative and all other affairs were under rigid control of the Allied forces. Most of the Japanese were in a servile spirit as the vanquished, and among Allied personnel there were not a few with an air of importance. In striking contrast, Dr. Deming showed his warm cordiality to everybody. His high personality deeply impressed all those who learned from him and became acquainted with him. He loved Japan

---

[1]Dr. Koraku Yoshida, "Sources of Japanese Productivity: Competition and Cooperation," *Review of Business*, St. John's University, Winter 1985.
[2]Kenichi Koyanagi, *The Deming Prize*, JUSE, Tokyo, 1960. Used by permission of W. Edwards Deming.

and the Japanese from his own heart. The sincerity and enthusiasm with which he did his best for his courses still lives and will live forever in the memory of all the concerned. Dr. Deming again visited Japan in the summer of 1951 and in January, 1952, both times invited by the JUSE. In 1951, he gave a seminar course on sampling survey and two 8-day courses on quality control, and in 1952 he offered an after clinic on sampling techniques. Featuring all these educational activities was his deep love and high humaneness. Herein, lies why we loved and respected, and still love and respect, him. And this is the very reason why the Deming Prize was instituted and has since been managed with recommendable results.

Chapter Four
The Deming Prize

Introduction

The documents in this chapter have been extracted, by Dr. Deming, from *The Deming Prize*, written by Kenichi Koyanagi and published by The Union of Japanese Scientists and Engineers, Tokyo, 1960.

The Decision of JUSE to Invite Dr. Deming in 1950

After the Surrender, industrial activities were at a stand-still as Japan had almost exhausted all her economic resources for war purposes and most of her major plants and production facilities had been reduced by American air raids to piles of ashes or skeletons of scrap. It appeared highly difficult for us to recover productive activities from this state of things and thereby to restore an industrial country on a new peaceful basis. Toward the end of 1945, making of civilian goods was started here and there and industrial production recovered step by step from 1946 through 1947. But products were all deplorably poor in quality because the seller's market prevailed for every kind of goods and social order still remained unrestored. There were indeed a large number of able engineers, but most of them were in such moral depression that they could hardly give full scope to their ability.

Under these conditions, it was expected that the introduction and dissemination of statistical quality control methods would bring about remarkable results in improving the quality of industrial products. Moreover, statistical ideas and methods offered Japanese engineers a splendid tool with which they could grasp the exact status of engineering jobs ahead of them and analyze and interpret any complicated problem, and work. The Civil Communication Section, SCAP, urged Japanese communication equipment makers to adopt quality control methods, offering educational service for this purpose. The Japan Management Association and some other private organization started dissemination activities in this field.

Independent from these organizations, The Union of Japanese Scientists and Engineers (JUSE) also commenced in March, 1948, pioneering services in statistical quality control as part of its regular activities. In that year, with Dr. Motosambure Masuyama as tutor, a series of lectures was sponsored on the subject "Statistical Analysis of Small Sample," and a six-man research group started the collection of necessary literature and initiated research work. The group members were: Shingenori Baba, Shigeru Mizuno, Masao Goto, Eizo Watanabe, Shin Miura, and Kenichi Koyanagi.

With the help of not only these members but also Dr. Masuyama, Dr. Tatsuo Kawata, Dr. Shigeti Moriguti and some other statisticians, the JUSE sponsored the first quality control seminar in September, 1949. This seminar has since been open for engineers as JUSE Basic Course, and it now is in its 18th session. The engineers who have taken this course now reach more than 3,500. With this course as a basis, moreover, several seminar courses have been held successively on such new ideas and techniques of business administration as sampling survey, marketing research, and operations research. These courses indeed greatly contributed to the improvement of industrial management, but there was little hope that good results could be expected due to lack of experience and material. In the years following 1945, Japan was still under Allied occupation, and her international relations were under strict restrictions. Thus, it was considerably difficult for us to get foreign literature and material on quality control, though these were in dire need for the Japanese engineers quite unexperienced in the application of modern quality control methods to industrial administration.

For all this, we managed to get copies of the American War Standards Z1.1, Z1.2, Z1.3 and some works by Dr. W. A. Shewhart, E. S. Pearson and some other authors, and studied them with great zeal. Reading these literatures, we came to know the name of Dr. Deming. Toward the end of 1949, we happened to learn from Dr. Moriguti that Dr. Deming would re-visit Japan some time in May, 1950, as advisor in sampling techniques to GHQ, SCAP.

Though he was quite a layman in statistics and had never met Dr. Deming, Managing Director Kenichi Koyanagi of the JUSE thought that a lecture course by a famous statistician like Dr. Deming could bring about epochal results. For he had been well aware that Dr. Deming was one of the American Pioneers in statistical quality control, making immense contributions to the education and dissemination of quality control methods. Thus, Mr. Koyanagi wrote a letter, dated March 8, 1950, to Dr. Deming, asking for the following two favors:

1. To give a QC lecture course for several days to the Japanese research workers, plant managers and engineers who had just started learning or taking an interest in quality control methods, and

2. To contribute a message to the inaugural number of the monthly journal "Statistical Quality Control" to be published by the JUSE.

In his very kind reply of April 21, 1950, Dr. Deming willingly accepted the two proposals and gave valuable suggestions about the projected course. As it is of great significance for the succeeding dissemination of quality control methods in Japan, Dr. Deming's letter is quoted in full as follows:

Dr. Deming's Letter of Acceptance

Washington
22 April 1950

My dear Mr. Koyanagi,

I felt deeply honored by your invitation to give lectures this summer and to assist with your proposed course in the statistical theory of control of quality and its applications. First of all, let me say that your plan for an intensive course lasting 5 to 7 days, 7 hours per day, is excellent. I myself have organized such courses in this country a number of times, and the results have been very good. Such courses enable people to attend who could not go to a regular university course.

It will be possible, I am sure, for me to assist you with this course by giving some lectures on statistical theory and demonstrations of applications, from 2 to 4 hours daily. However, I should explain before being too definite that my time will be under the direction of Mr. Kenneth Morrow, Research and Programs Division, Economic and Scientific Section, SCAP. I am sure, though, that Mr. Morrow will be delighted to have me give assistance to such a course in statistics in Tokyo while I am there. I shall speak to him about the matter and give you definite word as soon as possible.

In this country we found that 8 days was a minimum for the people who had not studied elementary statistical theory. I should think that in Tokyo the 7-day period would probably be much better than the 5-day period. If possible you might even extend the time to 8 days. Another suggestion which you might wish to consider is the possibility of requiring some preliminary study. Each student might be supplied with some preliminary papers to study before he comes to take the actual course. For example the registration fee might be made large enough to cover a pamphlet like the one titled

"Control chart method of controlling quality during production" which was published by the American Standards Association. I shall send a copy to you by sea. If students were thoroughly familiar with the contents of that article, and would also study something about statistical distributions, they could accomplish as much in 5 to 7 days as they could accomplish in 8 days without preliminary studies.

As for remuneration I shall not desire any. It will be only a great pleasure to assist you.

With regard to dates I might say that my ETA is about the 1st of June. I am not just sure how long I shall be able to stay in Tokyo, but I hope to be there during June and July, and possibly a part of August. I believe that the best time for your course would be the last part of June or the first week in July.

I had wondered if I should give a general course in sampling while I am in Tokyo. It would cover the sampling of human populations, agriculture, and industrial product, including quality control. It might meet 3 times per week, and it would follow my new book, which will soon appear. Possibly this course should be given at the University. I shall attach an outline of the course in order to give you an idea concerning the type of course that I have in mind. As my stay in Tokyo would be short, some of the topics would be covered only briefly.

Please be assured of my earnest desire to help you in every possible way. Please accept my kindest regards and best wishes for the success of your course and for your journal.

Sincerely yours,

W. Edwards Deming
Advisor in Sampling

Other Arrangements for the 1950 Lectures

As for preparations for the proposed course, communications were frequently exchanged between Dr. Deming and Mr. Koyanagi. A number of materials, including AS Z 1.2 and Z 1.3 were sent to the latter. Thus, the first 8-day course on quality control was finally opened in Tokyo during July 10–18, 1950. Dr. Deming gave his lessons to 230 students on the "Elementary Principles of the Statistical Control of Quality." Cooperating with deep gratitude and high enthusiasm in this course were a number of Japanese experts who had been taking the leadership in the JUSE-sponsored educational activities. They helped in every possible way the students to learn Dr. Deming's teachings.

Moreover, Dr. Deming gave a valuable lecture to a group of top-managers and inspected a number of manufacturing plants, offering practical instructions (See Chapter 3).

Thanks to the kind collaboration of the Japanese lecturers and of Mr. Masamichi Kano, able interpreter, the JUSE compiled a brochure, *Elementary Principles of the Statistical Control of Quality*, based upon a transcript of Dr. Deming's lectures. Fortunately, this brochure enjoyed a wide circulation among quality-minded engineers. Royalties due to Dr. Deming amounted to a sizeable amount, and Mr. Koyanagi naturally offered to pay them. But Dr. Deming declined to receive them and donated them to Mr. Koyanagi to be used freely for any conscientious purpose. With the royalties donated as a foundation, Mr. Koyanagi mapped out a plan to institute a prize with thanks to Dr. Deming's friendship and in commemoration of his service.

The Institution of the Deming Prize

In December, 1950, the JUSE Board of Directors formally resolved to create the Deming Prize in commemoration of Dr. Deming's contributions to Japanese industry and for encouragement of quality control development in Japan as follows:

The Deming Medal
Presented to the Annual Deming Prize Winner
by the Union of Japanese Scientists and Engineers

a) The Deming Prize shall be instituted as proposed by Managing Director Koyanagi.

b) The Deming Prize Committee shall be established for management of the prize, members of which shall be commissioned from all the quarters concerned.

c) Dr. Deming shall be recommended as honorary chairman, and the president of the JUSE shall assume the chairmanship of the Deming Prize Committee.

d) Affairs of the Deming Prize Committee shall be administered by the JUSE.

e) Funds for the Deming Prize shall be provided mainly from royalties on the afore-mentioned work of Dr. Deming. The JUSE shall transfer all the revenues from this publication to the Deming Prize fund and pay necessary expenses if there is any deficit.

f) Public donations shall be accepted for the Deming Prize fund. (For instance, the Nihon Keizai Shimbun Sha—better known as Nikkei—annually donates some money as a sub-prize. Some donations have been offered by Dr. Deming, Professor Shigeru Mizuno and Mr. Koyanagi.)

g) The Deming Prize shall be divided into two categories:

(1) The Deming Prize for research and education to be awarded to those who have made excellent researches in theory and application of quality control.

(2) The Deming Prize for application to be awarded to the corporations or plants which have attained recommendable results in practice of quality control.

In accordance with these rules, the Deming Prize Committee was soon organized, and the prize has been awarded every year since 1951.

The Deming Prize is a silver medal, with Dr. Deming's profile engraved on the surface, designed by Professor Kiyoshi Unno of Tokyo University of Fine Arts and other artists. A sum of money is to be given as a sub-prize to the recipients of the prize. Since 1953, funds for the sub-prize have been donated by the Nihon Keizai Shimbun Sha. Incidentally, since 1954 the same newspaper company has been donating funds necessary for the Nikkei Quality Control Literature Prize, which is to be awarded to the authors of recommendable literature on quality control.

Regulations for the Deming Prize

The Deming Prize Committee has revised the necessary rules as occasions demand. Since March 1957, the regulations are as follows.

1. The Deming Prize is a prize instituted in commemoration of the friendship and contributions of Dr. W. Edwards Deming, who has visited Japan for instructions in application of statistical quality control methods to industry.

2. The Deming Prize shall be awarded to:
   a) Those who have achieved excellent researches in the theory or application of statistical quality control,
   b) Those who have made remarkable contributions to the dissemination of statistical quality control methods, and
   c) The corporations, plants, etc. which have attained recommendable results in the practice of statistical quality control (the prize for application).
   d) In the case of small enterprises, a prize for application is also awarded.

3. The Deming Prize fund shall be provided mainly from royalties due to Dr. Deming on his *Elementary Principles of the Statistical Control of Quality* and other works published in Japan. Public donations and others, if any, shall be accepted to cover the deficit.

4. The Deming Prize shall be awarded once a year. The awarding of the Deming Prize shall be put in charge of the Deming Prize Committee.

5. The President of the Union of Japanese Scientists and Engineers shall assume the chairmanship of the Deming Prize Committee, and the Chairman shall commission other members.

6. The Deming Prize Committee Regulations shall be stipulated otherwise.

7. Affairs pertaining to the Deming Prize and the Deming Prize Committee shall all be entrusted to the Secretariat of the Union of Japanese Scientists and Engineers. The Deming Prize fund shall be put in charge of the Union of Japanese Scientists and Engineers.

Nikkei Quality Control Literature Prize Regulations

1. The Nikkei Quality Control Literature Prize shall be awarded in accordance with the rules hereby stipulated.

2. The Nikkei Quality Control Literature Prize shall be awarded once a year to the authors of literature on statistical quality control published in the past calendar year.

3. The Nikkei Quality Control Literature Prize shall be awarded for literature (including figure tables and others of similar nature) recognized highly conducive to the improvement and development of quality control.

4. Candidates for prize winners shall be recommended as follows:
   a) Recommendations shall be made by the authors of literature themselves or other parties.
   b) Recommendations shall be made by the prescribed form, attached with the literature concerned and other data.
   c) Recommendations shall be made by May 15 every year.
   d) The date of close for the recommendation can be changed by the resolution of the sub-committee when necessary.
   e) Recommendations shall be submitted to the Deming Prize Committee.

5. The screening of candidates recommended for the Nikkei Quality Control Literature Prize shall be made by the Deming Prize Committee. For this purpose, the Deming Prize Committee shall set up a sub-committee as per Article 6 of the Deming Prize Committee Regulations.

6. The Nikkei Quality Control Literature Prize shall consist of a certificate of merit and a prize money.

7. The prize money for the Nikkei Quality Control Literature Prize shall be covered by donations from the Nihon Keizai Shimbun Sha.

8. The number of winners and amount of the prize money for the Nikkei Quality Control Literature Prize shall be determined every year by the Deming Prize Committee.

9. Affairs pertaining to the Nikkei Quality Control Literature Prize shall be considered as part of the Deming Prize Committee's business and entrusted to the Secretariat of the Union of Japanese Scientists and Engineers.

Deming Prize Committee Regulations

Organization and Management of the Committee

1. The President of the Union of Japanese Scientists and Engineers shall assume the chairmanship of the Deming Prize Committee.

2. The chairman shall commission committee members for the succeeding year, immediately after the annual awarding ceremony of the Deming Prize.

   If necessary the chairman shall commission men of knowledge and experience as temporary members and to hear their opinions.

3. Committee meetings shall be convened by the Chairman.

4. The resolutions of committee meetings shall be decided by a majority vote of members present. When votes are evenly divided, the Chairman shall have the casting vote.

5. Committee meetings shall not be in session unless more than one half of the members are present.

6. The Deming Prize Committee shall be allowed to set up a sub-committee for deliberations on a special matter.

7. The temporary members shall have no voting right.

Duties of the Committee

8. a) The Deming Prize Committee shall assume responsibilities for the enforcement of the Deming Prize Regulations.

    b) The Deming Prize Committee shall assume responsibilities for the enforcement of the Nikkei Quality Control Literature Prize Regulations.

9. The Deming Prize Committee shall receive the widest possible recommendations as for winner candidates, natural or juridical persons, and screen them as per the prescribed regulations.

    When the screening of winner candidates is finished, the Deming Prize Committee shall make a public statement on its final decision and award the prize in public.

    The Deming Prize Committee reserves privileges to any of past winners of the prize for application to ask to publish their progresses in the matter awarded.

10. The number of winners and the scope of the prize shall be decided every year by the Deming Prize committee.

11. The amount of the prize money as a sub-prize shall be decided by the Deming Prize Committee.

12. As to the screening of winner candidates, preliminary deliberations shall be made by the sub-committee set up for each of the items stipulated in Article 2 of the Deming Prize Regulations.

13. Amendment, revision or abolition of the Deming Prize Regulations and the Deming Prize Committee Regulations shall be put in charge of the Deming Prize Committee.

14. The resolutions adopted at committee meetings shall be entered in the minute-book of the Deming Prize Committee and kept in custody.

15. If it becomes necessary to make a field inspection in the course of screening winner candidates, travel expenses may be provided.

16. Various expenses of the Deming Prize Committee shall be covered by the Deming Prize Fund.

Message to the Ceremonies for the 10th Annual Award for the Deming Prize in Japan

W. Edwards Deming

The phenomenal growth of Japanese Industry since 1950 has attracted attention the world over. The quality and dependability of many Japanese products has earned admiration and respect everywhere, and has created a market any place in the world where high precision and dependability are in demand.

Japanese quality, as we know it today, has its origin in events that date from the summer of 1950. It may be worthwhile to recall the economic state of Japan at that time. Physical plant and morale of the technical and professional men was at an all-time low. Japanese manufacturers faced, furthermore, a new and strange situation. Gone were the days when they could manufacture goods of any quality and sell or barter them in other parts of Asia. Their wares must now earn acceptance in new markets, against the handicap of a reputation for inferior quality. It was not the nature of the Japanese people to eat imported food bought on credit. Something had to be done.

Several hundred Japanese engineers and statisticians had received rudimentary training in 8-day courses in elementary statistical principles and methods in the summer of 1950. It was not enough that these people should hear of statistical methods, and understand something of their use. Statistical methods do not formulate goals. Statistical methods help one to achieve goals. It was necessary for top management to fix goals. It was also essential for them to know that statistical techniques and statistical thinking, diligently applied, could create a new industrial era. How to reach top management was the big question.

It is most fortunate that Mr. Ichiro Ishikawa, President of the Union of Japanese Scientists and Engineers, then President of the great Showa Denko, respected citizen and hard worker in scientific and civic organizations, came to understand the problems that confronted Japanese industry, and that he and Mr. Koyanagi, Managing Director of the Union of Japanese Scientists and Engineers, perceived what statistical methods could do for Japan.

Mr. Ishikawa, thereupon, invited a group of about 50 Japanese executives of manufacturing companies to the Industry Club, to learn, from a statistician, what statistical methods might do for Japanese industry. I faced this meeting with much fear. I was only a statistician. I was not an economist nor an executive. Yet I was to address a gathering of top-ranking executives of Japanese people to sense the opportunity to use these methods. A further meeting with the same group and a few others on Mt. Hakone on the 19th August 1950, gave opportunity for further examination of the uses of statistical methods in consumer-research, in production, and in marketing.

Statistical quality control was presented and taught at that time, to engineers and to top management, as THE APPLICATION OF STATISTICAL PRINCIPLES AND TECHNIQUES IN ALL STAGES OF PRO-

DUCTION DIRECTED TOWARD THE ECONOMIC MANUFACTURE OF A PRODUCT THAT IS USEFUL AND HAS A MARKET. I still use this definition. It starts with the consumer at one end, and with raw materials and the vendor of finished and semi-finished parts at the other end.

The rapid acceptance of statistical methods in Japan arose, in large part, from the fact that top management were convinced that these methods were vital for survival. This meant that younger people who learned statistical methods had a chance to try them.

I am no economist, nor even less an expert in marketing, but I can add and subtract, and it seemed to me that if Japanese wares could find markets in various parts of the world, the Japanese need not worry about raising enough food in their own country to live on. It might be smart to import even a greater proportion of their food than they did then, and to export Japanese wares to pay for it. The people in Chicago don't raise their own food; they export their product and buy food with the returns. Switzerland, with hard currency and with an enviable standard of living, imports a good fraction of its food, in trade for scenery, watches, and other products that are in demand all over the world.

It seemed to me, therefore, that the following 6 points were worthy of presentation for consideration of Japanese executives, in their plans for the future.

1. Japan need not feed herself with her own agricultural products. It might be better to manufacture goods and to trade those goods for food.

2. Japanese industry must now become competitive, in a world-market. Statistical methods could help Japanese manufacturers to raise the quality and dependability of their product, and to put it out at competitive prices.

Incidentally, if some manufacturers in my own country would meet competition with effort, and spend less time on lobbies to boost tariffs and to lower trade quotas, they might have less worry about Japanese competition and could give some of the rest of us the benefit of better quality and lower prices. Many people say that they believe in free enterprise in competition, but what they often mean is competition for the other fellow, not for themselves. Now in my own case, I believe in free enterprise, and I am not afraid of Japanese statisticians, English statisticians, French statisticians, or any others. If one of them is doing a better job, then the thing to do is to go over there, or bring him to my own country, and find out how he does it. I don't know of any statisticians' lobby to try to keep out Japanese statisticians, English statisticians, or any others. The more of them we import, the better off we are.

3. It would require 2 years and more to revise Japanese ideas of quality, precision, and uniformity. It would require another 5 years and more to establish a reputation for quality and precision, and uniformity. Plans for a new era would be long-range and would require patience. It would take a long time to overcome the reputation for inferior quality that Japanese products had built up before the war.

4. Japanese manufacturers must learn to use consumer-research in the design, manufacture and marketing of their products. This consumer-research must be done in other parts of the world, where the markets lie.

5. Concerted heavy action would be necessary. Spotty use of statistical methods, here and there, would not pull Japan out of the crisis. Top management throughout Japan must work together in a vast movement that would leave no doubt about the improved quality and dependability of Japanese products.

6. Japan was poor in natural resources, with little oil, little coal, iron ore, some wood. Japan was nevertheless rich in the greatest resource of all—skilled and willing labor. Technical knowledge of Japanese engineers, statisticians, and economists was unsurpassed. Scarcity of raw material need not be cause for discouragement if the aim of Japanese manufacturers was to turn out products of high quality and

precision. Any saving of coal, iron, petroleum, cotton, machinery, copper, and other scarce materials through the use of statistical methods or by any other technical advance was the equivalent of going out and finding deposits of coal, iron ore, copper, oil, etc.. This fact was of special appeal in Japan. Results in a number of plants, within a few months, emphasized the fact that the great savings of materials were possible, along with improved quality. One company learned how to save nearly 1/3d of their fuel; another one decreased the loss of scrap in one operation to 1/9th what it had been.

It was this firm faith in statistical methods and in Japanese people that led me to these bold statements. This was my story, and top management in Japan believed it. Mr. Ishikawa, Mr. Koyanagi, and the Japanese executives at the meetings believed the story. The reconstructions in basic philosophy, and in morale, and in aims, that has taken place in the decade has been no less phenomenal than the reconstruction of physical plant.

The educational facilities of the Union of Japanese Scientists and Engineers opened up studies of unsurpassed thoroughness and coverage, at all levels, from top management on down. Results became obvious in a few months. Definite improvement in the quality of many Japanese articles became cause for comment in various parts of the world within 2 years. Such rapid change bears eloquent testimony to remarkable teamwork and performance.

It is worthy of note that organization of Japanese companies, and the spirit of reception to new ideas gave statistical methods quicker chance of adoption than they have had in most other countries. This had been an important factor in the reconstruction of Japanese industry, and its adaptation to a competitive situation. Japan is now the place to go to study statistical methods in industry, not only for the theory, principles, and application but for organization as well.

One reason for the effective use of statistical methods in Japan and for proper organization, lies in the fact that the first courses in statistical methods there distinguished carefully between (a) statistical problems, and (b) engineering and consumer problems. They taught statistical theory as a tool to solve statistical problems, and not as a substitute for chemistry, engineering, production, psychology, consumer-research, or accounting, or other subject-matter.

What statistical methods do is to point out the existence of special causes. A point beyond limits on a control chart, or a significant result in an experiment or test, indicates almost certainly the existence of one or more special causes. Points in control, or showing no significance, indicate that only common causes of variation remain.

The statistical method does not find causes. Finding special causes, and eliminating them if economical to do so, is the responsibility of some-one who understands the machine or the production-methods. In many cases, this person is the operator of a machine.

When you find most of the special causes and eliminate them, you have left common causes of variability, which may be any or several of various types—poor light, humidity, vibration, poor food in the cafeteria, absence of a real quality program, poor supervision, poor or spotty raw material, etc.. Common causes are more difficult to identify than special causes are. Moreover, the removal of common causes calls for action by administration at a high level. Workers and foremen cannot change the lighting, nor write new contracts for raw materials, nor institute a quality program, yet these are examples of common causes of variation and of poor quality. Such action can be taken only by administration on a high level.

Statistical techniques thus turn the spotlight on the responsibilities for action in various levels and positions. They direct substantive knowl-edge to the problems where it can be most effective. If one understands something about the power of the statistical method, and understands where it will work, why it will work, and where it won't work, he has a good start. The rest is up to the individual student to educate himself from then on.

Japanese manufacturers may take extra glory in the fact that they did not look to their government nor to mine for assistance. Instead, they raised the money themselves to pay for the technical assistance that they received.

Japan has exported to the world something very important besides material product. Japan has exported statistical knowledge and methods of organization for use of statistical knowledge in industry. Nearly 1/3d of the abstracts selected for the INTERNATIONAL JOURNAL OF ABSTRACTS ON STATISTICAL METHODS IN INDUSTRY have come from Japan. Many books by Japanese statisticians have appeared. Some of these books extend to the frontiers of statistical theory; many are models of exposition. Japanese statistical journals, especially those on basic theory, are respected and are in demand in all centers of learning and research where people engage themselves in serious study. I may mention also, the work of Professor Kaoru Ishikawa's committee on the sampling of raw materials. This work has contributed greatly to vendor-purchaser relations and has saved tremendous sums of money for Japanese industry. The next step may be extension of the use of statistical methods in vendor-purchaser relations by small companies that depend on smaller companies for materials and parts, even those that depend on home-manufacturing. Application of statistical principles to home-manufacturing is a challenge, but I believe that it is possible.

Statistical methods, including theories of stochastic processes and extreme values, are providing better knowledge of chemistry and of physics, epidemiology, movement of goods and poisons in the soil, and better testing of materials for performance and reliability. Design of experiment, queuing theory, methods of simulation, linear programming, and other aids to management through statistical theory and mathematics are contributing to Japanese industry.

I close with commendation and admiration of the Japanese people for what they have accomplished, and with warm appreciation for the privilege of working with them these 10 years.

The Deming Prize Winners 1951-1992

1951	Motosaburo Masuyama
1952	Tetsuichi Asaka
	Kaoru Ishikawa*
	Masao Kogure
	Masao Goto
	Hidehiko Higashi
	Shin Miura
	Shigeru Mizuno*
	Eizo Watanabe
1953	Toshio Kitagawa
1954	Eizaburo Nishibori*
1955	Shigeiti Moriguti
1956	Yasushi Ishida*
1957	Ziro Yamauti*
1958	Takeshi Kayano
1959-1960	Kenichi Koyanagi*
	Genichi Taguchi
1961	Takeo Katoh*
1962	Ikuro Kusaba
1963	Noboru Yamaguchi
	Sadakichi Shimizu*
1964	No Listing
1965	Masumasa Imaizumi
1966	Masashi Asao
	Kiyomi Kadokawa
	Kazufumi Seki*
	Tadasu Fujita
1967	Jiro Kondo
1968	Shinobu Toshima*
1969	Tadakazu Okuno
1970	Tatsuo Sugimoto
1971	Teiichi Ando
	Yoshio Kondo
	Shoichi Shimizu
1972	Kotaro Itoh*

1973	Koichi Ohba*
1974	Koji Kobayashi
1975	Taro Yamamoto
	Yoshitsugu Ohmae
1976	Katsuyoshi Ishihara
1977	Osamu Furukawa
1978	Yoji Akao
1979	Hajime Makabe
1980	Shoichiro Toyota
1981	Hajime Karatsu
1982	Hiroshi Shiomi
1983	Minoru Toyoda
1984	Tatsuo Ikezawa
1985	Yoshinobu Nayatani
1986	Ryoichi Kawai
1987	Ryuichi Kobayashi
1988	Ren-ichi Takenaka
1989	Hitoshi Kume
1990	Shoichiro Kobayashi
1991	Kenji Kurogane
1992	Masao Nemoto
	*: Deceased

Corporation Deming Prize Winners 1951-1992

1951	(Fuji Iron and Steel Co., Ltd.) Nippon Steel Corp.
	Showa Denko K.K.
	Tanabe Sciyaku Co., Ltd.
	(Yawata Iron & Steel Co., Ltd.) Nippon Steel Corp.
1952	Asahi Chemical Industry Co., Ltd.
	The Furukawa Electric Co., Ltd.
	(Nippon Electric Co., Ltd.) NEC Corp.
	Shionogi & Co., Ltd.
	Takeda Chemical Industries, Ltd.
	(Toyo Spinning Co., Ltd.) Toyobo Co., Ltd.
	Kyushu Cloth Industry Co., Ltd.
1953	Kawasaki Steel Corp.
	Shin-etsu Chemical Industry Co., Ltd.
	Sumitomo Metal Mining Co., Ltd.

	(Tokyo Shibaura Electric Co., Ltd.) Toshiba Corp.
1954	Nippon Soda Co., Ltd.
	Toyo Bearing Mfg. Co., Ltd.
	(Toyo Rayon Co., Ltd.) Toray Industries, Inc.
1955	Asahi Glass Co., Ltd.
	Hitachi, Ltd.
	(Honshu Paper Mfg. Co., Ltd.) Honshu Paper Co., Ltd.
1956	Fuji Photo Film Co., Ltd.
	(Konishiroku Photo Industry Co., Ltd.) Konica Corp.
	Mitsubishi Electric Corp.
	Tohoku Industry Co., Ltd.
1957	(None)
1958	Kanegafuchi Chemical Industry Co., Ltd.
	Kureha Chemical Industry Co., Ltd.
	Matsushita Electronics Corp.
	(Nippon Kokan K.K.) NKK Corp.
	Nakayo Communication Equipments Co., Ltd.
1959–1960	Asahi Special Glass Co., Ltd.
	Kurake Spinning Co., Ltd.
	Nissan Motor Co., Ltd.
	Towa Industry Co., Ltd.
1961	Nippondenso Co., Ltd.
	Teijin Ltd.
	Nihon Radiator Co., Ltd.
1962	Sumitomo Electric Industries, Ltd.
1963	Nipoon Kayaku Co., Ltd.
1964	(Komatsu Mfg. Co., Ltd.) Komatsu Ltd.
1965	(Toyota Motor Co., Ltd.) Toyota Motor Corp.
1966	Kanto Auto Works, Ltd.
	Matsushita Electric Industrial Co., Ltd.
	- Electric Components Division
1967	Shinko Wire Co., Ltd.
	Kojima Press Industry Co., Ltd.
1968	(Bridgestone Tire Co., Ltd.) Bridgestone Corp.
	Yanmer Diesel Engine Co., Ltd.
	Chugoku Kayaku Co., Ltd.
1969	Shimpo Industry Co., Ltd.
1970	Toyota Auto Body Co., Ltd.

1971	Hino Motors, Ltd.
1972	Aisin Seiki Co., Ltd.
	Saitama Chuzo Kogyo K.K.
1973	Sanwa Seiki Mfg. Co., Ltd.
	Saitama Kiki Mfg. Co., Ltd.
	*Mitsubishi Heavy Industries Co., Ltd.
	- Kobe Shipyard
1974	Horikiri Spring Mfg. Co., Ltd.
	Kyodo Surveying Co., Ltd.
1975	Ricoh Co., Ltd.
	K.K. Takebe Tekkosho
	Tokai Chemical Industries, Ltd.
	Riken Forge Co., Ltd.
	*Sekisui Chemical Co. Ltd.
	- Tokyo Plant
1976	Sankyo Seiki Mfg. Co., Ltd.
	Pentel Co., Ltd.
	Komatsu Zoki, Ltd.
	Ishikawajima-Harima Heavy Industries Co., Ltd.
	- Aero-Engine & Space Operations
	*Kubota Iron & Machinery Works, Ltd.
	- Engine Tech-Research Dept.
	*Kubota Iron & Machinery Works, Ltd.
	- Sakai Works
1977	(Aisin-Warner Ltd.) Aisin AW Co.
	*Japan Aircraft Mfg. Co., Ltd.
	- Atsugi Works
1978	Tokai Rika Co., Ltd.
	Chuetsu Metal Works Co., Ltd.
1979	(Nippon Electric Kyushu, Ltd.) NEC Kyushu Ltd.
	Sekisui Chemical Co., Ltd.
	(Takenaka Komuten Co., Ltd.) Takenaka Corp.
	Tohoku Ricoh Co., Ltd.
	Hamanakodenso Co., Ltd.
	*The Japan Steel Works, Ltd.
	- Hiroshima Plant
1980	Kayaba Industry Co., Ltd.
	Komatsu Forklift Co., Ltd.
	Fuji Xerox Co., Ltd.
	The Takaoka Industrial Co., Ltd.

Kyowa Industrial Co., Ltd.
*(Kobayashi Kose Co., Ltd.) Kose Co., Ltd.
- Manufacturing Division

1981   Aiphone Co., Ltd.
Kyosan Denki Co., Ltd.
(Tokyo Juki Industrial Co., Ltd.) Juki Corp.
-Industrial Sewing Machine Division
*Matsushita Electric Works, Ltd.
- Hikone Factory

1982   Kajima Corp.
(Nippon Electric Yamagata Ltd.) NEC Yamagata Ltd.
Rhythm Watch Co., Ltd.
Yokogawa Hewlett-Packard Co., Ltd.
Aisin Chemical Co., Ltd.
Shinwa Industrial Co., Ltd.

1983   (Shimizu Construction Ltd.) Shimizu Corp.
The Japan Steel Works, Ltd.
Aisin Keikinzoku Co., Ltd.
*Fuji Electric Co., Ltd.
- Matsumoto Plant

1984   Komatsu Zenoah Co., Ltd.
The Kansai Electric Power Co.
Yaskawa Electric Co.
Anjo Denki Co., Ltd.
Hokuriku Kogyou Co., Ltd.

1985   Nippon Carbon Co., Ltd.
Nippon Zeon Co., Ltd.
Toyoda Gosei Co., Ltd.
Toyoda Machine Works, Ltd.
Comany Inc.
Hoyo Seiki Co., Ltd.
Uchino Komuten Co., Ltd.
Texas Instruments Japan Ltd.
- Bipolar Dept.

1986   (Hazama-Gumi, Ltd.) Hazama Corp.
Toyoda Automatic Loom Works, Ltd.
Nitto Construction Co., Ltd.
Sanyo Electric Works Ltd.

1987   Aichi Steel Works Ltd.
Aisin Chemical Co., Ltd.

	Daihen Corp.
	NEC IC Microcomputer Systems, Ltd.
1988	Aisin Keikinzoku Co., Ltd.
	Asmo Co., Ltd.
	(Fuji Tekko Co., Ltd.) Fuji Univance Corp.
	(Joban Hawaiian Center) Joban Kosan Co., Ltd.
	- Spa Resort Hawaiians
	*Suntory Ltd.
	- Musashino Brewery
1989	Aisin Sinwa Co., Ltd.
	Itoki Kosakusyo Co., Ltd.
	Maeda Corp.
	NEC Tohoku, Ltd.
	TOTO Ltd.
	Florida Power & Light Company, USA
	Ahresty Corp.
	Toyooki Kogyo Co., Ltd.
	*Kobe Steel Ltd.
	- Chofu-Kita Plant
	*Maeta Concrete Industry, Ltd.
	- Honsha Plant
1990	Aisin Hoyo Co., Ltd.
	Amada Wasino Co., Ltd.
	NEC Shizuoka, Ltd.
	*Suntory Ltd.
	- Yamanashi Winery
1991	NEC Kansai, Ltd.
	Nachi-Fujikoshi Corp.
	Hokusin Industries, Inc.
	Philips Taiwan, Ltd.
	Sin'ei Industries Co., Ltd.
	Niigata Toppan Printing Co., Ltd.
1992	Aisan Industry Co., Ltd.
	Jatco Corp.
	*Toppan Printing Co., Ltd.
	Electronics Division - Kumamoto Plant
	*Nissan Motor Co., Ltd.
	-Oppama Plant

( ):   Name of Company at the time of awarding

*:   Winners of the Factory Quality Control Award of the Deming Prize Committee

Japan Quality Control Medalists

1970	(Toyota Motor Co., Ltd.) Toyota Motor Corp.
1973	(Nippon Electric Co., Ltd.) NEC Corp.
1975	Nippon Steel Corp.
1977	Aisin Seiki Co., Ltd.
1980	Toyota Auto Body Co., Ltd.
1981	Komatsu Ltd.
1982	(Aisin-Warner Ltd.) Aisin AW Co., Ltd.
1985	The Takaoka Industrial Co., Ltd.
1990	Aisin Seiki Co., Ltd.
1991	Aisin AW Co., Ltd.
1992	Aisin Chemical Co., Ltd.
	Takenaka Corp.

( ): Name of Company at the time of awarding

IN APPRECIATION FOR YOUR VISION AND LEADERSHIP
IN THE FIELD OF STATISTICAL CONTROL OF QUALITY

YHP **YOKOGAWA HEWLETT·PACKARD**

November 19, 1982

Kenzo Sasaoka
President

This replica of the Deming Medal was presented to Dr. Deming by Yokogawa Hewlett-Packard in 1982. It is made up of the names of all employees written in the Japanese alphabet.

Chapter Four

Chapter Five
The Second Order Medal of the Sacred Treasure

In May 1960, Dr. Deming was awarded the Second Order Medal of the Sacred Treasure, the highest award Japan can bestow on a foreigner. The award was authorized by Emperor Hirohito and given to Dr. Deming by Prime Minister Nobusuke Kishi at the opening assembly of the International Statistical Institute conference in Tokyo. Here is Dr. Deming's own record of the award ceremony, taken from his journal, *Sixth Trip to Japan.*

> <u>Tuesday 31 May</u>. H.I.H. The Crown Prince addressed the opening assembly of the International Statistical Institute. We had seats in the front row. I surreptitiously snapped a few pictures of the Crown Prince, and they turned out to be good. There was an embarrassing silence as he departed: the ushers could not immediately open the door for his exit, though they succeeded eventually. The announcement of the award of my medal came in the course of the ceremony.

The actual award took place in a small room. Prime Minister Kishi pinned a small emblem on my lapel. The medal itself is about 3 inches in diameter, heavy with much gold, with a certificate in Japanese, signed by the Prime Minister. The design of my medal is mirror, jewels, and swords. The mirror is about the size of a dime, platinum or paladium, then jewels (rubies?) in a circle, and radial swords, all set in solid gold, in a beautiful lacquered box, a delightful work of art. I can say that nothing ever pleased me so much as this recognition. The citation stated that the Japanese people attribute the rebirth of Japanese industry, and their success in marketing their radios and parts, transistors, cameras, binoculars, and sewing machines all over the world to my work there.

Dr. Deming always wears the small lapel pin.

In 1950, Dr. Deming told the top Japanese managers that in spite of the total devastation of their factories and plants, they could capture world markets *because of the quality of their manufactured products* within five years. While his prediction may have seemed overly optimistic, his ideas made sense to the Japanese leaders. They also had great respect for this foreign scholar, who unlike some of his fellow-countrymen, treated them with respect and humanity. And, really having nothing to lose, they embraced the Deming philosophy with enthusiasm and dedication almost beyond Dr. Deming's belief: "They changed the economy of the world."

A more subtle sign of the respect of the Japanese for Dr. Deming is found in his travel diary of 1955. There he observed that this was his 3d invitation to Japan at the expense of Japanese companies. "So far as I know, this is the only instance where a man from an occupying power was actually invited back and paid by the people that were occupied, to continue the same work that he was doing under the occupation (1947–1950)."

The Second Order Medal of the Sacred Treasure

Chapter Five

Chapter Six
The 1950 Lecture
to Japanese Top Management

We are in a new industrial age, created largely by statistical principles and techniques. I shall try to explain how these principles and techniques are helping Japan to increase her export trade.

International trade is an essential component of peace and prosperity. International trade depends on—

   a. Quality at the right level (I shall say more on this later.)

   b. Uniform quality and dependable performance (It is a fact that trade depends more on uniformity than on high levels of quality.)

   c. Competitive price (which requires efficient production)

   d. International standardization

e. Meaningful specifications—tests that will distinguish economically and reliably between good and bad quality

f. Manufacture in sufficient quantity to warrant business

g. International language of communication of quality. (The buyer, even though separated by oceans from the seller, must be able to express the quality desired in a language that both buyer and seller understand. Equally important, the seller must be able to express the quality of the product that he is able to produce and sell, in a language that they both, understand. Of course, this problem is not simple, because the needs of the buyer must be met by the product and quality that the producer is capable of making, and for which the buyer has purchasing power.)

Statistical techniques have brought new meaning into all these requirements of international trade. As I said, we are in a new industrial age. Most of you have heard of the quality-control charts and acceptance sampling. The quality-control chart is a very simple device, much used now in Japan. It is so simple that a shop foreman can learn to use it in a few hours or days, he can and will immediately start to improve the quality and uniformity of his product, and to turn out a greater amount of product every day. His machines will be idle less time every day, and he will waste less material. He will turn out more good product every day, and not so much rejected product. All this he will do without new machines or more space.

The international language that is so essential for the communication between buyer and seller of the quality-characteristics of a product is provided by the same statistical techniques that are used for improved testing, production, and inspection. Those of you who are familiar with the control charts and acceptance sampling will see at once how true this is: the control chart, when the production process has been brought to a state of control, shows indisputable proof of quality and uniformity, to anyone in any part of the world.

Actually, as most of you know, in recent Japanese experience, the simple statistical techniques of the control chart have brought forth increases in production that range from 5% to 100%, *without expansion of plant.* Some firms are saving 10% of their raw material, compared with their performance of a year ago. In some cases, the savings are much greater. One large steel company reported they were able to cut their fuel bill by a third. All these achievements, and more, were reported at the convention held in Osaka the 22d September, last, at the occasion of the Deming award.

In one large spinning mill that I visited last summer in Japan, three-quarters of the girls who had been engaged in rework and repair a year before had been moved into production, because of improved quality and lesser number of rejections.

The gain in production and profit, although considerable from such achievements, are the least of the gains. The gains from a better competitive position through improved quality to lower the price are much greater, though more difficult to measure.

Acceptance sampling is another simple technique by which quality is guaranteed to the consumer at minimum expense for testing.

In these ways, and in many others ways, statistical techniques help greatly to meet the requirements for increased international trade. I shall now define what I mean by statistical quality control.

Statistical quality control is the application of statistical principles and techniques in all stages of production directed toward the most economic manufacture of a product that is maximally useful and has a market.

Now let me tell you what I mean by statistical techniques applied in all stages of production. In any manufacturing plant, raw materials come in, and product flows out. Eventually, your product is used by people who will judge your product. Your raw materials may indeed be raw, or they may be sub-assemblies or piece-parts from another manufacturer. Your finished product may indeed be finished, or it may be raw material for some other manufacturer.

Anyway, there will be a chain of production, and to make the problem simple enough for me to deal with in one lecture, I shall draw a diagram (See Fig. 6.1 on next page).

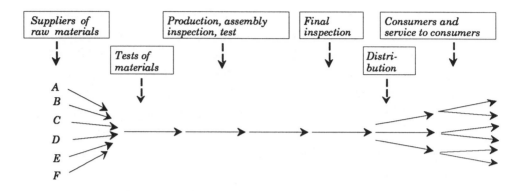

Figure 6.1
Chain of Production

By statistical quality control, I mean statistical work in all these stages of production. Statistical techniques are essential in all these stages. It is really impossible for manufacturers to compete and to build up their export trade to the fullest usefulness to themselves and to the rest of the world without using the best techniques: otherwise their quality will not be good enough or uniform enough, or their price will be too high.

Through full use of statistical quality control, from raw material to the consumer, a manufacturer may expect to achieve in some measure the following advantages:

1. Increased production, without investment in capital equipment or expansion of plant

2. Savings on raw materials and fuel (a particularly vital advantage when scarcity of materials threatens production)

3. Better operating efficiency: (a) idle time of machines decreased; fewer rejections; less scrap and re-work; (b) better prediction of the market, through consumer research, by which the purchase of materials, and the expansion and contraction of the plant, are carried out rationally, resulting in better economy than would be possible otherwise.

4. Decreased inspection, but with increased assurance of dependable quality

5. Quality, uniformity and price, better suited to the market

6. Greater precision of dimensions when required (as when parts are to be interchangeable)

7. Better design, through consumer research, carried out by modern methods of sampling and design of experiment

8. Stronger competitive position, through ability to meet world requirements in price, quality and uniformity; and to furnish statistical proof of quality and uniformity in an international language.

I must now ask you to think with me in broad terms just what good quality and economic production really mean. Some people think in terms of price alone. Perhaps others think in terms of quality alone. Some people think of economic production as saving 10% in the cost of some operation. All these ideas are important, but we must go deeper.

In the first place, *price has no meaning except in terms of the quality of the product.* But that is not enough. "GOOD QUALITY" and "UNIFORM QUALITY" *have no meaning except with reference to the consumer's needs.*

Therefore, next I shall speak to you in terms of the entire production line, which begins with the producers of your raw materials, and ends with the consumer—the man who uses your product.

Incidentally, the consumer is more important than raw material. It is usually easier to replace a supplier of raw material with another one than it is to find a new consumer. And a non-consumer, one who has not yet tried your product, is still more important to you, because he represents *a possible additional user of your product.* For this reason I shall speak to you of *consumer research*, because I believe in the importance of consumer research to Japanese industry, particularly for its export trade.

A moment's digression on the newness of statistical techniques, of statistical quality control, may be interesting. The use of control charts began on a big scale in America only in 1942 and 1943. Acceptance sampling, however, began much earlier; about 1926. The techniques for the proper design of tests of raw materials, designs and finished products began about 1820, although their use in industry was not recognized extensively until about 1935. Suitable techniques of sampling and questioning for economical and reliable consumer research have been built only within the last 10 years.

Some manufacturers think of consumer research (or market research) as analysis of complaints from purchasers and users. Certainly, no one can deny the great importance of the analysis of consumers' complaints. No matter how silly and unjust a complaint may be, it is still important to a manufacturer, because it shows him *where he has failed in public relations*—that is, failed to make clear to the public just what quality they have a right to expect when they buy his product. A legitimate complaint helps the manufacturer to improve his quality, provided he has real quality control, and can be used by the manufacturer in tracing the cause of trouble all the way back to production and raw material.

Surely you will agree that complaints are only a part of the problem of public relations—communication with the consumer and the non-consumer.

Complaints come from a very biased sample of consumers. Complaints do not provide communication with the other consumers nor with the non-consumer.

For reliable and economical communication with the consumers and non-consumers of a product, it is necessary to carry out *statistical tests and surveys*. I shall now speak to you about this particular aspect of quality control, and I shall remind you that its main purpose is *re-design* of the quality of your product, and *adjustment* of the plant, *contraction or expansion* of the output of particular products *to meet rationally predicted changes in demand*. These are important requirements of trade, domestic and international.

What is consumer research? I have mentioned several times the need for statistical surveys for consumer research. As the importance of the consumer has been left out of the chain of production in many parts of the world where industry needs expansion, I shall append a few remarks on the subject.

Consumer research is an integral part of production. As I said earlier, the terms "good quality" and "quality control" have no meaning except with reference to the consumer's needs. Without consumer research, the product has little chance of being maximally useful, or made in the most economical quantities. In fact, a manufacturing concern can hardly hope to stay in business today without vigorous consumer research.

The main use of consumer research is to feed consumer reactions back into the design of the product, so that management can anticipate changing demands and requirements, and set economical production levels. Consumer research takes the pulse of the consumer's reactions and demands, and seeks explanations for the findings.

Consumer research is not merely selling. Real consumer research, geared to design and production, is an indispensable modern tool for modern problems.

Consumer research is communication between the manufacturer and the users and potential users of his product, like this:

$$\text{manufacturer} \; \rightleftarrows \; \left\{ \begin{array}{l} \text{the user} \\ \text{and} \\ \text{the non-user} \end{array} \right.$$

This communication may be carried out today only by sampling procedures. On the basis of this communication, by which the manufacturer discovers how his product performs in service and what people think of his product, why some bought it, why some do not, or would not buy it again, the manufacturer is able to re-design his product, to make it better—better in the sense of meeting the needs of the people who may buy it, and of quality and uniformity best suited to the end-uses, and to the price that people can pay. Consumer research acts as a governor or servo-mechanism which by probing into the future market regulates both the design of the product and the amount of production.

In the olden days, before the industrial era, the tailor, the carpenter, the shoemaker, the milkman, the blacksmith knew his customers by name. He knew whether they were satisfied and what he should do to improve appreciation for his product. With the expansion of industry, this personal touch was lost. The wholesaler, the jobber, and the retailer have now stepped in, and in effect have set up a barrier between the manufacturer and the ultimate consumer. But sampling, a new science, steps in and pierces that barrier. The manufacturer of today, but for a sampling, would be out of touch with the people who use his product, or those who might use it.

THE OLD WAY

Manufacturers used to think of manufacturing in three steps, as shown in Fig. 6.2. Success depended on guess-work—guessing what type and design of product would sell, how much of it to make. In the old way, the three steps of Fig. 6.2 are completely independent.

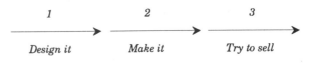

Fig. 6.2
The Old Way

THE NEW WAY

In the new way, management introduces, through consumer research, a 4th step, and runs through the four steps in a *cycle*, over and over as in Fig. 6.3, and not in the *line* of Fig. 6.2.

1. Design the product (with appropriate tests)
2. Make it, test it in the production line and in the laboratory

3. Put it on the market
4. Test it in service, through market research, find out what the user thinks of it, and why the non-user has not bought it
5. *Re*-design the product, in the light of consumer reactions to quality and price

Continue around and around the cycle

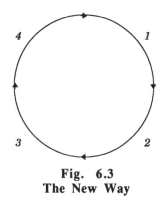

Fig. 6.3
The New Way

This 4th step in Fig. 3 was impossible until recently—i.e., it could not be carried out economically or reliably. Modern statistical techniques, such as sampling and design of experiment, combined with the arts of questioning and interviewing, provide information on consumer reactions with economy and reliability. Intelligent manufacturers have always been interested in discovering the needs and the reactions of the user and the potential user, but until recently they had no economical or reliable way of investigating them.

The 4th step, communication between the manufacturer and the user and the potential user, gives the public a chance. It gives the user a better product, better suited to his needs, and cheaper. *Democracy in industry*, one might say.

A still better way is to begin the manufacturing and marketing of a product on a pilot scale, and to build up its production on a sound economic basis, only as fast as market conditions indicate, re-designing the product from time to time in the light of consumer needs and reactions. The cycle is best taken on a spiral, as in Fig. 6.4.

It is not to be supposed that the first three steps are the same in the figures that display the old and new ways. Con-

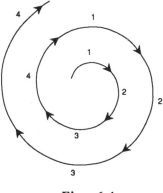

Fig. 6.4
The Spiral Cycle

sider, for example, design in Step 1. Proper design today means not only attention to color, shape, size, hardness, strength, and finish, but attention also to a suitable degree of uniformity—enough, but not so much that the article is priced out of the market. In consumer research, the 4th step, the manufacturer studies the requirements of uniformity, as well as of color, shape, size, hardness, etc.. Then, through statistical procedures he achieves uniformity with economy, and his control charts furnish proof of uniformity.

Consumer research is a continuous process by which the product is continually improved and modified to meet changing requirements of the consumer. Consumer research, intelligently used, enables the manufacturer to run his factory on an even keel, neither greatly over-producing nor under-producing. He does not let out 300 men one month and try to recover them the next. Consumer research used in this way is a powerful factor in economical production. Again, it is only one of the indispensable statistical tools of production.

Will you think of some important area in your own manufacturing plan, where some article is being made, shaped, assembled, soldered, or welded? Are the results uniform? Are they 100% successful? Are there any failures? Are these articles inspected? Are any articles rejected afterward in inspection?

Now I ask this question: Do you know how many (what percentage) of these articles were failures or were rejected last week, or on any day last week? Were any records kept? If so, *was any use made of the records*?

Inspection of a product in its various stages of manufacture and assembly is a good idea, but it is not enough. Inspection is not quality control, and quality control is not inspection. Quality control is *action*. My friend Mr. Harold F. Dodge of the Bell Telephone Laboratories once said: "You can not inspect quality into a product." He meant that you must *build* quality: you must make the product so that it has quality in it, if you want quality. Quality is not built by making a great number of articles, hoping that some of them will be good, and then sorting out the bad ones. Your company, or anyone else's whether it is in Tokyo or Chicago, will go bankrupt if it attempts to operate in that way today.

Here you will learn something about the use of statistical techniques for trimming the costs of manufacturing, and in improving the quality and uniformity of your product. As I said earlier, you can not learn the entire subject in 8 days. You will learn some elementary principles. I hope that you will continue your statistical studies for many years. If you are going to succeed today as engineers, executives, or economists, you must know and use a lot of statistical theory.

If I succeed in inspiring you to continue your studies, then my efforts in this course will be successful, and I shall be happy.

Chapter Six

Chapter Seven
What Happened in Japan?

This chapter is taken directly from the reprint of Dr. Deming's article, "What Happened in Japan?". It was written about 1966 and forms of it have appeared in *SANKHYA* (Calcutta), series B, vol. 28: 1966 and *Industrial Quality Control,* Vol. 24, No. 2, August 1967: pp. 89–93.

This article contains the genesis of much that is today commonly referred to as Deming Philosophy: Deming Theory, The Fourteen Points, Deadly Diseases, and Profound Knowledge. To study the original teaching, within the original context, is helpful to those seeking a deeper understanding of Dr. Deming's teachings and how it can and should be applied. Once you understand the history of the quality movement, it is easier to understand why these methods and ideas are important to the future welfare of American industry.

What Happened in Japan?

W. EDWARDS DEMING

Consultant in Statistical Surveys, Washington

> Dedicated to my friend and colleague
> WALTER A. SHEWHART
> 1891–1967
> whose works have raised the quality
> of living the world over.

Introduction and Purpose of This Article

The competitive position of many Japanese products, according to the testimony of their own manufacturers, has been achieved largely through understanding and use of the statistical control of quality in the broad sense (*vide infra*). Statistical techniques were not wholly responsible for what happened, as deeper perspective of later paragraphs will bring forth, but statistical techniques certainly played an important role in the miracle. The first step was to fire up desire on the part of management to improve quality and to impart confidence that improvement was possible; that utilization of statistical techniques would help.

The purpose of this article is to offer some observations on the causes of success in Japan, from the viewpoint of the statistical control of quality, with the thought that energetic application of statistical techniques in other parts of the world, including the United States, might have healthy impact. Appreciation of what happened in Japan might also be taken seriously on programs of scientific and professional societies that are interested in statistical methods applied to production.

Nine Features of Quality in Japan

As I see it, there are nine main reasons for the success and speed of application of the statistical control of quality by Japanese manufacturers:

1. Genuine and resolute determination on the part of management to improve quality.

2. Confidence in their ability to lead Japanese industry forth from the bad reputation that Japanese products had built up in the past, confidence in Japanese scientific ability, and confidence in Japanese skills. Confidence also, I might add, in statistical methods.

3. They were Japanese, with industrial experience, and with an inbred pride of workmanship.

4. Japanese top management, statisticians, and engineers learned the statistical control of quality in the broad sense of Shewhart, as defined further on.

5. Management took immediate interest and learned something about the techniques of the statistical control of quality as well as about the possible results, and still more about what their own responsibilities would be. Proper arrangements for contact with top management, at the outset, was one of the fortunate features of statistical education in Japan.

6. Statistical education became a continuing process. Statistical methods can not be installed once for all and left to run, like a new carpet or a new dean. They require constant adaptation, revision, extension, new theory, and new knowledge of the statistical properties of materials. Perhaps the main accomplishment in the eight-day courses that began in 1950 was to impart inspiration to learn more about statistical methods.

7. The Japanese learned the difference between a statistical problem and one in engineering, chemistry, management, or marketing. They learned that statistical knowledge is not a substitute for knowledge of engineering or of other subject-matter, and that knowledge of engineering does not solve statistical problems.

8. Japanese manufacturers took on the job themselves. They did not look to their government nor to ours for help. When they arranged for consultation, they sent a ticket and a cheque. They gave financial and moral

support to statistical education, mainly through the Union of Japanese Scientists and Engineers.

9. Suggestions and technical information have a fairly clear channel from lower to higher levels of supervision and management. A Japanese executive is never too old or too successful to listen to the possibility of doing it a better way.

One ought also to mention the stimulus of a prize offered annually in the name of an American statistician to the Japanese manufacturer who in the opinion of the Committee on Awards, has made the greatest advance in quality of his product during the past calendar-year. Many companies compete for the prize, often laying plans years in advance. Although only one company, or at most two, can receive the prize, the continual competition of many companies has had an important leavening effect in quality.

Lectures to Top Management

Lectures to management, beginning in 1950, brought up a few simple questions to think about. I am not an economist, nor a business-man, only a statistician, but some conclusions seemed inescapable. Why was it necessary to improve quality of Japanese products? Because Japanese products must now become competitive: the market in Asia was lost. The market for poor quality in the western world is a losing game.

It is not necessary to raise all your own food, it seemed to me. Chicago doesn't. Switzerland doesn't. It may be smarter for Japan to import food and pay for it with exports. There is a market for quality. How do you build quality, and a reputation for quality?

No country is so able as Japan, I pointed out, with its vast pool of skilled and educated industrial manpower, and with so many highly proficient engineers, mathematicians, and statisticians, to improve quality. Statistical methods could help: in fact, realization of any goal to raise quality to a sufficiently high level would be impossible without statistical methods on a broad scale. Seeing their serious determination, I predicted at an assembly of Japanese manufacturers in Tokyo in July 1950 that in five years, manufacturers in other industrial nations would be on the defensive and that in ten years the reputation for top quality in Japanese products would be firmly established the world over.

Management must assume the responsibility to optimize the use of statistical methods in all stages of manufacture, and to understand the statistical control of quality as a never-ending cycle of improved methods of manufacture, test, consumer research, and re-design of product. Lectures described in simple terms management's responsibility to understand the capability of the process, management's responsibility for common causes (*vide infra*), and the economic loss from failure to accept these responsibilities.

Japanese manufacturers took these arguments seriously to the point of doing something about them with concerted effort. A little fire here, and a little there, would be too slow. Concerted effort meant cooperation amongst competitors, assistance to vendors, and—probably for the first time in Japan—immediate attention to the demands of the consumer, and need for consumer research on a continuing basis, with feed-back for re-design.

Results were spectacular, even after only one year, especially in productivity per man-hour, with little new machinery. One steel company saved 28 percent on consumption of coal per ton of steel. A huge pharmaceutical company put out three times as much finished product per unit of input of raw material. A big cable company reduced greatly the amount of paper and re-work on insulated wire and cable. Many companies reduced accidents to a permanent low level. Improvement in quality and dependability came in due course, and in five years, as predicted, many Japanese products had earned respect to the point of fear in markets the world over.

Definition of the Statistical Control of Quality

The Japanese never knew the statistical control of quality in any way but in the broad sense introduced by Shewhart.[1] The statistical control of quality was defined in plain English in 1950 and ever after in big letters like this:

---

[1]W.A. Shewhart, *The Economic Control of Quality of Manufactured Product* (Van Nostrand, 1931): *Statistical Method from the Viewpoint of Quality Control* (The Graduate School, Department of Agriculture, Washington 1939). "Nature and Origin of Standards of Quality," *Bell System Technical Journal*, xxxvii. 1958: pp. 1–22. No attempt is made here to give a full list of Dr. Shewhart's papers.

THE STATISTICAL CONTROL OF QUALITY IS
THE APPLICATION OF STATISTICAL PRINCIPLES
AND TECHNIQUES IN ALL STAGES OF PRODUC-
TION, DIRECTED TOWARD THE ECONOMIC MANU-
FACTURE OF A PRODUCT THAT IS MAXIMALLY
USEFUL AND HAS A MARKET.

Translated into action, this definition of the statistical control of quality means:

1. Use of statistical methods to construct meaningful specifications of raw materials, piece-parts, assemblies, and performance of finished product, by appropriate statistical design.

2. Assistance to suppliers. Any raw material or piece-part is someone's finished product. Improvement of quality of incoming materials from vendors or from a previous operation is one of the most important requirements in a program of quality.

3. Control of process. Detection of special causes by statistical methods ($\overline{X}$- and R-charts, run-charts, design of experiment, and other techniques). Distinction between special causes and common causes, with examples. Separation of responsibility for finding and removing:

    a. Special causes of variability (local).
    b. Common or general causes of variability (upper management).

4. Use of acceptance sampling where appropriate.

5. Consumer research. Test of product in service.

6. Re-design of product.

7. Tests of new product, in the laboratory and in service.

8. Use of proper theory for finding optimum levels of inventory, and for economy in distribution.

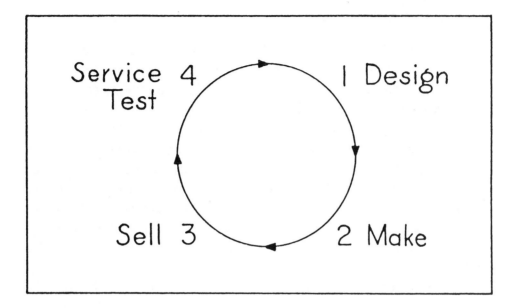

Figure 7.1
Cycle of Applied Statistical Methods

The statistical method shown in the figure was taught as a continuing process, in a never-ending cycle:

1. Design a product
2. Make it
3. Try to sell it
4. Test it in service
5. Repeat Step 1. Re-design the product on the basis of tests in service.
6. Repeat Step 2
7. Repeat Step 3, etc..

Special (Assignable) Contrasted with Common (General) Causes of Variation or of Wrong Level

One of the important uses of statistical techniques is to help an engineer or scientist to distinguish between two types of cause, and hence to fix (with adjustable risk of being wrong) the responsibility for correction of undesired variability or of undesired level.

Confusion between common causes and special causes is one of the most serious mistakes of administration in industry, and in public administration as well. Unaided by statistical techniques, man's natural reaction to trouble of any kind, such as an accident, high rejection-rate, stoppage of production (of shoes, for example, because of breakage of thread) is to blame a specific operator or machine. Anything bad that happens, it might seem, is somebody's fault, and it wouldn't have happened if he had done his job right.

Actually, however, the cause of trouble may be common to all machines, *e.g.*, poor thread, the fault of management, whose policy may be to buy thread locally or from a subsidiary. Demoralization, frustration, and economic loss are inevitable results of attributing trouble to some specific operator, foreman, machine, or other local condition, when the trouble is actually a common cause, affecting all operators and machines, and correctable only at a higher level of management.

The specific local operator is powerless to act on a common cause. He can not change specifications of raw materials. He can not alter the policy of purchase of materials. He can not change the lighting system. He might as well try to change the speed of rotation of the earth.

A mistake common amongst workers in the statistical control of quality, and amongst writers of textbooks on the subject, is to assume that they have solved all the problems once they have weeded out most of the special causes. The fact is, instead, that they are at that point just ready to tackle the most important problems of variation, namely, the common causes.

Special Causes of Variation

Variation of any quality-characteristic is to be expected. The question is whether the variation arises from a special cause, or from common causes. A point outside limits on a control chart indicates the existence of a special cause. Special causes are what Shewhart called assignable causes. The name is not important; the concept is.

Statistical techniques, based as they are on the theory of probability, enable us to govern the risk of being wrong in the interpretation of a test. Statistical techniques defend us, almost unerringly, against the costly and demoralizing practice of blaming variability and rejections on to the wrong person or machine. At the same time, they detect almost unerringly the existence of a special cause when it is worth searching for.

What statistical tests do, in effect, is not just to detect the existence of a special cause, or the absence of special causes; they do more; they indicate the level of responsibility for finding the cause and for removing it. The contribution that statistical methods make in placing responsibility squarely where it belongs (at the local operator, at the foreman, or at the door of higher management) can hardly be over-estimated.

This aspect of the statistical control of quality was not appreciated, I believe, in the earlier history of statistical methods in American industry, and is even now neglected. The Japanese had the benefit of advanced thinking on the matter.

Common Causes of Variation and of Wrong Spread, Wrong Level

If we succeed in removing all special causes worth removing, then henceforth (until another special cause appears), variations in quality behave as if they came from common causes. That is, they have the same random scatter as if the units of product were being drawn by random numbers from a common supply. The remaining causes of variability are then common to all treatments, to all operators, to all machines, etc..

Some common causes are in the following list. The reader may supply others, appropriate to his own plant and conditions.

- Poor light
- Humidity not suited to the process
- Vibration
- Poor instruction and poor supervision
- Lack of interest of management in a program for quality
- Poor food in the cafeteria
- Inept management
- Raw materials not suited to the requirements
- Procedures not suited to the requirements
- Machines not suited to the requirements
- Mixing product from streams of production, each having small variability, but a different level

Common causes are usually much more difficult to identify than specific causes, and more difficult to correct. In the first place, carefully designed tests may be required to identify a common cause. Then problems really commence. Would it be economically feasible to change the specifications for incoming material? to change the design of the product? to install new machinery? to change the lighting? to put in air-conditioning? Only management can take action on these things. If the trouble lies in management itself, who is going to make the correction?

Although the detection and removal of special causes are important, it is a fact that some of the finest examples of improvement of quality have come from effort directed at common causes of variation and at causes of wrong level. One example, interesting because it is outside the usual sphere of industrial production, is the improvement of quality and decrease in the cost of statistical data put out by the Census in Washington. For many years, effort has been directed at common causes of the system that lead to error and to high cost, as well as elimination of special causes. The result today is quality, reliability, and speed of current statistical series that are the envy of other statistical organizations in the U.S. and abroad, and at costs that are about a third of what private industry in this country pays out for similar surveys in consumer research.

Other Statistical Techniques

Consumer research was taught as an integral part of the statistical control of quality. In fact, small surveys of household inventories and requirements of pharmaceuticals, sewing machines, bicycles, and the like, constituted part of the course in sampling in the summer of 1951. These have been designated by the Japanese as the first studies in consumer research to be carried out by Japanese companies with the aid of modern methods of sampling.

Shewhart charts were taught in Japan as statistical tools for the economic detection of the existence of special causes of variation, not as tools that actually find the cause. However, emphasis was on action, find the cause and remove it, once a point goes outside limits. Once statistical control is established, then do something about common causes.

Problems in statistical estimation are very important in industrial production, as in decisions on whether one type of machine is sufficiently better than another to warrant the cost of replacement, or to warrant the higher cost of purchase of a better machine. Consumer research presents hosts of problems in estimation. Determinations of the iron-content of a shipload of ore is a common problem in estimation.

In a problem of estimation, one is not seeking to detect the existence of a special cause. He is not trying to discover whether there is a difference such as p_1-p_2 of x_1-x_2 between two processes, or between two machines, standard and proposed. One knows in advance, without spending a nickel on a test, that there is a difference; the only question is how big is the difference?

Statistical calculations using data from two samples (coming from two treatments, two operators, two machines, two processes) provide a basis on which to decide, with a prescribed risk of being wrong, (a) whether it would be economical to proceed as if the two samples came from a common source, or (b) whether it would be more economical to assume the converse, and to proceed as if the difference has its origin in a special cause, not common to the samples, which makes one of the treatments, operators, machines, or processes different from the other. Essential considerations in fixing the probability of being wrong lie in the economic losses to be expected (a) from the failure of being too cautious—failure to make a change that would turn out to be profitable, or (b) from making a change that turns out to be costly and unwarranted.

The teaching of statistical methods in Japan did not confuse statistical estimation, nor Shewhart charts, with statistical tests of hypotheses.

The effectiveness of mass education in statistical methods in Japan was more pronounced and more rapid than results observed in the U.S.. In the first place, Japan was in 1950 in desperate circumstances. Every minute must count. Second, management was more responsive. Third, practically everyone in attendance at technical sessions in Japan had studied calculus.

A vigorous system of courses for continuation and advancement in theory was instituted by the Union of Japanese Scientists and Engineers. The levels are varied. The duration, days, and hours meet the requirements of engineers who must come from distant points, as well as for those that live in or near Tokyo. Some idea of the thoroughness of the courses for continuation and advancement may be gained by perusal of bulletins from the Union of Japanese Scientists and Engineers.[2]

An additional point of strength came from the formation of committees to work on new theory, and to investigate various areas of application, such as the sampling of bulk materials (mainly ores), design of experiment, queueing theory, and other problems. The impact of the work of these committees has substantially changed much industrial practice in Japan.

---

[2]Kenichi Koyanagi, "Statistical Quality Control in Japanese Industry," a paper delivered at the national convention of the American Society for Quality Control in Syracuse, 1952. Also, his paper, "Some Case Histories of Increased Production and Improved Quality Through Simple Techniques in Japanese Industry," and another, "Education Activities for Industrial Statistics in Japan," both presented at the 29th Congress of the International Statistical Institute, Rio de Janeiro, 1955; "Quality Emphasis in Japan's Postwar Trade," C.I.O.S., International Management Congress, New York, September 1963.

Publication of a journal *Statistical Quality Control* (in Japanese) was started by the Union of Japanese Scientists and Engineers; the journal is now in its 18th year. *Research Reports*, a journal now in its 17th year, has a high reputation amongst mathematical statisticians the world over. A journal specifically for foremen has been started, and one for engineers.

Some idea of the importance of these Japanese publications may be had by noting that in the *International Journal of Abstracts*, a third of the citations refer to Japanese journals.

Chapter Seven

Chapter Eight
Walter A. Shewhart

Walter A. Shewhart was a great friend, mentor, and colleague to Dr. Deming. They met in the fall of 1927 and spent much time working together thereafter. Their working-friendship was beyond value to the profession. The first article in this chapter was written by Dr. Deming in 1967, as a memorial to his friend, Walter A. Shewhart. It has appeared in the April, 1967 issue of "The American Statistician" and was reprinted in the August, 1967 issue of "Industrial Quality Control," the forerunner of "Quality Progress," which was published by the American Society for Quality Control. This article is followed by the introduction Dr. Deming wrote for the 1980 edition of Dr. Shewhart's book, *Economic Control of Quality of Manufactured Product.* The last section is the dedication Dr. Deming wrote for the book, *Statistical Method from the Viewpoint of Quality Control.* This book was based on the series of four lectures given by Dr. Shewhart at the Graduate School of the Department of Agriculture. These lectures were edited by Dr. Deming and published in 1939.

Walter A. Shewhart, Ph.D.
1891–1967

*Another half-century may pass
before the full spectrum of Dr. Shewhart's contributions
has been revealed in liberal education, science, and industry.*

W. Edwards Deming

A Tribute to Walter A. Shewhart
On the Occasion of the 100th Anniversary of his Birth

I write as one outside the Bell System who had the privilege of working intimately with Dr. Shewhart over a period of years. This could happen only because he was always glad to help anyone. Actually, he never thought of himself as helping anyone: he was simply glad to talk and absorb thoughts from anyone who was genuinely struggling to improve his understanding of the statistical method—interchanging ideas was his way to put it. And to Dr. Shewhart it was the statistical method in the singular, not in the plural. Statistical methods are necessary, but they are the tools and pass-words by which the statistician works and communicates in applying the statistical method.

It was Dr. Shewhart who emphasized the theory of probability as the tool of the statistician. It is his knowledge and use of the theory of probability that distinguishes the statistician from the expert in chemistry, agriculture, bacteriology, medicine, production, consumer research, engineering, or anything else. Otherwise, the statistician would be merely another chemist, another agricultural scientist, or something else.

Quality control meant to him use of statistical methods all the way from raw material to consumer and back again, through redesign of product, re-working of specifications of raw materials, in a continuous cycle as results come in from consumer research and from other tests.

He was quick to see that quality must mean not necessarily high quality, but dependable and economic quality, which in turn meant quality suited to the purpose. But what quality is suited to the purpose? Statistical methods for discovery of what product is needed, what quality is needed, and for learning how a product performs in service and in the laboratory are thus necessary ingredients of the statistical control of quality.

The world knows him for the Shewhart control charts, and the world lives better for them. They are, however, only one of his statistical contributions. He leaves a rich legacy that it will take years to absorb. For example, his Rules 1 and 2 on the presentation of data:

Rule 1. Original data should be presented in a way that will preserve the evidence in the original data for all the predictions assumed to be useful.

Rule 2. Any summary of a distribution of numbers should not give an objective degree of belief in any one of the inferences or predictions to be made therefrom that would cause human action significantly different from what this action would be if the original distribution had been taken as a basis for evidence.

Then there is his Criterion of Meaning:

Every sentence in order to have definite scientific meaning must be practically or at least theoretically verifiable as either true or false upon the basis of experimental measurements either practically or theoretically obtainable by carrying out a definite and previously specified operation in the future. The meaning of such a sentence is the method of its verification.

The above rules and criterion of meaning were to him a necessary ingredient of industrial research for the reason that, as he stated, industrial research is more exacting than pure science. His faith in the power of the statistical method in all human enquiry was unshakable.

He acknowledged an everlasting debt to C.I. Lewis' *Mind and the World Order* (Scribner 1929), which he recommended to me. I had the usual difficulty with it, and I recall saying to Dr. Shewhart at the end of the seventh reading that so far it had meant nothing to me. "Stay with it," he said, "I read it fourteen times before it began to mean anything." I wonder how he came upon it in the first place, and how he knew how important it was that he should pursue it.

Although operational definitions, his criteria of meaning, and his Rules 1 and 2 for the presentation of data, have been known to scientists for several generations, no one to my knowledge has stated them so well as Shewhart. One sees in them C.I. Lewis in the background.

Hypothesis is necessary. Some knowledge must be *a priori*, even if shown later by observation to be untenable. Without theory (hypothesis), data are meaningless or nonexistent. There is thus no true value of anything: true value is undefinable operationally. There are, however, numerical values that people can use with confidence if they understand their meaning (for the tensile strength of a batch of wire, for example, or for the proportion of the labor force unemployed last month).

There was to Shewhart no such thing as a random sample. There was and is, however, such a thing as a sample selected by a random operation. There may be a concept of randomness, but one can not communicate it. What one can communicate is an operational definition of a random operation (for example, proper use of random numbers). Likewise, one can only define yellow, green, tired, unemployed, one inch, in terms of an operation. The particular operation will vary with the needs of the subject-matter.

There is accordingly no such thing as factual information, distinguished from (*e.g.*) judgments. Physical measurements are no exception. There are no facts except as man makes them. Man gets marks on a piece of paper in response to a stimulus. Such marks on paper and tabulations made from them are useful only if the method of investigation is suited to the purpose.

Although his explanations could be simple and clear in a face-to-face discussion, his greatest papers remain as difficult for the reader as they were for him to write. As he told me once, when he writes, he must make it foolproof. I replied in a particular instance that he had made it so foolproof that no one would understand it.

His book of 1931 will remain a monument, but it was his book *Statistical Method From the Viewpoint of Quality Control* (The Graduate School, Dept. of Agriculture, Washington 1939), based on his four lectures given in Washington in 1938, that exposed Shewhart to the statistical world. People then began to understand something about his contributions.

To appreciate a mite of his greatness, one must read not only the two books just mentioned, but his article, "Nature and origin of standards of quality," *Bell System Technical Journal*, xxxvii, 1958, pages 1–22. (Although this article was published in 1958, he actually wrote it in 1935.) One can only ask why schools of business don't require this article to be read by all professors and students. Why don't people engaged in consumer research and in advertising research read it? Some day they will.

There was a time when some people pushed the idea of probability limits on the control-chart, instead of Shewhart's 3-sigma limits. No one could appreciate more than Shewhart the ability of the theory of probability to adjust the limits to the requirements, but he had the uncanny prescience to see that because of fluctuations of level that must continually occur in a production-process, the 3-sigma limits would do the job. He saw further that statistical control is not a matter of estimation nor of testing a hypothesis, but rather a rule of behavior that will strike a balance for the net economic loss from two sources of mistake: (1) looking for special causes (he called them assignable causes) too often, or overadjusting; (2) not looking often enough.

Although use of the control chart for detection of special (assignable) causes of variability is extremely important, reduction of special causes is only the start on the road to quality. There is of course, besides special causes, the important problem of common causes of variability.

Although the writing of papers and books was difficult for him, and his efforts often went wide of the mark, nevertheless one of his great powers lay in his perseverance in communication by letter. He used this power to work through committees. He knew the importance of getting a strong man at the head of a committee, and he was adept at pushing him in the right direction, without himself being visible. He made his points not so much by giving his own point of view but by asking questions—embarrassing questions. Establishment of Committee E-11 on statistical methods in the American Society for Testing and Materials is an example of this type of accomplishment. The American Standards, *Guide For Quality Control* and *Control Chart Method of Analyzing Data*, written by a small committee under the guidance of Harold Dodge, and published by the American Standards Association in 1941 and 1942 (known as the Z-pamphlets from their code-numbers Z1.1, .2, .3) is another example. The Z-pamphlets met immediate acceptance, and are still best sellers. They were translated and adopted by standardizing bodies in practically all industrial nations of the world. The Shewhart statistical series published by Wiley is another example. He sought out the great thinkers and invited them to write. That an author might disagree with Shewhart's point of view made no difference to Shewhart, so long as a book would stimulate people to think.

A contribution of a technical nature is the formula

$$\bar{n} = \frac{\sigma_w}{\sigma_b} \sqrt{\frac{c_1}{c_2}}$$

for the optimum number of tests per unit, or for the optimum number of segments to cover in a block or other area. His book of 1931 and Tippett's book *The Methods of Statistics*, published also in 1931, both gave this formula, for the first time, I believe.

As a statistician, he was, like so many of the rest of us, self-taught, on a good background of physics and mathematics. He respected advanced knowledge of statistical theory, and studied daily, but he was not always happy the way people recommended statistical techniques for use.

As a man, he was gentle, genteel, never ruffled, never off his dignity. He knew disappointment and frustration, through failure of many writers in mathematical statistics to understand his point of view. He also knew success. He was President of the American Statistical Association in 1945, and was twice President of the Institute of Mathematical Statistics, 1937 and 1944. One of the highlights of his life was an invitation from Karl Pearson to give lectures at University College in London in 1932. A visit to Japan later in life where he saw spectacular results of statistical methods applied in the broad sense of Shewhart must have been great satisfaction to him. He went to India three times as a guest of Professor Mahalanobis at the Indian Statistical Institute, and received therefrom in 1962 the honorary degree D. Sc..

Economic Control of Quality of Manufactured Product

Written by
W. A. SHEWHART, PH.D.

Dedication Written by W. Edwards Deming

People who are interested in serious study of quality control will welcome the reprinting of Dr. Shewhart's great work, *The Economic Control of Manufactured Product*, long out of print.[1] This book did more than lay a foundation; it touched quality control in all aspects—specifications, problems with inspection of incoming materials and with inspection all along the line, improvement of the process, operational definitions, problems in the definition of quality. The consumer, to Shewhart, was the most important part of the production-line. Without the consumer, production ceases.

Quality aimed at, to meet the needs of the consumer, must be stated in terms of specified quality-characteristics that can be measured. It is necessary to predict what quality-characteristics of a product will produce satisfaction in use.

Quality, however, to the consumer, is not a set of specifications. The quality of any product is interaction between the product, the user, his expectations, and the service that he can get in case the product fails or requires maintenance. The needs of the consumer are in continual change. So are materials, methods of manufacture, and products. Quality of a product does not necessarily mean high quality. It means continual improvement of the process, so that the consumer may depend on the uniformity of

---

[1]Walter A. Shewhart, Ph.D. *Economic Control of Quality of Manufactured Product.* Originally published in 1931 by D. Van Nostrand Company, Inc. Republished in 1980 as a 50th Anniversary Commemorative Reissue by American Society for Quality Control, Milwaukee.

a product and purchase it at low cost. Chapters IV and XVIII in Shewhart's book are a masterpiece on the meaning of quality.

To Shewhart, quality control meant every activity and every technique that can contribute to better living, in a material sense, through economy in manufacture. His book emphasizes the need for continual search for better knowledge about materials, how they behave in manufacture, and how the product behaves in use. Economic manufacture requires achievement of statistical control in the process and statistical control of measurements. The cost and inadequacy of inspection are well known. The ultimate aim of quality control should accordingly be elimination of inspection except for small samples for assurance of continuation of statistical control and for comparison of measurements between vendor and purchaser, manufacturer and customer, etc..

As the Japanese learned in 1950, productivity moves upward as the quality of process improves. One requires only 4th grade arithmetic to see this. If action of the process (as by introduction of operational definitions for a quality-characteristic) decreases defectives from 8% to 4%, any school boy can understand that this means at least 4% greater productivity. Waste is cut to half. It is important to note that this gain is accomplished with no outlay for new equipment. Besides, there is the long-run benefit that better quality achieves in the market-place, plus improvement in morale of the work-force. The next step is further improvement of the process for further reduction of the proportion defective, and further gain in productivity.

Tests of variables that affect a process are useful only if they predict what will happen if this or that variable is increased or decreased. It is only with material produced in statistical control that one may talk about an experiment as a conceptual sample that could be extended to infinite size. Unfortunately, this supposition, basic to the analysis of variance and to many other statistical techniques, is as unrealizable as it is vital in much experimentation carried out in industry, agriculture, and medicine.

Statistical theory as taught in the books is valid and leads to operationally verifiable tests and criteria for an enumerative study. Not so with an analytic problem, as the conditions of the experiment will not be duplicated in the next trial. Unfortunately, most problems in industry are analytic.

The needs of industry for something better from statisticians always bothered Shewhart. No wonder. As he often said, the requirements of industry are more exacting than the requirements for research in pure science. Industry requires statistical methods that are efficient. Good data are costly. Why waste information that can help to improve a process when efficient methods are known and are simple?

The scientific importance of controlled measurements in research has let Dr. Heihachi Sakamoto of Keio University to classify the problems of statistics into three types: enumerative, analytic, and methods by which to achieve statistical control.

Anyone who has tried to draw random samples of poker chips from a bowl, as Shewhart tried, and as Tippett tried, or anyone who has tried to bring use of a simple instrument into statistical control, can and should raise questions about how one can use some of the statistical methods taught today. It was in fact Tippett's difficulties with home-made cards that led him, at the suggestion of Karl Pearson, to construct his well known table of random numbers, and be rid of cards and poker chips forever.

Chapters XII and XIII form an excellent text on statistical methods. For example, the formula

$$\text{Opt } n_2 = \frac{\sigma_E}{\sigma_T} \sqrt{\frac{a_1}{a_2}}$$

for the optimum number of measurements to take on a selected unit is on page 389. Here σ_E is the standard deviation between measurements, σ_T the standard deviation between units, a_1 is the cost to select a unit and make it available for measurement, a_2 the cost of each measurement. Curiously, Tippett published the same formula, the same year, in his book, *The Methods of Statistics*, now in the Wiley statistical series. The power of statistical theory is well illustrated by the uses made of this formula by these two authors: Shewhart was sampling wire; Tippett was sampling soils in England.

Although considerations of probability and distributions are basic to the control chart, Shewhart perceived that control limits must serve industry in action. A manufacturing process, even in statistical control, wavers. Control limits can thus not be associated with any exact probability of looking for trouble (an assignable cause) when there is none, nor with failure to look for trouble when an assignable cause does exist. It was for such reasons that he used 3-sigma limits. Experience of 50 years shows how right he was.

Another contribution from Shewhart is his recognition of the need for operational definitions. An operational definition is one that is communicable. How can an operator carry out his job if he does not know what the job is? How can he know what the job is if what he produced yesterday was right, but the same thing is wrong today? Inspection, no matter whether the operator inspects his own work or relies on someone else to do it for him, must have operational definitions for quality-characteristics. A system of measurement, whether by machine or visual, must exhibit statistical control. Otherwise, production can only remain in chaos.

An operational definition translates a concept (round, random, safe, conforming, good) into a test and a criterion—yes, it is sufficiently round, sufficiently safe, or it is not. The test-method and the criterion to have meaning for business or legal purposes can only be stated in statistical terms: likewise a standard for safety, reliability, or performance.

There was never before greater need for statistical methods in industry and in research. The whole world is talking about safety in mechanical and electrical devices (in automobiles, for example), safety in drugs, reliability, due care, pollution, poverty, nutrition, improvement of agricultural practice, improvement in quality of product, break-down of service, breakdown of equipment, tardy busses, trains, and mail, need for greater output in industry and in agriculture, enrichment of jobs. The consumer requires month by month ever greater and greater safety, and he expects better and better performance of manufactured articles. The manufacturer has the same problems in his purchases of materials, assemblies, machines, and use of manpower. He must, in addition, know more and more about his own product. What is due care in manufacturing?

These problems can not be understood and can not even be stated, nor can the effect of any alleged solution be evaluated, without the aid of statistical theory and methods.

Study of Dr. Shewhart's great book will assist production and will bring better living to people the world over. It is fitting and proper that the American Society for Quality Control should reprint this monumental work.

June 1980

Statistical Method
from the Viewpoint of Quality Control

Written by
WALTER A. SHEWHART

Foreword written by W. Edwards Deming

The present book gave Dr. Shewhart an opportunity to elaborate on a number of principles that he had already stated and applied in his great book *The Economic Control of Manufactured Product* (Van Nostrand, 1931) and in a number of papers. The origin of the present book lies in four lectures delivered at my invitation in Washington in 1938 under the auspices of the Graduate School of the Department of Agriculture.[2]

---

[2]Walter A. Shewhart, Ph.D. *Statistical Method from the Viewpoint of Quality Control*. Originally: Washington: Graduate School of the Department of Agriculture, 1939. Dover edition published in 1986; an unabridged republication of the original work. The new foreword has been written by W. Edwards Deming for this edition, and he holds the copyright.

The important principles explained here include Dr. Shewhart's rules for presentation of data (pp. 89–92). Any conclusion or statement, if it is to have use for science or industry, must add to the degree of belief for rational prediction. The reader may reflect on the fact that the only reason to carry out a test is to improve a process, to improve the quality and quantity of the next run or of next year's crop. Important questions in science and industry are how and under what conditions observations may contribute to a rational decision to change or not to change a process to accomplish improvements. A record of observations must accordingly contain all the information that anyone might need in order to make his own prediction.

This information will include not merely numerical data, but also, (for example): the names of observers, the type of apparatus or measurement system used, a description of materials used, the temperature and humidity, a description of efforts taken to reduce error, the side effects and other external factors that in the judgment of the expert in the subject matter may be helpful for use of the results.

Omission from data (as of a test or a run of production) of information on the order of the observations may well bury, for purposes of prediction (*i.e.*, for planning), nearly all the information that there is in the test. Any symmetric function loses the information that is contained in the order of observation. Thus, the mean, the standard deviation—in fact any moment—is in most applications inefficient, as it causes the loss of all information that is contained in the order of observation. A distribution is another example of a symmetric function. Original data plotted in order of production may provide much more information than is contained in the distribution.

Dr. Shewhart was well aware that the statistician's levels of significance furnish no measure of belief in a prediction. Probability has use; tests of significance do not.

There is no true value of anything. There is, instead, a figure that is produced by application of a master or ideal method of counting or of measurement. This figure may be accepted as a standard until the method of measurement is supplanted by experts in the subject matter with some other method and some other figure. There is no true value of the speed of light; no true value of the number of inhabitants within the boundaries of *(e.g.)* Detroit. A count of the number of inhabitants of Detroit is dependent upon the application of arbitrary rules for carrying out the count. Repetition of an experiment or of a count will exhibit variation. Change in the method of measuring the speed of light produces a new result.

All this has been known for generations. What Dr. Shewhart demonstrates in this book is the importance of these principles in science and industry, whether it be manufacturing or service, including government service. The requirements of industry are more exacting than the requirements of pure science.

As with many contributors to science, literature, and the arts, Dr. Shewhart is best known for the least of his contributions—control charts. Control charts alone would be sufficient for eternal fame (even though, because of poor understanding of teachers and books, many students' applications seen in practice are faulty and may be doing more harm than good). The fact is that some of the greatest contributions from control charts lie in areas that are only partially explored so far, such as applications to supervision, management, and systems of measurement, including the standardization and use of instruments, test panels, and standard samples of chemicals and compounds.

The great contribution of control charts is to separate variation by rational methods into two sources: (1) the system itself (chance causes, Dr. Shewhart called them), the responsibility of management; and (2) assignable causes, called by Deming special causes, specific to some ephemeral event that can usually be discovered to the satisfaction of the expert on the job, and removed. A process is in *statistical control* when it is no longer afflicted with special causes. The performance of a process that is in statistical control is predictable.

A process has no measurable capability unless it is in statistical control. An instrument has no ascertainable precision unless observations made with it show statistical control. Results obtained by two instruments can not be usefully compared unless the two instruments are in statistical control.

Statistical control is ephemeral; there must be a running record for judging whether the state of statistical control still exists.

Every observation, numerical or otherwise, is subject to variation. Moreover, there is useful information in variation. The closest approach possible to a numerical evaluation of any so-called physical content, to any count, or to any characteristics of a process is a result that emanates from a system of measurement that shows evidence that it is in statistical control.

The expert in the subject matter holds the responsibility for the use of the data from a test.

Another half-century may pass before the full spectrum of Dr. Shewhart's contributions has been revealed in liberal education, science, and industry.

W. E. D.

WASHINGTON
June 1986

Chapter Eight

Chapter Nine
Principles of Professional Practice

Principles of Professional Statistical Practice

By W. Edwards Deming
Washington

I. Purpose and Scope

1. Purpose. Application of statistical theory has found wide acceptance and has made notable contributions in agriculture, medicine, industry, accounting, administration, and consumer research. It has made equal contributions to the natural and social sciences. Sampling and survey-design, along with statistical theory of response and non-response, form the structural framework of government statistical series of diverse types, and of censuses of population, agriculture, and commerce.

Statistical theory grows year by year more difficult and abstract, more and more a specialism, more and more powerful in application. Statistical theory is transferable. The specialist in statistical methods may find himself applying the same basic theory in a dozen different fields in a week, rotating through the same projects the next week. Or, he may work day after day primarily in a single substantive field.

Either way, the statistician requires certain principles of practice for effective use of statistical knowledge. Knowledge of statistical theory is necessary but not sufficient. Statistical theory does not provide a road-map toward effective use of itself. The purpose of this paper is to propose some principles of practice, and to explain their meaning in some of the situations that the statistician encounters.

The statistician has no magic touch by which he may come in at the stage of tabulation and make something of nothing. Neither will his advice, however wise in the early stages of a study, ensure successful execution and conclusion. Many a study, launched on the ways of elegant statistical design, later boggled in execution, ends up with results to which the theory of probability can contribute little.

Even though carried off with reasonable conformance to specifications, a study may fail through structural deficiencies in the method of investigation (questionnaire, type of test, technique of interviewing), to provide the information needed. The statistician may reduce the risk of this kind of failure by pointing out to his client[1] in the early stages of the study the nature of the contributions that he himself must put into it.

The purpose here is not to describe any new statistical techniques, nor old ones. Neither is it to convince anyone that statistical theory is important, nor how to become a successful statistician. Instead, the aim is to find and illustrate principles of practice by which statisticians may make effective use of their knowledge. Statistical practice is mostly a collaborative venture between statistician and experts in subject-matter. Logical princi-

---

[1]The word client will denote the expert or group of experts in a substantive field (medicine, engineering, production, marketing, psychology, agriculture, or other) who are responsible to the man that will pay the bill for the study.

ples of statistical practice will give greater effectiveness to the high returns that come from creative imagination on the part of the expert in the subject-matter with a logical and critical mind, and with a spice of ingenuity coupled with an eye for the simple and the humdrum (to borrow words from Bradford Hill [16]).

Previous writings on the subject have helped to clarify the position of statistical inference in legal evidence, and have pointed to the need for principles of practice and for principles for presentation of data [1], [5], [6], [7], [8], [9], [11], [12], [13], [15], [21], [25], [27]. This paper, in recognition of the need, attempts to lay out a road-map to meet it.

The recommendation offered here is simple in principle, *viz.*, to have logical rules concerning the division of responsibilities between the substantive and statistical aspects of a study, and to come to an understanding at the outset of an engagement, with everyone concerned in the study, on just what these principles mean in operation.

What is the logic behind a proper division of responsibilities? How important is this division? How does the statistician work with other experts and hold firm to the responsibilities that he prescribes?

In order to stay within the bounds of my own experience, the suggestions to be offered here will relate specifically to only a portion of theoretical statistics, namely, professional practice in sampling and in the design of experiments. The purpose of this paper will be served if these suggestions provide some guidance in areas in which they are less directly applicable, or even if they only stimulate interchange of ideas that will lead to further work on professional standards.

Incidentally, it seems to me that the salaried statistician should have the same responsibilities and principles of workmanship as the consulting statistician, whether he is on a salary or acts as a consultant. The same principles apply also to the statistician who works as a member of a research team.

Of course in a small place, the same man must sometimes work both as statistician and as engineer or other expert. The rules of statistical practice nevertheless remain the same. One should, to be effective, depend on statistical theory as a guide to valid and efficient plans for sampling and experimentation, and for safe statistical inferences. Substantive knowledge (engineering, medicine, marketing, psychology, or other) is no substitute for statistical theory.

2. What is a professional man? Professional practice stems from an expanding body of theory and from principles of application. A professional man aims at recognition and respect for his practice, not for himself alone, but for his colleagues as well. A professional man takes orders, in technical matters, from standards set by his professional colleagues as unseen judges; never from an administrative superior. His usefulness and his profession will suffer impairment if he yields to convenience or to opportunity. A professional man is one who feels an obligation to provide services that his client may never comprehend or appreciate.

A professional statistician will not follow methods that are indefensible, merely to please someone, nor support inferences based on such methods. He ranks his own name and profession as more important than convenient assent to interpretations not warranted by statistical theory. He can be a trusted and respected public servant.

His career as an expert witness will shatter in shipwreck if he indicates concern over which side of the case the results seem to favor. "As a statistician, I couldn't care less," is the right attitude in a legal case, or in any other report.

He will not deliberately attempt to carry out work that lies beyond his competence, but will, on request, recommend other specialists.

He will, if asked, render all possible assistance to another statistician in order to improve statistical service.

One further point. The practicing statistician of imagination and probity will meet problems that, for best results, require new theory, or even a new line of attack. He will too often not have time to arrive, either by himself or with help, at what he believes to be a better solution than the one that he proceeds to use. In such cases, the practitioner has an obligation to bring the problem to the community of his colleagues, as by publication of a letter to the editor, or by a more formal note or paper.

II.   Logical Basis for Division of Responsibilities

3.   Limitations of statistical theory.   The limitations of statistical theory serve as signposts to guide a logical division of responsibilities between statistician and client. We accordingly digress for a brief review of the power and the limitations of statistical theory.

We note first that statistical inferences (probabilities, tests of significance, estimates, confidence limits, fiducial limits, etc.), calculated by statistical theory from the results of a study will relate only to the material, product, people, business establishments, etc., that the frame was in effect drawn from, and only to the environment of the study, such as the method of investigation, the date, weather, rate of flow and levels of concentration of the components used in tests of a production-process, range of voltage or of other stress specified for the tests (as of electrical equipment).

Empirical investigation consists of observations on material of some kind. The material may be people; it may be pigs, insects, physical material, or records of transactions. The aim may be enumerative, which leads to the theory for the sampling of finite populations. The aim may be analytic, the study of the causes that make the material what it is, and which will produce other material in the future. A definable lot of material may be divisible into identifiable sampling units. A list of these sampling units, with identification of each unit, constitutes a frame. In some physical and astronomical investigations, the sampling unit is a unit of time. We need not detour here to describe nests of frames for multi-stage sampling. The important point is that without a frame there can be neither a complete coverage of a designated lot of material, nor a sample of any designated part thereof. Stephan introduced the concept of the frame, but without giving it a name [26].

Objective statistical inferences in respect to the frame are the speciality of the statistician. In contrast, generalization to cover material not included in the frame, nor to ranges, conditions, and methods outside the scope of the experiment, however essential for application of the results of a study, are a matter of judgment, and will depend on knowledge of the subject-matter [10].

For example, the universe in a study of consumer behavior might be all the female homemakers in a certain region. The frame therefore might be census blocks, tracts, or other small districts, and the ultimate sampling unit might be a segment of area containing households. The study itself will of course reach only the people that can be found at home in the segments selected for the sample. The client, however, must reach generalizations and take action on his product or system of marketing with respect to all female homemakers, whether they be the kind that are almost always at home and easy to reach, or almost never at home and therefore in part omitted from the study. Moreover, the female homemakers that the client must take action on belong to the future, next year, and the next. The frame only permits study of the past.

For another example, the universe might be the production-process that will turn out next week's product. The frame for study might be part of last week's product. The universe might be traffic in future years, as in studies needed as basis for estimating possible losses or gains as a result of merger. The frame for this study might be records of last year's shipments.

Statistical theory alone could not decide, in a study of traffic that a railway is making, whether it would be important to show the movement of (for example) potatoes, separately from other agricultural products in the northwest part of the U.S.: only the man that must use the data can decide that one.

The frame for a comparison of two medical treatments might be patients or other people in Chicago with a specific ailment. A pathologist might, on his own judgment, without further studies, generalize the results to people that have this ailment anywhere in the world. Statistical theory provides no basis for such generalizations.

No knowledge of statistical theory, however profound, provides by itself a basis for deciding whether a proposed frame would be satisfactory for a study. For example, statistical theory would not tell us, in a study of consumer research, whether to include in the frame people that live in trailer-parks. The statistician places the responsibility for the answer to this question where it belongs; *viz.*, with his client: are trailer-parks in your problem? Would they be in it if this were a complete census? If yes, would the cost of including them be worthwhile?

Statistical theory is indispensable in discussions with the client on what precision to expect in tabulation plans for certain areas or classes or on the question of how much difference the inclusion of (*e.g.*) people that live in trailer-parks could make in the results. The statistician may be helpful by just happening to know where to look for figures on the magnitude of a specific group of people (though familiarity with sources of information is not the statistician's primary obligation). Or he may suggest an inexpensive study that will provide rough estimates of the magnitude and importance of questionable classes. He may know by experience that investigation of certain areas or classes encounters considerable difficulty; and he may, to be helpful, raise a question, for the client's decision, on the possibility of omitting them. Such activity, however helpful to the client, is not an assumption of his responsibilities.

Statistical theory will not of itself originate a substantive problem. Statistical theory can not generate ideas for a questionnaire, nor for a test of hardness, nor specify what would be acceptable colors of dishes or of a carpet; nor does statistical theory originate ways to teach field-workers or inspectors how to do their work properly, nor what characteristics of workmanship constitute a meaningful measure of performance. This is so in spite of the fact that statistical theory is essential for reliable comparisons of questionnaires and tests.

Definitions and questions to use in the Current Population Survey, carried out monthly by the Bureau of the Census, by which a man in the sample is declared and recorded as unemployed or under-employed are substantive problems. They belong to the experts in the labor force. In contrast, statistical design to test alternative choices of questions on employment and unemployment, and the design of the sample, and the design and interpretation of controls for supervision, are statistical [14].

Statistical theory takes no cognizance of substantive requirements. The role of the statistician tapers off as the results are extended, projected, or generalized beyond the frame.

4. Contributions of statistical theory to subject-matter. It is necessary, for statistical reliability of results, that the design of a survey or experiment fit into a theoretical model. Part of the statistician's job is to find a suitable model that he can manage, once the client has presented his case and explained why he needs statistical information and how he could use the results of a study. Statistical practice goes further than merely to try to find a suitable model (theory). Part of the job is to adjust the physical conditions to meet the model selected. Randomness, for example, in sampling a frame, is not just a word to assume: it must be created by use of random numbers for the selection of sampling units. Re-calls to find people at home, or tracing illegible or missing information back to source-documents, are specified so as to approach the prescribed probability of selection.

Statistical theory has in this way profoundly influenced the theory of knowledge. It has given form and direction to quantitative studies, by moulding them into the requirements of the theory of estimation, statistical test of hypothesis, and other techniques of inference. The aim is, of course, to yield results that have meaning in terms that man can understand.

Any statistician could offer endless illustrations. A few reminders suffice here. The two risks that management must accept and specify numerically for the application of the theory of probability (queueing theory), introduced independently by Molina [19], [20], and Erlang [18] to minimize the net economic loss from too much equipment or service, or from too little, is an example. Use of the theory of probability, following Shewhart, to minimize the net economic loss from the risks of blaming a common cause of variation on to a specific possibility (operator, machine, or other local source) and the cost of the converse error, is appreciated the world over [22], [23], [24]. The purchaser's plan of acceptance-sampling forms the only meaningful language in which to communicate the average quality desired of a stream of product.

Such techniques are building a theory of management. The principles of mini-max, along with use of biased estimates to minimize the mean-square-error, are examples of more recent contributions to knowledge. The theory of probability is making profound impact on the study of genetics. The average book-dollar of investment, in the evaluation of the current-cost-new of property and equipment, has made impact on accounting methods.

Statistical theory has contributed important refinements to methods of testing in many lines of work (industrial, physical, psychological) by requiring that an acceptable system of tests and criteria must exhibit randomness in the Shewhart sense. It is only with the aid of statistical theory that one may construct and measure reliably and economically the repeatability of proposed tests. In fact, the words repeatable, reproducible, precise, reliable, good, round, hard, etc., as characteristics of performance or of material, have no operationally verifiable meaning except in terms of statistical tests and criteria.

Further, the statistician is often effective in assisting the substantive expert to improve accepted methods of interviewing, testing coding, and other operations. Tests properly designed will show how alternative test- or field-procedures really perform in practice, so that rational changes or choices may be possible. It sometimes happens, for example, that a time-honored or committee-honored method of investigation, when put to statistically designed tests, shows alarming inherent variances between instruments, between investigators, or even between days for the same investigator. It may show a trend, or heavy intraclass correlation between units, introduced by the investigator. Once detected, such sources of variation may then be corrected or diminished by new rules, which are of course the responsibility of the substantive expert.

Use of a random sample of x and y coordinates at which to test a surface (as of enamel) for control of a process for finishing surfaces, or for evaluation of deterioration, in place of a judgment selection of points or complete reliance on a general view of the whole surface, is a simple example of a contribution to test-methods.

Statistical techniques provide a safe supervisory tool to help to reduce variability in the performance of man and machine. The effectiveness of statistical controls, in all stages of a survey, for improving supervision, to achieve uniformity, to reduce errors, to gain speed, reduce costs, and to improve quality of performance in other ways are well known. A host of references could be given, but two will suffice here [3], [4].

5. Statistical theory as a basis for division of responsibilities. We may now, with this background, see where the statistician's responsibilities lie.

In the first place, his specialized knowledge of statistical theory enables him to see which parts of a problem belong to substantive knowledge (sociology, transportation, chemistry of a manufacturing process, laws), and which parts are statistical. The responsibility as logician in a study falls to him by default, and he must accept it. As logician, he will do well to designate, in the planning stages, which decisions will belong to the statistician, and which to the substantive expert.

This matter of defining specifically one's area of responsibility is a unique problem faced by the statistician. Businessmen and lawyers who engage an expert on corporate finance, or an expert on steam power plants, know pretty well what such experts are able to do, and have an idea about how to work with them. It is different with statisticians (one who uses theory to guide his practice) and the popular idea that a statistician is skilful in compiling tables about people or trade, or is one who prophesies the economic outlook of the coming year, and which way the stock market will drift. They may know little about the contributions that the statistician can make to a study, or how to work with him.

Allocation of responsibilities does not mean impervious compartments in which you do this and I'll do that. It means that there is a logical basis for allocation of responsibilities, and that it is necessary for everyone involved in a study to know in advance what he will be accountable for.

A clear statement of responsibilities will be a joy to the client's lawyer in a legal case, especially at the time of cross-examination. It will show the kind of question that the statistician is answerable for, and what belongs to the substantive experts.

Statisticians have something to learn about professional practice from law and medicine.

6. Assistance to the client to understand the relationship. The statistician must take the time and the trouble in the early stages to understand the client's problem, and what it means to him. One way to go about this is to direct the client's thoughts toward possible uses of the results of a statistical study of the entire frame without consideration of sampling, which only confuses the client's thinking in the early stages. As groundwork, there will be, of course, consideration of possible frames. Then follows the question of how the client proposes to investigate any unit, however it be selected from the frame.

Once these matters are cleared, the statistician may outline one or more statistical plans and explain to the client in his own language what they mean in respect to possible choices of frame and environmental conditions, choices of sampling unit, skills, facilities and supervision required. The statistician will urge the client to foresee possible difficulties with definitions, or with the proposed method of investigation. He may illustrate with rough calculations possible levels of precision to be expected from one or more statistical plans that appear to be feasible, along with rudimentary examples of the kinds of tables and inferences that might be forthcoming. These early stages are often the hardest part of the job.

It is good practice in most work to make the point that prediction of the precision or protection that any statistical plan will deliver is dependent on assumptions concerning the numerical values of certain statistical characteristics of the sampling units in the frame, and dependent on the performance of investigators. These assumptions relate to conditions to be encountered; hence the precision predicted may differ somewhat from the actual precision delivered.

The aim in statistical design is to hold accuracy and precision to sensible levels, with an economic balance between all the possible uncertainties that afflict data—built-in deficiencies of definition, errors of response, no-response, sampling variation, difficulties in coding, errors in processing, difficulties of interpretation.

A general theory that would embrace an economic balance of all sources of uncertainty does not exist, or might be unwieldy if it did exist. Hence, to strive toward an economic balance of all uncertainties, the statistician usually ascribes subjective weights to the importance of the various sources of uncertainty, and seeks to allocate effort toward reduction of each source, in accordance with these weights.

Professional statistical practice requires experience, maturity, fortitude, and patience, to protect the client against himself or against his duly appointed experts in subject-matter who may have in mind needless but costly tabulations in fine classes (5 year age-groups, small areas, fine mileage-brackets, fine gradations in voltage, etc.), or unattainable precision in differences between treatments, beyond the capacity of the skills and facilities available, or beyond the meaning inherent in the definitions.

These first steps, which depend on guidance from the statistician, may lead to important modifications of the problem. Advance considerations of cost, and of the limitations of the inferences that appear to be possible, may even lead the client to abandon the study, at least until he feels more confident of his requirements. Protection of the client's bank-account, and deliverance from more serious losses from decisions based on inconclusive or misleading results, or from misinterpretation, is one of the statistician's greatest services.

Joint effort does not imply joint responsibility. Divided responsibility for a decision in a statistical survey is as bad as divided responsibility in any venture—it means that no one is responsible.

Although he acquires superficial knowledge of the subject-matter, the one thing that the statistician contributes to the problem, and which distinguishes him from other experts, is knowledge and ability in statistical theory.

III. SUMMARY STATEMENT OF RECIPROCAL OBLIGATIONS AND RESPONSIBILITIES

7. Responsibilities of the client. The client will assume responsibility for those aspects of the problem that are substantive. Specifically, he will stand the ultimate responsibility for:

    a. the type of statistical information to be obtained;

    b. the methods of test, examination, questionnaire, or interview, by which to elicit the information from any unit selected from the frame;

    c. the decision on whether a proposed frame is satisfactory;

    d. approval of the probability model proposed by the statistician (statistical procedures, scope and limitations of the statistical inferences that may be possible from the results);

e. the decision on the classes and areas of tabulation (as these depend on the uses that the client intends to make of the data); the approximate level of statistical precision or protection that would be desirable in view of the purpose of the investigation, skills and time available, and costs.

The client will make proper arrangements for:

f. the actual work of preparing the frame for sampling, such as serializing and identifying sampling units at the various stages;

g. the selection of the sample according to procedures that the statistician will prescribe, and the preparation of these units for investigation;

h. the actual investigation; the training for this work, and the supervision thereof;

i. the rules for coding; the coding itself;

j. the processing, tabulations and computations, following procedures of estimation that the sampling plans prescribe.

The client or his representative has the obligation to report at once any departure from instructions, to permit the statistician to make a decision between a fresh start or an unbiased adjustment. The client will keep a record of the actual performance.

8. Responsibilities of the statistician. The statistician owes an obligation to his own practice to forestall disappointment on the part of the client, who if he fails to understand at the start that he must exercise his own responsibilities in the planning stages, and in execution, may not realize in the end the fullest possibility of the investigation, or may discover too late that certain information that he had expected to get out of the study was not built into the design. The statistician's responsibility may be summarized as follows:

a. to formulate the client's problem in statistical terms (probability model), subject to approval of the client, so that a proposed statistical investigation may be helpful to the purpose;

b. to lay out a logical division of responsibilities for the client, and for the statistician, suitable to the investigation proposed;

c. to explain to the client the advantages and disadvantages of various frames and possible choices of sampling units, and of one or more feasible statistical plans of sampling or experimentation that seem to be feasible (*vide supra*, "Assistance to the client...");

d. to explain to the client, in connexion with the frame, that any objective inferences that one may draw by statistical theory from the results of an investigation can only refer to the material or system that the frame was drawn from, and only to the methods, levels, types, and ranges of stress presented for study. It is essential that the client understand the limitations of a proposed study, and of the statistical inferences to be drawn therefrom, so that he may have a chance to modify the content before it is too late;

e. to furnish statistical procedures for the investigation—selection, computation of estimates and standard errors, tests, audits, and controls as seem warranted for detection and evaluation of important possible departures from specifications, variances between investigators, non-response, and other persistent uncertainties not contained in the standard error; to follow the work and to know when to step in (*vide infra* "Necessity for the statistician to keep in touch");

f. to assist the client (on request) with statistical methods of supervision, to help him to improve uniformity of performance of investigators, gain speed, reduce errors, reduce costs, and to produce a better record of just what took place;

g. to report on the statistical reliability of the results (*vide infra*).

9. **The statistician's report or testimony.** The statistician's report or testimony will deal with the statistical reliability of the results. the usual content will cover the following points:

a. a statement to explain what aspects of the study his responsibility included, and what it excluded. It will delimit the scope of the report;

b. a description of the frame, the sampling unit, how defined and identified, the material covered, and a statement in respect to conditions of the survey or experiment that might throw light on the usefulness of the results;

c. a statement concerning the effect of any gap between the frame and the universe for important conclusions likely to be drawn from the results. (A good rule is that the statistician should have before him a rough draft of the client's proposed conclusions.)

d. evaluation of the margin of uncertainty, for a specified probability level, attributable to random errors of various kinds, including the uncertainty introduced by sampling, and by small independent random variations in judgment, instruments, coding, transcription, and other processing;

e. evaluation of the possible effects of other relevant sources of variation, examples being differences between investigators, between instruments, between days, between areas;

f. effect of persistent drift and conditioning of instruments and of investigators, changes in technique;

g. non-response and illegible or missing entries;

h. failure to select sampling units according to procedure prescribed;

i. failure to reach and to cover sampling units that were designated in the sampling table;

j. inclusion of sampling units not designated for the sample but nevertheless covered and included in the results;

k. any other important slips and departures from procedure prescribed;

l. comparisons with other studies, if any are relevant.

In summary, a statement of statistical reliability attempts to present to the reader a lower limit (or an upper limit) above which (or below which) he may assume rationally, with a stated risk, that the results of bigger samples would fall, if freed of important persistent operational blemishes. It should present any information that might help the reader to form his own opinion concerning the validity of conclusions likely to be drawn from the results.

Evaluation of the statistical reliability of a set of results is not mere calculation of standard errors and confidence limits. The statistician must go far beyond the statistical methods in textbooks. He must evaluate uncertainty in terms of possible uses of the data. Some of this writing is not statistical, but draws on assistance from the expert in the subject-matter.

The aim of a statistical report is to protect the client from seeing merely what he would like to see; to protect him from losses that could come from misuse of the results. A further aim is to forestall unwarranted claims of accuracy that the client's public might otherwise accept.

My own code of professional conduct specifies that the client shall not mention verbally or in print the statistician's participation in a study without approval. Any printed description of the statistical procedures that refer to this participation, or any evaluation of the statistical reliability of the results, must be prepared by the statistician as part of the engagement. If the client prints the statistician's report, he will print it in full.

In my opinion, the statistician should not recommend to the client that he take any specific administrative action or policy. Use of the results that come from a survey or experiment are entirely up to the client. The statistician, if he were to make recommendations for decision, would cease to be a statistician.

Actually, ways in which the results may throw light on foreseeable problems will be settled in advance, in the design, and there should be little need for the client or for anyone else to re-open a question. However, problems sometimes change character with time (as when a competitor of the client suddenly comes out with a new model), and open up considerations of statistical precision and significance of estimates that were not initially in view.

The statistician should reserve the right, I believe, to describe in a professional or scientific meeting the statistical methods that he develops in an engagement. He will not publish actual data or substantive results or other information about the client's business without his permission. In other words, the statistical methods belong to the statistician: the data to the client.

A statistician may at times perform a useful function by examining and reporting on a study in which he did not participate. A professional statistician will not write an opinion on another's procedures or inferences without adequate time for study and evaluation.

IV. SUPPLEMENTAL REMARKS

10. Necessity for the statistician to keep in touch. The statistician, when he enters into a relationship to participate in a study, accepts certain responsibilities. He does not merely draft instructions and wait to be called. The people whom he services are not statisticians. They can not always know when they are in trouble. The statistician will ask questions and will probe on his own account with the help of proper statistical design, to discover for himself whether the work is proceeding according to the intent of the instructions. He must expect to revise the instructions a number of times in the early stages. He will be accessible by mail, telephone, telegraph, facsimile machines, or in person, to answer questions and to listen to suggestions.

He may of course arrange consultations with other statisticians on questions of theory or procedure. He may engage another statistician to take over certain duties. He may employ other skills at suitable levels to carry out independent tests or re-investigation of certain units, to detect difficulties and departures from the prescribed procedure, or errors in transcription or calculation.

It must be firmly understood, however, that consultation or assistance is in no sense a partitioning of responsibility. The obligations of the statistician to his client, once entered into, may not be shared.

11. What is an engagement? Dangers of informal advice. It may seem at first thought that a statistician ought to be willing to give to the world informally and impromptu, if he so desires, the benefit of his knowledge and experience, without discussion or agreement concerning participation and relationships. Anyone who has received aid in sickness from a doctor of medicine who did his best without a chance to make a more thorough examination, or perhaps even by telephone, can appreciate how important the skills of a professional man can be, even under handicap.

On second thought, most statisticians can recall instances in which informal advice backfired. It is the same in any professional line. A statistician who tries to be a good fellow and give advice under adverse circumstances is in practice and has a client, whether he intended it so or not; and he will later on find himself accountable for the advice. It is important to take special precaution under these circumstances to state the basis of understanding for any statements of recommendations, and to make clear that other conditions and circumstances could well lead to different statements.

12. When do the statistician's obligations come to a close? The statistician should make it clear that his name may be identified with a study only so long as he is active in it and accountable for it, as by continued responsibility for evaluation of the statistical reliability of results. This obligation will require regular receipt of reports of statistical controls for the detection of non-sampling errors, and continual assistance on problems that come up, including procedures by which to add to the frame new areas or other new material, and for sampling these additions. A statistical procedure, contrary to popular parlance, is not installed. One may install new furniture, a new carpet, or a new dean, and they stay in place, but not a statistical procedure. It does not stay installed without constant vigil. Experience shows that a statistical procedure deteriorates rapidly when left completely to nonprofessional administration.

A statistician may draw up plans for a continuing study, such as for the annual inventory of materials in process in a group of manufacturing plants, or for a continuing national survey of consumers. He may nurse the job into running order, and conduct it through several performances. Experience shows, however, that if he steps out and leaves the work in nonstatistical hands, he will shortly find it to be unrecognizable. New people come on to the job. They know better than their predecessor how to do the work. Or, they may not be aware that there ever were any rules or instructions, and make up their own.

What is even worse, perhaps, is that people that have been on a job a number of years think that they know it so well that they can't go wrong. This type of fault will be observed, for example, in a national monthly sample in which households are to be re-visited a number of times: when left entirely to nonstatistical administration, it will develop faults. Some interviewers will put down their best guesses about the family, on the basis of the preceding month, without an actual interview. They will forget the exact wording of the question, or may think that they have something better. They will become lax about calling back on people not at home. Some of them may suppose that they are following literally the intent of the instructions, when in fact (as shown by a control), through misunderstanding, they are doing something wrong. Or, they may depart willfully, thinking that they are thereby improving the design, on the supposition that the statistician did not really understand the circumstances. A common example is to substitute an average-looking sampling unit, when the sampling unit designated is obviously unusual in some respect [2].

In the weighing and testing of physical product, men will in all sincerity substitute their judgment for the use of random numbers. Administration at the top will fail to rotate areas in the manner specified. Such deterioration may be predicted with confidence unless the statistician specifies statistical controls that provide detective devices and feed-back.

13. The single consultation. In my own experience, I have found it wise to avoid a single consultation with a commercial concern unless satisfactory agenda are prepared in advance, and satisfactory arrangements made for absorbing advice offered. This requirement, along with an understanding that there will be a fee for a consultation, acts as a shield against a hapless conference which somebody calls in the hope that something may turn up. It also shows that the statistician, as a professional man, although eager to teach and explain statistical methods, is not on the lookout for chances to demonstrate what he himself might be able to accomplish.

Moreover, what may be intended as a single consultation often ends up with a request for a memorandum. This may be very difficult to write, especially in the absence of adequate time to study the problem. The precautions of informal advice apply here (*vide supra*).

14. The statistician's obligation in a muddle. Suppose that the plans for a study were properly formalized and rehearsed, the field-work under way. Then the statistician discovers that the client or his duly appointed representatives have disregarded the instructions for the preparation of the frame, or the selection of the sample, or that the field-work seems to be falling apart. "We went ahead and did so and so before your letter came, confident that you would approve," is a violation of relationship. That the statistician may approve the deed done does not mitigate the violation.

What should the statistician do in a muddle? It may still be possible to repeat some of the work, and thus to salvage the job. It is the client's decision on whether he can stand the expense or the delay. If little can be done to put the study back on the rails, the statistician is technically in the position of trying to do something with a non-probability sample (next section). Morally, he must ask himself how he can balance his responsibilities to his client and to his profession. If it appears to the statistician that there is no chance that the study will yield results that he could take professional responsibility for, then he must make this fact clear to his client, at a sufficiently high management-level. It is a good idea for the statistician to explain at the outset that such situations, while extreme, have been known.

The statistician should do all in his power to help the client to avoid such a catastrophe. There is always the possibility that the statistician himself may be partly to blame for not being sufficiently clear nor firm at the outset concerning his principles of participation, or for not being on hand at the right time to ask questions and to keep himself apprised of what is happening. Unfortunate circumstances may teach the statistician a lesson on participation.

15. Assistance in interpretation of non-probability samples. It may be humiliating, but statisticians must face the fact that many accepted laws of science have come from theory and experimentation without benefit of formal statistical design. Vaccination for prevention of smallpox is one; John Snow's discovery of the source of cholera in London is another [16]. So is the law $F = ma$ in physics; also Hooke's law, Boyle's law, Mendel's findings, Keppler's laws, Darwin's theory of evolution, the Stefan-Boltz-Mann law of radiation (first empirical, later established by physical theory). All this only means, as everyone knows, that there may well be information in a non-probability sample.

One possible way in which the statistician may render assistance in a non-probability sample is to make rough estimates of precision by pulling out of the data a few replicates, but this is no help in estimating the bias of selection, which is of course the main problem.

Another point is that a plea for assistance in the interpretation of the results of a survey that had not the benefit of statistical design presents a good chance for the statistician to explain how much more effective the study would have been had it started off properly, and had it been carried off in reasonable accord with the statistical specifications.

Perhaps the main contribution that the statistician can make is to advise the experimenter with a non-probability sample against conclusions based on meaningless statistical calculations. The expert in the subject-matter must take the responsibility for the effects of selectivity and confounding of treatments. The statistician may make a positive contribution by encouraging the expert in the subject-matter to draw whatever conclusions he believes to be warranted, but to do so over his own signature, and not to attribute his conclusions to statistical calculations, nor to the kind help of a certain statistician.

V. ACKNOWLEDGMENT

A paper on this subject is too important to entrust to one point of view. Copies of three previous versions went out about 4 years apart to about 50 statisticians for criticism and comment, and I have held innumerable conversations on the matter with statisticians, and with lawyers and other clients. Every line of this manuscript has its origin in experience. The principles expounded here met almost universal acceptance, but with suggestions on emphasis and clarity. There is no difficulty with the logic of division of responsibility. What is at times difficult to comprehend is the consequences of applying the logic. Comments that have come from friends kind enough to read earlier drafts may assist readers of the final version to overcome the same difficulties.

For example, one esteemed friend, head of a statistical organization in a university, said that as a statistician he frequently does the coding in studies that he carries out (surveys on health and sickness), and that the role that I have drawn for the statistician may be too restrictive. In further conversation, however, he agreed firmly with the point of this paper, that although any of us may at times take it on to himself to see that the coding is done (just as any of us may compute, type, draw up forms, or wash the cups after coffee), the fact remains that only a qualified expert in the substantive field should be responsible for the rules for coding or for the substantive content of the investigation.

Another statistician, eminently distinguished, agreed with the views expressed here but said that he himself takes a deep interest in the questionnaire in a survey. Nothing in this paper precludes the statistician's interest in any aspect of a survey. Although the statistician is responsible for the statistical aspects of a study, he is under no obligation to proceed—in fact, has an obligation to call a halt—if he entertains serious doubts about the questionnaire or the method of investigation, or about the availability of he necessary skills and facilities for carrying out the work.

The only real note of dissent came from an esteemed colleague who in private conversation agreed with the entire content of the paper, and practices it, but had the feeling that a formal statement of responsibilities might alienate the substantive expert and weaken the bond of dependence. Personally, I have observed the opposite: a careful statement of what is expected of the substantive expert, and what he may expect for the statistician, cements the relationship, with mutual respect.

Another friend agreed with the paper, but thought that the statistician should try to do more than merely use statistical techniques; he should, forsooth, use techniques appropriate to the problem. For example, as he said, in vacuum-zone melting, longitudinal and transverse layers of a sheet of material may exhibit widely different tensile strengths, and the statistician is not at liberty to select samples in one direction or the other willy nilly as takes his fancy.

One could go on and on. In a study of performance and usage apparatus, the sampling unit must contain not only the main piece that sends or receives signals, but auxiliary apparatus as well. In a study of the psychological or social problems of families, it may not suffice to interview one member. The proper sampling unit may be the family, to complete the story on interaction and stresses. It may be necessary to interview other families in the same community.

Such remarks constitute good advice on how to improve statistical methods. However important, they would be out of scope here. Nothing in this paper relieves the statistician of his obligation to apply statistical methods appropriate to the problem, to the material to be investigated, and to the skills available.

It is a pleasure to mention in particular help for F.F. Stephan, William Kruskal, Frank Hoeber, John Tukey, Morris Hansen, William N. Hurwitz, Samuel Greenhouse, Churchill Eisenhart, Bradford F. Kimball, Nathan Keyfitz, Tore Dalenius, Josephine Cunningham, William G. Cochran, Harold Dodge, W.J. Youden, Bernard Greenberg, A.C. Rosander, Gerald J. Glasser, Leon Pritzker, Leslie Kish, Howard Jones, Edgar King, Richard Bingham, Charles Bicking, Cuthbert Daniel. The report of the Hotelling Committee on the teaching of statistics has provided guiding principles for practice as well as for teaching [17].

An unseen referee made a number of very helpful suggestions in the penultimate version, and suggested references. I express my thanks to him.

REFERENCES

[1] Brown, Theodore H. (1952). The statistician and his conscience. *Amer. Statist.* **6** No. 1 14–18.

[2] Bureau of the Census (1954). Measurement of employment and unemployment: Report of Special Advisory Committee on Employment Statistics. Washington.

[3] Bureau of the Census (1964). Evaluation and research program of the censuses of population and housing: 1960 Series ER60. No. 1.

[4] Bureau of the Census (1963). The current population survey and re-interview program. Technical paper No. 6.

[5] Burgess, R. W. (1947). Do we need a "Bureau of Standards" for statistics? *J. Marketing* **11** 281–2.

[6] Chambers, S. Paul (1965). Statistics and intellectual integrity. *J. Roy. Statist. Soc. Ser.* A **128** 1–16.

[7] Court, Andrew T. (1952). Standards of statistical conduct in business and in government. *Amer. Statist.* **6** 6–14.

[8] Deming, W. Edwards (1954). On the presentation of the results of samples as legal evidence. *J. Amer. Statist. Assoc.* **49** 814–825.

[9] Deming, W. Edwards (1954). On the contributions of standards of sampling to legal evidence and accounting. Current Business Studies, Society of Business Advisory Professions, Graduate School of Business Administration, New York University.

[10] Deming, W. Edwards (1960). *Sample Design in Business Research,* Chapter 3. Wiley, New York.

[11] Eisenhart, Churchill (1947). The role of a statistical consultant in a research organization. *Proc. Internat. Statist. Conferences* **3** 309–313.

[12] Freeman, William W. K. (1952). Discussion of Theodore Brown's paper, (see [1]). *Amer. Statist.* **6** No. 1 18–20.

[13] Freeman, William W. K. (1963). Training of statistician in diplomacy to maintain their integrity. *Amer. Statist.* **17** No. 5 16–20.

[14] Gordon, Robert A. et. al. (1962). Measuring employment and unemployment statistics: President's Committee to Appraise Employment and Unemployment Statistics. Superintendent of Documents, Washington.

[15] Hansen, Morris H. (1952). Statistical standards and the Census. *Amer. Statist.* **6** No. 1 7–10.

[16] Hill, A. Bradford (1953). Observation and experiment. *New England J. of Med.* **248** 995–1001.

[17] Hotelling, Harold et. al. (1948). The teaching of statistics (a report of the Institute of Mathematical Statistics Committee on the teaching of statistics). *Ann. Math. Statist.* **19** 95–115.

[18] Jensen, Arne et. al. (1948). The life and works of A. K. Erlang. *Trans. Danish Acad. Tech. Sci.,* No. 2 Copenhagen.

[19] Molina, Edward C. (1913). Computation formula for the probability of an event happening at least c times in n trials. *Amer. Math. Monthly* **20** 190–192.

[20] Molina, Edward C. (1925). The theory of probability and some applications to engineering problems. *J. Amer. Inst. Electrical Engineers* **44** 1–6.

[21] Morton, J. E. (1952). Standards of statistical conduct in business and government. *Amer. Statist.* **6** No. 1 6–7.

[22] Shewhart, Walter A. (1931). *Economic Control of Quality of Manufactured Product.* Van Nostrand, New York.

[23] Shewhart, Walter A. (1939). *Statistical Method from the Viewpoint of Quality Control.* The Graduate School, Department of Agriculture, Washington.

[24] Shewhart, Walter A. (1958). Nature and origin of standards of quality. *Bell Syst. Tech. J.* **37** 1–22.

[25] Society of Business Advisory Professions (1957). Report of Committee on standards of probability sampling for legal evidence. Graduate School of Business Administration, New York University.

[26] Stephan, Frederick Franklin (1936). Practical problems of sampling procedure. *Amer. Sociological Rev.* **1** 569–580.

[27] Zirkle, Conway (1954). Citation of fraudulent data. *Science* **120** 189–190.

Chapter Nine

Chapter Ten
Observations on Medical Care
and Hospital Management

Dr. Deming has had two significant personal experiences in hospitals during his career. It is of interest to note his observations on the quality of care for the patient and the overall quality of management within the hospital itself.

The first article is the latest: *Some Notes on Management in a Hospital*, published in the Journal of the Society for Health Systems, Vol. 2, No. 1, Spring 1990. The second is *St. Vincent's Hospital*, which tells his story of being mugged in New York, and the subsequent medical care that saved his life. He ends with an eloquent plea for blood donors.

The first article consists of his own observations as a patient. It asks significant and piercing questions: questions for which every health care practitioner, every hospital management team, and every group of hospital owners should be seeking answers.

SOME NOTES ON MANAGEMENT IN A HOSPITAL
W. Edwards Deming, Ph.D.

A hospital is an important component in a system of medical care. In a system that is operating efficiently, workers know how their work fits into the system. Everyone would feel important, and would work with people that likewise feel important.

Hard work and best efforts are not sufficient for optimization of a system. A system must be managed. The administrator of a hospital knows a lot about what happens in the hospital. So does a head nurse. A head nurse, for example, knows a lot that the administrator can not see. Likewise for any nurse that works there. The physicians that attend patients know a lot about the hospital that no one else knows. A patient in the hospital sees what no one else sees.

All these different observations, from different points of view, were they known, might be helpful to the management of a medical care system.

The notes attached were written by an observing, grateful patient. They show how best efforts of nurses, with their special skills and knowledge, are to a large extent squandered. The nurses must be discouraged, seeing a large portion of their efforts as fruitless. How can a nurse feel important under such conditions?

The author has hopes that publication of these notes written from a patient's point of view may make a contribution to improvement of the management of medical care.

A Hospital Patient's Notes

Well, here I am—flat on my back, literally and in other ways, right ankle resting on three pillows. Elevation is vital to treatment.

My nurse of the moment (R.N.) came in at about one o'clock to wrap my leg from the knee down in a hot towel and insulator. As a first step, she turned on the hot water in the washbowl, as she needed hot water for the towel (some nurses use the microwave for this purpose). She then departed, saying, "I'll be right back." A social worker dropped in about a half-hour later. I asked her if she would mind turning off the hot water to avoid more waste of water and energy. She did. In another half-hour, the nurse came back to put on the hot towel, turned on the hot water, and completed the job.

Dr. Sch ordered from the drug store (in the hospital) a paste for the itch caused by the sore leg. The drug store was out of one of the ingredients; must order it from the wholesaler, and can not make up the paste till Monday. As this is Saturday, no delivery from the wholesaler till Monday. I need it tonight. On prodding from Dr. Sch, the drug store sent someone out to another drug store to fetch the missing ingredient. The paste came up that evening.

It may seem unbelievable, but the same scenario took place some days later. My nurse of the afternoon ordered from the drug store a refill for the paste. No problem, except that there would be a delay, as (again) the drug store would have to order from the wholesaler one of the ingredients. Tomorrow will be Saturday, next day Sunday, Monday a holiday. They would send up a substitute, which would be in the form of a lotion, not paste.

On another day, my nurse of the moment (R.N.) came in three times between 8:30 a.m. and 10 a.m. to say that she would be right back to make my bed. I offered to get out of it so that she could make it up straightaway, but she may not have heard me. Each time: "I'll be right back." Anyhow, near noon she came back and actually did the job. Of course, I'll live, bed made or no.

I wonder: Why is a registered nurse making beds? It seems to me that making beds is not good use of her time. Her education and skills could be put to better use, so it seems to me. Are there not helpers to do this kind of work? But maybe there are reasons that I don't understand.

All the while, nurses are on a dog-trot, panting for breath, working at top speed, losing time, not for start-up, but for no start. I know all about it; this is my way.

I was wondering about these thermometers with a heavy electric cord attached. Speedy, yes, but impossible for a patient to hold correctly because of the heavy cord. The patient can only hold the thermometer against his cheek. The reading could be a whole degree low, I surmise. The aide that records temperature seemed to be totally indifferent. A reading, after all, is a reading.

The wash basin in my room has not enough space on it for a shaving mug, barely enough for a shaving brush. Bought at lowest price tag, I surmise.

The man that designed the shower had obviously never used one. The shower head, when not held by hand, can only dangle and flood the floor. There is a tiny shelf in the shower big enough to hold only a wafer of soap. There is only one bar to hold on to. Use of this shower would be a risky business without a friend close by for rescue. Somebody sold somebody a bill of goods.

Intravenous diffusion due at 6 a.m. The nurse came at 5:05 a.m. to insert the needle into the more or less permanent spigot, known as a Heparin Lock, in my left arm and departed. The infusion would run around 90 minutes. Meanwhile, some time after she left, in reaching for something on the shelf, I reached too far and pulled the needle out of the Heparin Lock. The nurse, when she came in around 6 a.m., saw what had happened. She was startled, but said not a word. She merely carried everything away, liquid and tube. I supposed that she would return and start over. Time went on. No return.

At 8:30 a.m. I reported to Meg, head nurse in charge of the shift, that the intravenous effusion had not been given. It might be important to me, and important to Dr. D., else why bother with it? Meg's first impulse was to call (at home and maybe asleep) the nurse that left the job undone. It seemed to me, I told her, that it matters not what the nurse might say. I know what happened, and what did not. I called Dr. Sch. His secretary said that she would notify him at once and that he would call Dr. D.

The infusion came straightaway. The head nurse returned to say that the nurse that was to give the infusion had recorded the infusion as given. It is possible that she recorded it in advance, with the intention to give it, and did not correct the record. Is this the regular procedure, to record intentions? Who would know?

An unsuspecting physician, looking at the record for his patient, would assume that the infusion had been given, and could draw wrong inferences about how the patient had been doing on the drug. In my case, as it turned out, no harm. But how would he know? A nurse, or a physician, has a right to suppose that the medication was delivered as ordered and as recorded.

What is the purpose of the record? To inform the physician about intentions, or to tell him what happened?

Dr. Sch assured me that he is running this lapse down in every detail, and that nothing like it will ever happen again here—the usual supposition: working on only an actual defect, not on its cause.

A little figuring told me that insertion of the needle at 5:05 a.m., for infusion to start at 6 a.m. (if she came back on time) would tie the patient in bed for over 2 1/2 hours: the first hour tied in bed, then 1 1/2 hours for the infusion, plus time added for the nurse to come to take the needle out of the Heparin Lock and take the whole thing away. This long time in bed, with 3/4 cup of liquid infused, could create great discomfort for a patient.

She (R.N.) would "be back in 20 minutes," to take the wrapping off the hot towel and insulation that she had just wrapped my leg in, and would apply the cream prescribed. One hour and five minutes later, almost time for my IV, I rang the bell to call her. She returned in 15 minutes, unwrapped my leg, and started the IV just about on time.

The food is superb. The lasagna yesterday noon was the best that I have had since the days of Iacominni's Restaurant in Akron. The baked chicken today was superb: wing attached, browned to perfection, and the sweet potato, all steaming hot. Excellent beef and barley broth.

Such food in a fine restaurant would cost $20. If only the food came on dishes with a white or light colored moulded pattern, instead of on battered brown. These trays and dishes were purchased at lowest bid, I surmise, or maybe were donated by a soup kitchen on purchase of new ones.

The Fettuccini Alfredo for dinner Monday night was the best ever, with three packets of Parmesan cheese, as good as any Fettuccini Alfredo that I ever had this side of Rome. The broccoli soup was delicious. The beautiful looking apple dumpling was hot and tempting. I had already eaten enough food, but with one taste, just for trial, the dumpling was irresistible, so I finished it whether I needed it or not.

Fifteen hours elapse between dinner and breakfast. I was hungry in the middle of the night, first night. Fortunately had candy bars on hand.

I have learned how to acquire and store up food like a squirrel if I get hungry during the night. I order for dinner milk as well as coffee, set the milk aside for use during the night. On hand, from friends, I have wonderful Scottish short bread from Scotland, Waverly crackers, and candy bars. Also, I order a ripe banana for breakfast every day, and put it in storage. I now have two bananas on hand, the number that I started with, but not the same bananas. FIFO is my system, first in first out.

An aide comes along around 9 o'clock at night to hand out juice or (I surmise) soft drinks, or milk, but I now have my own food.

The chair in this room is huge, would seat two people, takes up an exorbitant amount of space, heavy to move. Somebody had good intentions. It can be adjusted to go back as a foot-board moves into place, but need it be so big and heavy? Why not have a movable chair?

The coat hangers here are that maddening kind, found in most hotels. How I wish that I had known about them before I sent that check to this hospital a year ago: I should have designated $10,000 of it to go for new racks and honest coat hangers in the rooms.

I had a new full-size bar of good soap on the wash bowl. The girl that picks up trash must have thought that this kind of soap is not suited to my kind of skin. Anyway, the nurse of the moment brought to me for replacement a new bar of soap, tiny but appreciated.

My nurse of the moment put on a hot towel this afternoon. "I'll be back in 20 minutes, and if I don't come, please ring." Sixty-five minutes later I pressed the button. A helper came in and explained to me that this was not her kind of job, so she cancelled the light for the nurse and went off. Thirty minutes later I rang again for the nurse. The same helper came and observed again that the job was not in her line of duty, so again she cancelled the light and went off. The solution was simple, for me—merely discard the towel and insulation myself, with the rules or against the rules. The same event recurred another day.

This experience leads to questions and guidelines. Why should an aide, unable to perform the task, cancel the light? The nurse on duty for that light would not know that her patient needed a nurse. What if a nurse was suddenly vital to a patient? If he was in a single room, he would be left stranded. His nurse would not know that he had rung for her. In a room with two patients, the other patient might be able to fetch a nurse. Moral: If you are acutely ill, don't go into a private room unless you have your own private nurse on duty at all times.

Shirley, a registered nurse, came to see me as a friend. She made the remark that a Heparin Lock ought to be examined at the end of 48 hours and maybe changed. It has now been in eight days. Later, I asked one of the nurses how long it should stay in one place. A nurse came and changed it from left arm to right arm.

What is the moral of all this? What have we learned? One answer: the Superintendent of the hospital needs to learn something about supervision. Only he can make the changes in procedure and responsibility that are required.

Talks between physicians and nurses, even with the head nurse, accomplish nothing. The same problems that I have noted will continue. A physician can not change the system. A head nurse can not change the system. Meanwhile, who would know? To work harder will not solve the problem. The nurses couldn't work any harder.

Ceil, my secretary, runs back and forth from here to my study, only a mile away, to try to keep work moving. I have accomplished work on manuscripts due soon, and have caught up with a number of letters that have been dangling, also with some reading and re-reading in *Harper's*

Magazine, The Atlantic Monthly, and others. It is not easy to read and to write while in bed with leg up. I violate instruction now and then, in order to write or to sign a letter, sitting up on the side of the bed, leg dangling.

I estimated, on my prescribed four walks per day up and down the corridor, that from half to a third of the beds were unoccupied. Saturday and Sunday could have been even lower and with less bustle. Vacant beds raise the cost per patient.

ST. VINCENT'S HOSPITAL

Written at St. Vincent's Hospital, New York
13 October 1968

Please read the plea on the last page, even if you skip the first part.

The paragraphs below will explain why I seemed to disappear for a time. It will also explain to kind friends who have enquired, some of the details about the event that sent me here. Of course, everyone knows what a wonderful hospital this is, and I can well appreciate how lucky I am to receive such skillful and kind attention.

It happened the night of Tuesday the 24th of September. Having worked in Harrisburg that day with Blue Shield of Pennsylvania, I had arrived at my apartment at 509 Hudson Street in Greenwich Village in New York, at about 8 o'clock. After tidying things up a bit, and after a cup of tea with half a slice of bread, and a few telephone calls, I set out at about 9:40 for a walk, having in mind the possibility of going to a restaurant later. I was so foolish as to walk down Hudson Street and turn left on to Houston Street, which is commercial and secluded at that point on one side and with a high wall on the other to set off a small playground. A man had been trailing along behind me on Hudson Street, but I gave the matter no thought and did not observe that he turned when I did. Suddenly his left arm was around my neck while his right arm thrust a dagger into my chest in the short ribs, with the words, "Give me your money." Instead, I shook loose, and shoved him away. I can't remember exactly what happened, but I must have given him a terrific shove and perhaps a wallop, for when I ran and looked back, he was, to my relief, off in the other direction.

People keep asking me if he got my money. Not a cent. And I was freshly re-fueled, as I had expected to depart early Friday morning for Seattle on a legal case.

I was unaware at first that the encounter was serious. There was at first glance no blood; then only a spot on my shirt. My first thought was to walk back to my apartment and use the telephone to find a physician who would see me that time of night. I supposed that I'd go to work next day same as usual. Blood then began to flow in bigger quantities. Home remedies might not do, so I ran toward 6th Avenue and hailed a taxicab at the foot of Bedford Street. I told the driver that I had been stabbed: please take me to the nearest hospital. Some men directed him to St. Vincent's Hospital, but he became confused in the maze of streets in this part of the Village. He encountered by chance a police car, so I had a swift escort right into the emergency room.

Action was immediate. It seemed that everyone had been waiting for me. Dr. Lisa Santoro, a resident surgeon, was fortunately on hand: she has been wonderful. The bleeding seemed to me to be profuse, though this is not important, except that it must have contributed to the state of shock that I went into just before the operation, necessitating a blood transfusion, all of which I learned about days later. I think also what helped to wear me down was the long lists of questions in the emergency room—personal data, Medicare, medical history, and questions that the detectives asked.

It was almost funny, I thought, the care with which a group of people, a nun in charge, maybe a nurse or two, policemen, counted my valuables on another stretcher and made lists of the contents of my pockets, including even the subway tokens. I wondered if they would cast lots over it all and my clothes. I'd rather they'd get it than my assailant. But no, they sealed everything in envelopes. Some woman came from the cashier's office and started to explain something about costs. What you mean is that it costs money to run a hospital, I said to her. Yes, that was indeed the point. She needed a deposit of $250. Well, you have my money: help yourself to $250, and lying flat I signed some kind of paper.

An exploratory operation, Dr. Santoro explained, would be necessary. No one could tell from external appearances just what had happened inside. The X-rays of the chest, already developed, showed no great amount of internal bleeding, but the possibility of cuts in the pericardium, lung and liver, had to be explored in order to avoid regrettable mistakes in treatment. Dr. Burchell, noted surgeon, was on his way over.

An intern cut slits in my arm for a manometer and for glucose. He used a local anesthetic. I had no idea that one of them was so long: I didn't have a look at the arm with the bandage off till some days later.

I asked for a priest. An Anglican priest was not at hand, but a Roman Catholic priest came, heard my confession, gave absolution.

I remember the ride to the operating-room, and of Dr. Han (who received his medical education in Japan, I learned later) introducing himself to me: he would give me the anesthesia. It seemed to be slow in its action, as I could still for many minutes see through the mask. It must have been an oxygen mask, I believe now, in an attempt to offset oncoming shock. Apparently it was not enough, but I knew no more. It was by then 2 a.m.

I had supposed that I'd bounce back at once and have a telephone at my bed next morning: that then I'd call Lola and tell her all about it.

Instead, next morning, after the usual stop in the recovery room, I found myself under intensive care, and there I stayed three days—oxygen mask, needles stuck in me to record heart-beats, incisions in one arm for a manometer, glucose dripping continuously into a vein (and to continue four days), tube through one nostril and into my stomach. Readings for temperature, pulse, blood pressure almost hourly it seemed. I must have been a sight to behold. And there was Lola! Someone at the hospital had called her in Washington at 4 a. m. She could stay only a few minutes at a time. And toward evening, here came Diana and Linda, no easy accomplishment, Diana with five little children to dispose of, and Linda a school-teacher.

My first visitor, other than Lola, was Dr. Badanes. I had talked the nun in charge of the emergency room to let me try to call Mrs. Badanes to explain that I could not ride to the Rockland State Hospital next morning with her. Dr. Badanes himself answered the telephone. He was horrified. He had come all the way from East 86th Street to see me and it was a special trip for him, as he is not on the staff of St. Vincent's. His wife Jean came later, having been directed by Dr. Rainer to forget the Rockland State Hospital and to come down here instead to see what she could do for me. By some magic touch, she talked Lola's way into the Fifth Avenue Hotel near-by, already over-booked. The twin beds plus one rolled in took care of Diana and Linda.

Right after Dr. Badanes came, here was my wonderful friend Dr. Susan Goldfarb. She is a psychologist on the staff here and had by chance happened to hear about me in the physician's lounge.

It was almost funny. The nurses must have put me down as a VIP (Very Important Patient). Came Dr. Freyhan, Chief of Psychiatry here. My friend Dr. Zubin had called him to make sure that Dr. Deming has everything that this hospital has to offer. Then came the Chief of Surgery. The Chancellor of New York University had called the head of the Medical School of New York University to ask him to get in touch with the head of surgery here and for him to make sure that I lacked nothing. Came then Dr. Pasani, Chief of Obstetrics here. He teaches at New York University.

All this time I was on the critical list: no telephone, no visitors, no food (fortunately I was not hungry). The nurses gave me the names of people that had come or called on the telephone, and of course I was grateful.

All this is behind me. Those four days in intensive care seem now like a few minutes. What I'll always remember about them is not the unpleasantness of all the contraptions, but the devotion of those nurses, and my dismal failure to cough. They tried so hard every hour to produce a cough out of me, very necessary for my lungs under those circumstances, they explained, to keep them from filling up, but oh how it hurt. One of them gave me an injection, over my protest, to ease the pain, but sure enough, I came through with a good cough as her reward. Then there was the necessity to breathe deep, with more pain. Dr. Santoro explained how important it was to exercise my legs—stretch toes up and down 100 times a day, so I did 200. A blower helped a lot, I think, to keep my bellows in good condition, and I used it every 4 hours for days, though apparently all this was not enough.

Dr. Susan Goldfarb came with a book on Japan. She had sent a card the first day. I mentioned her earlier. Now I may have a few visitors, if spaced far enough between. Natalie Calabro and Leon Kilbert talked their way in. Ruth Stockton brought mail. Dr. and Mrs. Rainer came: also Dr. Abdullach and Dr. Vollenweider. I learned later that Dr. Kurnow, Dr. Glasser, George Miaoulis were all here the first day but could not get in. Only people that know Jean Badanes can appreciate her angelic way of doing things. Mr. M. El Shennawy has almost the same touch, and mailed envelopes for me. Al and Betty Watson have been wonderful. I shouldn't mention names, as I am omitting so many. Telegrams and calls came from many parts of the country.

Fear of infection gradually subsided. I went into a private room. The critical period passed. I was up and about on a regular diet, working on numerous papers and plans, seeing visitors, using the telephone on business mostly on long distance. The stitches came out. On the 9th day, I could leave the hospital but must stay close by a few days in the Fifth Avenue Hotel for observation.

I knew almost immediately on arrival at the hotel that something was wrong—terrific pain at the base of one lung, not so bad when I'd sit or stand. Anyway, I finished work on my testimony for a study of the effects on other railways of the proposed merger of the Illinois Central and the Gulf, Mobile and Ohio Railways. The final results had only just arrived from Chicago. I had organized my testimony pretty well before we went on our trip to Amsterdam, Zagreb, and Madrid (4–18 September), and had in the hospital gone as far as I could without the final results. Of course, by now I had talked by telephone every hour with the men in Chicago.

Anyway, I finished this testimony next day at the hotel and mailed it to Ceil for final typing to send onward to Chicago. Of course, there was as usual some polishing to do here and there later on by telephone.

Meanwhile I had called Dr. Burchell. He called back twice to say that there was still no space at the hospital. Finally one opened up. Back to the hospital. A lung-scan. A pulmonary embolism. Fortunately, some new medicine (Heparin) injected every six hours would speed up dissolution of the clot, and help to dissolve any others that might be lurking around. So I was again in the ward for intensive care, but only for a day. The pain was gone in eight hours.

That was nine days ago. Now I can take short walks around the room and in the corridor. Meanwhile, I've studied a lot, and have kept up with some of my work. I read the book *Topaz* which Mr. Schoeneman sent to me: also a good portion of Chaucer's *Canterbury Tales*, which Leon Kilbert brought.

Thanks to my secretary Ceil in Washington, and in spite of abominable mail service, I've been able to carry on a lot of other work too, especially on the Midwest Divisions case. Morris Hansen has fortunately worked with me on it from the beginning, and he has been taking care of it as only he could, ever since I've been here. He has come here from Washington twice to talk about some of the problems. Lola went back to Washington with him last Thursday evening. She may return and escort me home when the time comes.

I can never find a way to repay the goodness shown to me for so many cards, telegrams, letters, calls, flowers, books, and other acts of kindness.

And tomorrow I'll be 68. Miss Sybil Carof came night before last with cake and a candle and Schrafft's ice cream. I was feeling miserable and could eat none of it, but how thoughtful of her. She will come and give me another chance tomorrow night.

20th Oct. I've been home now four days, and am recovering rapidly.

PLEA—A PLEA FOR BLOOD

I did not know till Dr. Burchell explained it to me. There are two kinds of blood in the blood-bank, good and bad. He used three units of good blood on me. Bad blood, he said, is a last resort.

People like my friends and your friends can give good blood, and that is about the only source thereof. The medical history of a friend in not shrouded. His blood is almost always of good quality. In contrast, blood from a regular donor that takes pay for it is almost dependably pretty well washed up, like the donor himself, if I understood Dr. Burchell correctly.

In other words, good blood comes from friends and from their friends. Money can not buy it: it is not for sale.

I may have garbled some of the medical language here, but Dr. Burchell's point was very clear. He and other surgeons need good blood. Any type will do as replacement.

In short, I owe three pints of good blood, and there is only one way to repay them. Money won't do it. I had not appreciated these critical requirements. Maybe this plea would bring friends to offer blood. (Some did.)

Chapter Eleven
Observations on Teaching

Dr. Deming is an educator. For years, he has taught at New York University and Columbia University. Several thousand people attend his 4-day seminars each year. He tells those participants that they are there for education: to learn theory.

In both of his latest books, *Out of the Crisis* and *The New Economics for Industry, Education, Government*, Dr. Deming discusses his ideas on education. Chapter 31 of *The Deming Dimension* by Henry Neave also has a good chapter on this topic, and *Quality or Else*, by Dobyns and Mason, discusses how the Deming philosophy is being implemented in public education.[1]

---

[1]W. Edwards Deming. *Out of the Crisis*, MIT, Cambridge University Press, 1988.

W. Edwards Deming. *The New Economics for Industry, Education, Government*, MIT, Cambridge University Press, 1992.

Henry Neave. *The Deming Dimension*, SPC Press, Knoxville, TN, 1990.

Lloyd Dobyns & Clare Crawford-Mason, *Quality or Else*, Houghton Mifflin, Boston, 1991.

The two articles which follow were both written by Dr. Deming. The first is actually a letter to the editor of *The American Statistician*. The second is taken from his book, *Out of the Crisis*.

On Teaching

From The American Statistician
Vol. 26, No. 1, Feb. 1972

A Letter to the Editor

Dear Sir:

Memorandum on Teaching

There is much discussion today about student participation in affairs of the university, even in respect to evaluation of teachers and content of courses. Here are some of my thoughts on the matter.

It seems to me that the prime requirement for a teacher is to possess some knowledge to teach. He who does no research possesses not knowledge and has nothing to teach. Of course some people that do good research are also good teachers. This is a fine combination, and one to be thankful for, but not to expect.

No lustre of personality can atone for teaching error instead of truth. One of the finest teachers that I ever knew could hold 300 students spellbound, teaching what is wrong. The two poorest teachers that I ever had (though a third one ran neck and neck) were Professor Ernest Brown in mathematics at Yale and Sir Ronald Fisher at University College in London. Sir Ernest will be known for centuries for his work in lunar theory, and Sir Ronald for revolutionizing man's methods of inference. People came from all over the world to listen to their impossible teaching, and to learn from them, and learn they did. I would not trade my good luck to have had these men as teachers for hundreds of lectures by lesser men but "good teachers."

It is too late when the student finds out that the foundation that he built in college is shaky. He may fill in gaps by self study, but the place to lay the sure foundation is in school. The best insurance that a student can take out is to make sure that his professors do research.

The student is at a disadvantage when asked to evaluate a teacher. On what basis? Lustre of personality? Knowledge of the subject? Content of course? The teacher's interest in making sure that he is communicating to the students whatever it is that he is trying to say? A student can possibly judge the teacher's knowledge of the subject, but he can hardly be a judge of the content of the course. Not even the teacher has dependable knowledge about what ought to be taught. Learning today is preparation for 5, 10, 20 years in the future. A student naturally likes what he calls a good teacher, for whatever reasons. What use, then, could be made of student's evaluation of a teacher?

The problem of identifying a good teacher is not one in consumer research, though every statistician knows well the importance of consumer research. A university should be now, as in days gone by, a place where one may listen and learn from great men.

The only suitable judge of a teacher's knowledge are his peers. The only objective criterion of knowledge is research worthy of publication. Publication should of course be measured on some scale of contribution to knowledge, not by numbers of papers.

Suggestions from students concerning the content of a course or the competence of a teacher are accordingly, in my judgment, a reckless idea. I would counsel myself and my colleagues to take no notice of evaluation by students. For my own part, I could not teach under a system of evaluation by students.

W. Edwards Deming
Professor of Statistics
Graduate School of Business Administration
New York University

W. Edwards Deming
A Master Teacher at the Blackboard

An Excerpt from

Out of the Crisis

by W. Edwards Deming

CAES, MIT, 1986, Chapter 6, page 173

Remark on quality of teaching. How do you define quality of teaching? How do you define a good teacher? I offer comment only in respect to higher education. The first requisite for a good teacher is that he have something to teach. His aim should be to give inspiration and direction to students for further study. To do this, a teacher must possess knowledge of the subject. The only operational definition of knowledge requisite for teaching is research. Research need not be earthshaking. It may only be a new derivation of knowledge or principles already established. Publication of original research in reputable journals is an index of achievement. This is an imperfect measure, but none better has been found.

In my experience, I have seen a teacher hold a hundred fifty students spellbound, teaching what is wrong. His students rated him as a great teacher. In contrast, two of my own greatest teachers in universities would be rated poor teachers on every count. Then why did people come from all over the world to study with them, including me? For the simple reason that these men had something to teach. They inspired their students to carry on further research. They were leaders of thought—by name, Sir Ronald Fisher in statistics at University College, and Sir Ernest Brown in lunar theory at Yale. Their works will remain classic for centuries. Their students had a chance to observe what these great men were thinking about, and how they built roads into new knowledge.

Example: Another publishing house was preparing a new edition of its widely used series (elementary readers). One of us, asked to consult, objected in detail to the blandness of the stories proposed. The company's vice-president in charge of textbooks confessed that he, too, thought that the stories would bore young readers, but he was obliged to keep in mind that neither children nor teachers buy textbooks; school boards and superintendents do.

Chapter Eleven

Chapter Twelve
Childhood Memories

Compiled for my daughter Diana at her request
29 January 1987

My dear Diana,

You asked me to write some notes about my early childhood and about my parents. It is a pleasure to do this, but the notes will be scrappy, written on aeroplanes now and then, from memories as they come to the surface.

I was born in Sioux City on 14 October 1900. My brother, your Uncle Bob, came later on 11 May 1902. We lived on Bluff Street. I can hear my father tell me the number, 121. Years ago, possibly 1960 or 1965, I had the good fortune to see Bluff Street and No. 121. The chance arose when there was need of a field trip to that area for one of my clients, Young and Rubicam on Madison Avenue. I pointed out to Dorothy Ackerman of

Young and Rubicam that I would be the logical one to go to Sioux City. The agent there willingly hauled me to Bluff Street, and I saw right away a reason for the name. It is on a bluff, high above the Missouri River. There were three cottages, the middle one being, sure enough, No. 121.

W. Edwards Deming, Age 2

I remember nothing about Sioux City. We (my father and all of us) moved when I was about four (and Bob two) to the Edwards farm, 300 acres, situated near Polk City between Ames and Des Moines. It was known as the Edwards farm because my mother's father, Henry Coffin Edwards, owned it. He moved to some town in Missouri and we moved in. I surmise that we made the trip from Sioux City to Ames by train, and then by the interurban (the Ft. Dodge, Des Moines, and Southern Railway) which ran between Ames and Des Moines, off at Wagner's Corner, not far from the house on the Edwards farm. Iowa was crisscrossed by railways, now mostly abandoned. There were of course no trucks. Everything moved by train or by horse and wagon. A freight train would stop at a designated spot to pick up canisters filled with cream, to haul to the creamery.

The land was hilly, green grass, horses, cows, pigs, a pond between the house and the barn. Water came from a well. My brother Bob remembers a little colt named Goldie.

We (Bob and I) wore on the farm, in the summer, one piece suits like pajamas, contrived by my mother for simplicity, and we went barefoot in those suits all over the farm. We put on a clean suit every morning. We each had two suits, one to wear, the other for the washing machine. I remember the pleasant feeling of green grass under our feet, especially when in later years we tried to go barefoot, and did, amongst the cactus plants of Wyoming, spending most of our time pulling out cactus thorns. I remember little ducks on the pond on the Edwards farm, the worried mother hen clucking on the bank, unable to understand why her little chickens had lost their minds and gone into the water.

I remember something about our first day on the Edwards farm. It was late in the day. I remember using my Aunt Chub's toothbrush, which she had left behind. I had known nothing about toothbrushes up till then. Her real name was Laura, but she never used it. I wrote to her once as "My dear Aunt Laura," to learn over and over for many years to come the seriousness of this error. She was Chub, not Laura.

I entered school at Polk City, possibly at age 5. The teacher was a Miss Ashmore. I thought that she was pretty. Later in life, at around age 40, I arranged to meet her at a certain spot in Minneapolis, or so I thought, but we somehow fouled up the arrangement and never found each other, although we both declared later that we were there at the appointed time and place.

Only recently my brother Bob, your Uncle Bob, who lives in Silver City, New Mexico, told me on the telephone his recollection that in the winter he would meet me with the sled, as I returned from school. I would put him on the sled, and with a jerk, toss him off the rear end of the sled and into the snow; I five, he three, or six and four.

We had a telephone, with multiple rings. My parents said that the first sentence that I ever uttered was, "Papa telephone to Mr. Ander." (Mr. Anderson).

Pluma Irene Deming
Mother of W. Edwards Deming

I wrote with chalk in the barn the letters A, B, C, but backward. My cousin Howard Edwards, who years later owned the farm, protected that writing to show me, thinking that some time I would come to visit him, as I did in 1935. The government later on bought the farm from Howard at a fancy figure, for a park, and he moved to Polk City nearby. Vandals set the barn on fire, he wrote to me.

My mother gave music lessons. She had a grand piano, a Kimball. She played the organ for church, anyone could be sure. I remember her and three women practicing for a concert, and I can hear the tune but not the words, and I can't identify it by name.

A solo that someone sang, probably more than once, maybe a pupil of my mother went like this.

I also remember her voice singing *The Swallow*, one of her favorite songs.

I would scribble with a pencil on paper, saying that I was writing music. My mother would put it on the piano and play something, and declare that I had written great music.

William Albert Deming
Father of W. Edwards Deming

I stepped on a nail, barefoot and recognized instantly the opportunity to let out a big howl. Dr. Tyler came in his automobile, crank on the side. (I wonder what kind it was.) He administered toxin anti-toxin, and I probably howled again. I remember I woke up one morning with an odd feeling, sick. Dr. Tyler came. Diphtheria. Diphtheria was serious but by now there was inoculation against it, and Dr. Tyler had it, even though it had only recently been invented. Anyway, I was very sick for days, and a worry to my parents, but I obviously recovered.

My father used a straight razor, and your Uncle Bob took it into his head one day that the time had come when he too ought to shave, and so he did. I can still see the right side of his face solid red with blood, and my father jumping to quick action.

My father made two trips to Wyoming. I knew nothing about Wyoming, nor why he went. The lure was free land, it must have been. Free it was, but with a price of hardship unforeseen. Thousands of acres of land in tracts of 40 to 80 acres would be opened up around Garland (long since abandoned) for people to "file on." He never returned from the second trip, but sent for the rest of us to come to Cody.

One of his trips to Wyoming extended beyond Christmas, and I remember that my mother gave me a book of pictures to fill in with colored crayons. She explained that Santa Claus had brought it, but did not know where to leave it, so he sent it to papa, and now papa had sent it to me.

On one page was a man in bed, with these words: "He was in bed for more than three weeks, with sunken eyes and shallow cheeks." Another showed a boy in bed, "When I was sick and lay abed, I had three pillows at my head." Another page showed a zebra, escaped from a big toaster with a fire under it.

My father had obtained work in Cody (named after Buffalo Bill, Colonel Cody), in Mr. Simpson's law office, and sent for us. We changed trains in Omaha en route to Wyoming. I remember my mother's explanation that the Indian sitting across the waiting room in the station in Omaha was an Indian—my first Indian. He was, I remember faintly, dressed in Indian garb with fancy braids and necklaces. I was seven years old.

(Left to right)

W. Edwards Deming, his sister, Elizabeth Deming, and his brother, Robert Deming

Our train (Burlington) went through Alliance, headed toward Billings, but we got off at Tuluka (luka as in St. Luke) to take the train to Cody through the Big Horn Mountains. Tuluka was later abolished, and trains thereafter went all the way to Billings, with connexion from Frannie to Cody, two round trips a day. Frannie was named after a Frannie who ran a hash house for the railroad men at Frannie. There was already a north and south Burlington line from Billings to Denver. Frannie was a station on this line.

We lived first in Cody in Mrs. Hutsonpillar's boarding house; then moved to the central one of the three Watkins cottages, owned by Mrs. Watkins who occupied one of them. The location was just below the "bench," a plateau that extended west from Rattlesnake Mountain to Cody and beyond.

School was not far away. We sometimes went to school barefoot. Your Uncle Bob certainly did one day. Our parents had bought for him a new pair of shoes, and he went wading in them, ruined them. "He'll just have to go barefoot," my mother said, and so he did, and I recall that it was a cool morning.

My mother gave music lessons. I surmise that it was the same grand piano that she had on the farm in Iowa; that it had come (by rail of course) without other furniture, but I don't recall that anyone came to our house on the farm in Iowa to put the piano into a box for shipment. On Saturdays, my mother gave lessons in Corbett in a house not far from the station. Maybe it was the station agent's home. Bob and I went with her, usually. We would take the train from Cody and get off at Corbett. I remember that the train would sometimes steam into Corbett at night with no headlight, headed for Cody: that my mother said that she was going to buy a gallon of kerosene for the engine. The station for Cody was across the Shoshone River from the town of Cody, a hackride to and from. Harry would haul us in his hack (probably drawn by two horses, but I am not sure) to the station, and meet us at the train as we returned.

Corbett was the spot along the Shoshone River selected for a dam to raise the level of the river for the canal to the Ralston Reservoir, for storage of water for irrigation of the Powell Flat.

Cody was alive with saloons. I remember the big fire. Our mother wakened us in the night, "The town is on fire," and it was. Eleven saloons burned down.

My mother played the organ (pumping kind, gratis I am sure) at the Roman Catholic Church. We all loved Father Endres, a Belgian priest, in the saddle day and night, covering Cody, Corbett, Meeteetsee, Marquette (later submerged by the Shoshone reservoir), Clark's Fork, and I don't know what else. Later he was put in charge of St. Barbara's Church in Powell, after we moved there, but my mother then played the organ (pumping kind) for the Episcopal Church.

We lived in Cody about two years; then moved 22 miles to Camp Coulter, on the railway of course, between Frannie and Cody. The name Camp Coulter was later changed to Powell, in honor of the explorer, John Wesley Powell. My father had filed on a tract of 40 acres adjacent to the town. We lived at first (4 or 5 years) in a tar paper shack, long, like a railroad car. The kitchen had a long bench in it. I remember our father working on it. A pump for water from the well came up through it.

The water was dreadfully hard with alkali. I would haul on my bicycle now and then a bucket of soft water from the canal some distance away (half a mile or more).

Your Uncle Bob and I entered school. There were 23 children in the school, counting us, grades 1 to 7. The teacher was a Miss Eva Warrington. My father thought that I could handle the 3d grade, and I did, skipped the 2d grade.

Elizabeth arrived on 21 January 1909, "born in a tar paper shack," she always said, and so she was. Dr. Sturgeon was there.

In 1911 came from Grandfather by telegraph to the station agent at Powell tickets for mama and the three children to visit him and the rest of the family in Los Angeles and Ontario.

We were there all winter. We went first to Aunt Marie, 1357 East 47th Street. There was Uncle Will and their children, cousin Kelso, four years older than I was, and Agnes two years older. Aunt Chub lived with them. Uncle Will died in the flu epidemic of 1918.

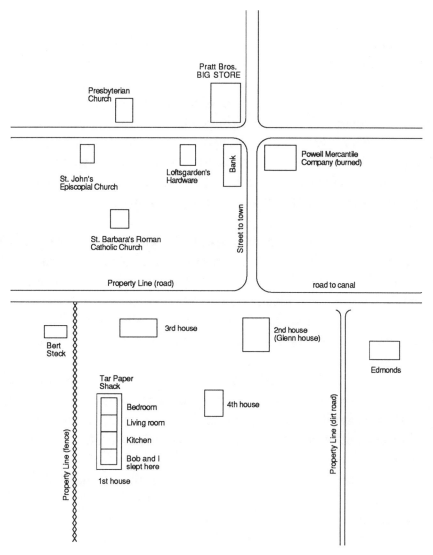

Pratt Bros.
BIG STORE

Presbyterian
Church

St. John's
Episcopial Church

Loftsgarden's
Hardware

Bank

Powell Mercantile
Company (burned)

St. Barbara's Roman
Catholic Church

Street to town

Property Line (road)

road to canal

3rd house

2nd house
(Glenn house)

Bert
Steck

Edmonds

Tar Paper
Shack

4th house

Bedroom

Living room

Kitchen

Bob and I
slept here

1st house

Property Line (fence)

Property Line (dirt road)

The Deming House and Property
Powell, Wyoming

Our mother was to Elizabeth, mama. Aunt Marie was "der mama" (probably "their mama"), and Aunt Chub was "der udder mama." Aunt Chub worked at the Broadway Department Store, $5 per week as I remember it, car fare 5 cents each way. The interurban to Long Beach ran not far away from Aunt Marie's house. My mother took me and your Uncle Bob to Long Beach one day, where I first saw the ocean. I remember eating lunch in a Japanese restaurant, and that the food was delicious.

We lived a month with Aunt Marie, then spent the rest of the winter with Grandfather and Grandmother at Ontario. We entered school.

We also entered Sunday School. We shopped around for one to our liking. Sunday School at the Episcopal Church was for study and for religion, a bit dull. We tried the Roman Catholic Sunday School, no improvement. We ended up liking best the Nazarene Sunday School—livelier, and with parties.

Tangerines were on the trees. Children as they walked to school, including Bob and me, helped ourselves. The teacher lined the pupils up one morning, and the man that saw us steal tangerines looked us all over, but could not be sure of identification. No more tangerines. I was scared.

The day came when we must return to Wyoming. "Take your last look at Paradise," my mother said, as the train pulled out of Ontario through groves of orange trees.

"You tell Will to build you a good house," Grandfather had said to our mother, and so he did, afterward known as the Glenn house, because after a few years in it, my father sold it to Dr. Glenn, an optometrist. His wife was beautiful, and his daughters too—Edna the oldest, then Mildred and Gertrude.

My father received a good education, thanks to his teacher, Mr. Walter E. Atkinson, who at my request wrote to me in 1934 an account of my father's determination for education. With no money in his pocket, he approached Mr. Atkinson, master of a private school near my father's home in Iowa, and Mr. Atkinson accepted him. It could be that my father was aware of the poor teaching in the public schools, and sought something better. His thirst for knowledge never ceased.

He was 19 when his father was killed in a runaway. His mother lived many years afterward, and my father was able to visit her a number of times. One way to get a free ride to Iowa was to accompany a carload of freight that required special attention.

He studied law while he worked in Sioux City. He never took the examination for the bar.

He was good in Latin and in arithmetic and in algebra, and always took delight in helping your Uncle Bob and me with our lessons when we came home from school.

One of his fondest hopes was that I would go forward with my education. He lived to see me with a college degree from the University of Wyoming 1921 in Electrical Engineering, M.S. 1925 from the University of Colorado in mathematics and physics, and my doctor's degree 1928 from Yale in mathematics and physics.

He was a good checker player. How he would have fared with experts I know not, but Bob and I were a great disappointment to him. Our checker-playing was so bad that it was no fun for him to play with us. I played chess with some of the boys in the same house in college, which is of course different from checkers. How I found time to play chess, I know not now.

I remember my father pacing the floor one evening—in which house I can not be sure of now, maybe in the tar-paper shack—recounting the debts that he owed, and the accumulated total, some accumulated in Cody and still unpaid. He was despondent. Credit would run out. My mother charged 50 cents for a music lesson. I am sure that was about the only cash income that we had. Some people could not pay. Mr. Charlie Robinson, Eileen's father, one time when my father was in Canada, paid for Eileen's lessons with a quarter of beef. It was tough as leather. My mother wrote to him to come and get it: she had too much respect for old age, she said to try to eat it. I had a job at Mrs. Judson's Hotel—Mrs. Haney, she was then, Frank Haney's wife, but she was still to most people Mrs. Judson—filling the boiler in the morning before school and again in the evening; after school, bring in kindling and coal for morning, and what else I don't now remember. It was not a hotel: no room, only meals. Mrs. Judson paid me $1.25 per week. I held on to the money except for contributions to the family for necessaries. Once in a while I could treat the family to Sunday dinner at Mrs. Judson's, 25 cents per meal.

My father took on the sale of Canadian Pacific lands, during the span between 1913 and 1918 (guess work) and was gone for weeks at a time. My mother went with him at least once, by train of course. It was not an easy trip. It was necessary to stay overnight in two places, possibly Billings and Lethbridge: no night trains north and south. As my father remarked, train service was good east and west, but bad north and south.

One time in the middle of the night in the house that Dr. Glenn bought, when my father was in Canada, my mother called to us (your Uncle Bob and me). I heard her, and went to her room. She was sure that someone was in the house. It was not quite finished, and anyone could walk in. Your Uncle Bob kept on sleeping. My mother kept on calling him, and he finally awakened and came. My mother took us by the hand, Elizabeth in her arms, and led us to the Edmonds house, not far away. Mr. Edmonds (Henry D.) took his revolver and went to our house to look around: came back with the report that he could find no trace of anyone there. He thought that the noise could have come from a rat. Some of the native rats were large and could well move timbers or furniture.

My mother watched the Cody paper, I remember, when my father was on one of his trips to Canada, expecting to see our lot advertised for sale for failure to pay taxes. Somehow, my father paid the taxes, and the way cleared for other worries.

When we lived in the Glenn house, we had a cat named Collar Button, black all over except for a white collar button. She was good at catching mice. I remember making a number of trips up and down the stairs in the dim light of a kerosene lamp, being careful not to step on a black piece of cloth or fur on one step. Later, with more light, I perceived that the dark spot was Collar Button, dozing in peace.

I never thought much about why my father sold our second home to Dr. Glenn. Maybe he got a good deal. Anyway, we had to move out. We endured a few months in cramped quarters in two rooms downtown rented from Mrs. Steinberger. There was not room for our grand piano. My father boxed it up and sent it to Chicago for renovation. It must have been sad for my mother to give lessons on a pumping organ. Meanwhile, we built the third home, not far from the original tar paper shack. I say we because I helped, and your Uncle Bob, too. I remember working on the roof and having an argument with my father. Your Uncle Bob and I were pretty good hack carpenters.

Later, around 1919 I think, my father built the fourth home. I arrived on the train in June 1919 (could have been 1920) from college to find our family in the fourth house. My father and mother may have met me at the station with an automobile, maybe with horse and buggy—can't remember except that we went to house No. 4 which I had not yet seen.

My father bought an automobile, a Metz. It was a disgrace to anybody that made such a thing and to anybody that owned one—no end of trouble and expense. The transmission was a large flat disk attached to the engine and a fiber wheel that rubbed against it, low gear near the centre, higher and higher gear as it moved out. A great idea, except that it didn't work.

Kerosene lamps furnished light. There was no electricity in Powell till around 1918. There were lamps with wicks straight across, maybe 3/4 inch, and those with a wick in a circle, a Rochester burner, which gave much more light. People sometimes carried kerosene lanterns at night.

Then came a new era of light, the gasoline lamp with a pump. Light came from a mantle, very fragile. There were five gasoline street lights along the main street of the town. At about age 14, I took on the job to light them, $10 per month, not bad, though one time I took a job out in the country irrigating for Mrs. Northrop, and forgot about the street lights. I rode a horse into town to light the lamps, after dark. The horse came out all right, but I was sore for days from the ride.

Each street light had a tank for gasoline at the bottom. I would pump up the tank, then hoist myself up on the lamp post to light the lamp. I must have needed a step ladder to put on a new mantle.

A runaway team smashed one of the lights. It never was restored, as I recall it. The town council decided that the town could no longer afford lights every night; there would be lights hereafter only Saturday and Sunday nights. My pay went down to $8 per month.

Some of us boys in Powell took a dislike to Dr. Llewelyn. I'm not sure now why. One possible reason is that he did not like cats. Anyway, a Dr. Mains had come to town. I sprained my thumb. I was to play a piano solo at High School. Desperate, I decided to go to a doctor. "I'll go to Dr. Mains," I said to myself, to get even with Dr. Llewelyn. I walked up the steps in the evening to the home of Dr. Mains, rang the bell. Here were Dr. Mains and Dr. Llewelyn playing cards. They both looked at my thumb. Dr. Mains wrote out a prescription to rub into it, and whatever it was, it was wonderful. I played the piano solo, and could not blame the thumb. Dr. Mains charged me 50 cents, as I remember it. He died in the flu epidemic of 1918. He did his best, driving his Model T Ford from house to house; contracted the flu himself, and Dr. Llewelyn could not save him.

My mother died in August 1920 at the Mayo Clinic in Rochester. She died from a blood clot a week after an operation. My father had left her, doing so well, to go down to Masillon, Iowa (not sure) to visit his mother. I was working in a government office in Powell for Mr. Hosig when the telephone rang for me, and your Uncle Bob said to me, "Come over to the office right away." He had the telegram in hand. My mother had died. We had a hard time finding our father, but we did. He brought her body from Rochester, and we buried her in the Powell cemetery.

He was heart broken. I remember that Elizabeth (only eleven when our mother died) wrote to the Dean of Women at the University of Wyoming, "He sits at the dining room table and sobs and calls for her, but she does not come."

He married Grace Peterson in 1925. Her husband Pete had died years before. Grace and my mother were good friends.

A letter came in 1930 from Grace to say that my father was worse. I had been worried. He was in the hospital at Powell. I left Washington at once; arrived in Powell, and went to the hospital. He was in pain most of the time. Possibly it was diverticulitis, though Elizabeth says that it was cancer of the stomach. He died in agony three days after I arrived. Your Uncle Bob lived in Los Angeles. I sent a telegram to him and he came at once.

I was at the time in the government service at the Fixed Nitrogen Research Laboratory, in the Ohio Building rented by the Department of Agriculture from the American University. Your mother worked for me there, and we published some papers together on physical properties of compressed gases. She loaned me a suitcase for the journey to Powell.

After our mother died, my father sent Elizabeth to Ivinson Hall in Laramie, an Episcopal School, owned by the Diocese, to study music. This was about 1922. Elizabeth was 13. I was teaching engineering at the University of Wyoming, and studying mathematics under Professor Stromquist, a real mathematician. It was at that time that Elizabeth's back started to hurt. The diagnosis a few years later was a beginning Marie-Strumpell arthritis. It gave her screaming pain years later, but it finally burned out, leaving her stooped in the shoulders.

My mother's mother was Elizabeth Grant, a relative, so I have been told, of General Grant. She died of erysypalis at the age of 24, my mother being then three years old. She caught it, I think, taking care of people so afflicted. She is buried in Streator, Illinois, so someone told me (probably cousin Agnes, deceased) who kept track of the family. My mother told me that she remembered her mother rocking her when she was three years old.

Elizabeth Grant had money: designated it, or a good portion of it, for advanced education of her two daughters, they being my Aunt Marie, two years older than my mother, and my mother.

In accordance with Elizabeth Grant's will, my Aunt Marie and my mother, around 1892 as near as I can figure it, took the train from where? (Missouri? Streator?) to San Francisco, Aunt Marie to study art, my mother to study music. They stayed the first few weeks (maybe three months) with an uncle, who sent to Grandfather Edwards a bill for their board and room.

I married Agnes 14 June 1922. We were married in her home in Rock Springs by the Episcopal priest. We lived in Golden, near Denver, where at the foot of Mt. Lookout, I had taken a job teaching physics at the Colorado School of Mines, appointed to the job, I suspect, mostly because of my ability on the flute. Professor A.E. Bellis was head of the Physics Department at the Colorado School of Mines, and director of the band, and needed a flute player. I had studied physics under him at the University of Wyoming, so he knew me. He had directed the band at the University of Wyoming, and I played drums and timpani one year in the band, switched to piccolo next year, after lugging my drums and timpani from station to auditorium in a number of towns, when the band took a trip. I could put the piccolo in my pocket. I alternated the piccolo with a flute; was not good on either one. His letter to me, offering the job, ended with the words, "... especially as you are somewhat talented on the flute," as I recall it.

Living in Golden, I studied mathematics by correspondence with Professor Charles E. Hutchinson at the University of Colorado, Boulder, and went to summer school there in the summers of 1922, 1923, and 1924, to study differential equations and other mathematics. One course was taught by Professor Abraham Cohen of the Johns Hopkins University, and I studied the kinetic theory of gases under Professor Pietenpol, and vector analysis under Professor Oliver C. Lester, Dean of the Graduate School, Theory of Functions under Professor George Light.

Dean Lester offered me a job at Boulder. I took it, and we moved to Boulder in the summer of 1924. It was Dean Lester that told me that I should go to Yale and study mathematical physics under Leigh Page. This advice far exceeded any stretch of my imagination, but I was grateful, would do my best. He obtained for me an instructorship at Yale which paid $1000 per year, and we lived on it. I worked summers of 1925 and 1926 at the Hawthorne Plant of the Western Electric Company in Chicago, and a great experience it was.

I finished in June 1927 the work for my doctor's degree in mathematical physics. We boxed up our meagre household belongings and sent them to Littlefield, Alvord and Company in Washington, for storage, and boarded the train for Powell, to see my father. I had received a number of offers for jobs; decided to go to the Fixed Nitrogen Research Laboratory, mentioned earlier; began work there 1 August 1927. My doctorate was awarded in June 1928.

Chapter Thirteen
Those Good Years at Wyoming U.

By W. Edwards Deming, '21; LL.D., '58

Taken from the book by this title, edited by
Ralph McWhinnie, published in 1965.

Those LEAN YEARS is a better title for my campus experiences. It was in 1917 that I took the train from Powell to start off to Laramie. Laramie was a big place, to me. I had been to Billings once or twice, so I was already accustomed to big-city life. I saw Cheyenne, only two hours between trains. I was brave enough to walk up and down a bit, keeping the Union Pacific station in view.

Of course there were no taxis at the station in Laramie, or if there were, I certainly couldn't afford one. Powell had no taxis: not even electric lights. In fact, I had made $10 per month for years lighting the four or five gasoline street lights at home (five it was till a runaway team demolished one).

W. Edwards Deming, Age 19

Hand luggage and I arrived on foot at the University. On my first night, I obtained a room at Appleby's, and stayed there two or three nights until I got located. I remember inquiring if the city water was fit to drink. I ended up in what was known as the Men's Commons: a large square frame house with no architectural imagination. The lower part was dining room and kitchen. The upstairs and possibly a third floor provided rooms for the boys, two, three, or four to a room, but only one to a bed, as I remember it. The food was good—at least I don't remember originating any complaints.

First of all I had to be on the lookout for a job. Subsistence would be the problem. I had some savings, but believed in conservation. I had thought that it would be simple to make dollars and have some left over every week. Just to be sure, I arrived a day or two ahead of school to get in on the ground floor. Wages had been good in Powell, as a result of inflation from the War. I had been earning (collecting rather) $5 a day for irrigating. It turned out, though, that in Laramie things were different. I learned the hard way something important—competition. The best that the boys could do was 25 cents an hour if they could find work at all.

I called on the President of the University, Dr. Aven Nelson, a man with a kind heart, as all know who remember him. He suggested that I consult the head janitor, Mr. John Prahl. John put me to work almost immediately. He gave me five different jobs during the week, with odd items part of Saturday. One morning I was to sweep the rural school. Another morning I was to wipe the tile floor in the main hall, and the other three gave me acquaintance with more buildings. On my first experience with the tile floor in the main hall, what I did was to scatter soapy water from a bucket all over the floor. I was very thorough: every square inch got soaped. No one had told me to wipe it up. I thought that it would dry up. When the students began to arrive, somewhere around eight, the floor was a hazard. The report came back to me from a dozen sources during the day that John Prahl was looking for me.

In big snow storms I made extra money shovelling snow so that students could get around. On Saturdays and in Christmas vacation, some of us cut ice on the pond for the Union Pacific Railroad. The pond was a gravel-pit some miles out, and the ice was three to four feet thick. I suppose that in a cold winter it would be six to seven feet thick.

I don't remember much about classes except that mathematics went all right, and that I had a dreadful time with English. It is a pleasure to remember Professor Ridgeway in mathematics and his kindness to help everybody. He must have had a heterogeneous lot of boys and girls. It is a good thing that I went to college at that time, and that there were no entrance examinations.

I don't know why I elected to move away from the Commons. Possibly there was too much noise, as I tried to be a studious young man. I do remember moving from one place to another. It became fashionable to move. I remember that I was able to engage a room, put my stuff into the trunk, engage a van or a wheelbarrow, and settle myself in good order in a new room, all in the space of two hours. When I wished to move back to the Men's Commons, Mr. Burage, in his capacity as Registrar General, Comptroller, Secretary of the Board of Trustees, and overall supervisor without portfolio, reminded me that I had deserted the Men's Commons once, and would have to do penance a while to get back in.

Another job was behind the soda fountain at a drug store. Somehow or other, I muddled through, though customers must have been amazed at the new concoctions. Some boys obtained work on the Union Pacific Railway on night shifts at various jobs. Two or three boys would take on a job together. The railway was very accommodating in that respect. It was a hard deal, being on the job eight hours at a stretch, even if only every other night. I preferred shorter hours and shorter pay.

The refinery, when it came to town much later (1919 or 1920) when I was about to graduate, provided work for a number of people. One summer I stayed in Laramie and worked for Mr. A. Hitchcock repainting and staining the new Commons on the inside, and working at the refinery cleaning out the boilers. The work was not very heavy, but I remember being pretty tired at the end of the 16th hour.

One cold winter I became acquainted with a Mr. Cook, as I remember it, editor or some official in the *Laramie Boomerang*. I wondered if he had any odd jobs, and if he agreed that an ad in the Boomerang would be the best he could think of. Ad or no ad, he had some railway ties to saw up for firewood, and would pay two cents per cut, he to furnish the saw and the ties. It was a long way through a tie—two, four, six cents, etc. I made 80 cents one evening in the cold.

My main source of income the 2d year was to rustle clothes for dry cleaning for J. Bezensky, bless his soul. He would pay me 25 cents per suit. All that I had to do was to find someone who had a suit that needed cleaning or pressing, and who had something to wear meanwhile. I would take the suit to the cleaner and deliver it. That went on for a year and a half, after which I became prosperous with other work.

Once I had done some work somewhere around the University and submitted a bill for $58. I later met Mr McWhinnie (who was then student helper in the Registrar's office under Mr. Burrage), and he wondered if I was good in arithmetic. I thought about the matter a while, trying to guess why he inquired. Then I discovered by recomputation that the bill should have been $76. I supposed that it would be impossible to do anything about it, but when the cheque came, it was for $76. He just thought that he would have a little fun letting me squirm meanwhile.

One indoor sport was tubbing. There would be summary court martials of one kind or another for some offense such as shouting or complaining, or I don't know what—sometimes merely on general principles—and a man would be put into cold water, and as one boy remarked, "Thanks, boys, I was going to take a bath anyway."

There were many diversions such as singing in the choir at the Cathedral under the direction of Mr. Roger Frisbie, who was indeed a fine organist and choir master. I was on the job there Sunday morning and again at night, and at rehearsal once a week. Then there was the band under Professor Bellis. It was slyly whispered about that if one did good work in the band, he would be sure to pass his courses in physics. Unfortunately, I took the basic course in physics before I joined the band, so I had to earn the grade. I had had musical education, but elected to play drums and timpani in the band. The band took a trip on the Union Pacific to Hanna, Rawlins, Rock Springs, and Green River, and by the time I had hauled all those drums and timpani from the train to the concert hall and back again in all those towns, I decided that it would be better to play a smaller instrument, whereupon next year I played the piccolo.

There were barn dances at the agricultural farm once in a while. I had nerve enough once to ask a girl for a date, and was almost overwhelmed by her acceptance. We missed the hay rack, maybe by design, and walked. Jaunts to the surrounding hills, such as to Pilot Knob, were one means of recreation, free to all.

If I might make some criticism of education as it fell to my lot in college, the criticism would be that too much time was spent on so-called practical work. My field was electrical engineering, and I know of course that there have meanwhile been changes in education for engineers, but I will voice the criticism nonetheless. We spent too much time in manipulating tools of one kind or another—chipping, filing, hacking, sawing, gluing, and learning various arts and trade such as mechanical drawing and descriptive geometry. What we should have been doing was to spend more time on electrodynamics, thermodynamics, mathematics, English, French, German and basic subjects like economics, which I had to fill in later.

Anyway, those "lean years" were good years for me.

Chapter Fourteen
Work at the Hawthorne Plant
and the Department of Agriculture

I worked at the Hawthorne plant in Chicago the summers of 1925 and 1926, four months each summer. I had been a student at the University of Colorado in mathematical physics; obtained there in 1925 the degree M.S. I worked at the Hawthorne plant on transmitters: did nobody any good, but it was a great experience. On arrival on the fifth floor, Mr. Chester M. Coulter, whom I reported to, made it clear to me as most important—don't get caught on the stairway when the whistle blows. Those women would trample you to death: there would be no trace of you. There were 46,000 people that worked at the Hawthorne plant, and I think that 43,000 of them had high heels. I did not get caught.

My pay was $18.25 (in cash) per week during the first summer at the Western Electric Company, out of which I saved $10 or $11 per week, needed at Yale. My pay the second summer was $24.

If we intended to work overtime (and I did, for enjoyment of the work), Mary would write out a supper ticket, worth 75 cents in the company's cafeteria. There were gold dollars in those days. Five-dollar gold pieces were in circulation. A five-dollar gold piece looked much like a one-cent piece, if the one-cent piece were new or polished. One had to be careful not to confuse one for the other, especially on Sunday. Anyway, the manager of the cafeteria, in his effort to show a profit in his domain, would suggest this and that food to us, trying to build up our purchases to 75 cents, but we could not eat so much. Someone in one of my seminars from the A.T.&T. Network wrote a note to me in 1983 to say that I could not eat 75 cents worth today either in the company's cafeteria.

What I learned at the Hawthorne plant made an impression for the rest of my life. The men were talking about uniformity of the telephone apparatus, and about Dr. Walter A. Shewhart, saying that they did not understand what he was doing, but that it was important. Advertisements told the public that the old adage "as alike as two peas" should now be "as alike as two telephones."

The head of all development was Dr. H. Rossbacher. He would get upset if someone would remark that some piece of work was too theoretical. Dr. Rossbacher would come back with the remark that all that we have accomplished here has been through work that someone had declared to be too theoretical. The word practical is greatly overworked, he said. No one knows what is practical. It is necessary to understand theory.

There was a Dr. Hal Fruth there. I did not work for him, nor with him, but we almost immediately became fast friends. One of our conversations affected my life. Dr. Fruth said to me, "You are on your way to Yale. You will get your degree." Dr. Fruth was right in one respect. I had been accepted to Yale, but I was not sure about the degree. Some people go to Yale but do not get their degrees. Anyway, he assured me that when I finished my degree at Yale, Western Electric would offer me a job. This was comforting. He said that Western Electric might offer me $5,000 per year. This was more money that I had ever expected to earn (gold dollars, remember). Dr. Fruth explained to me that it was not difficult to find men worth $5,000 per year but that we are not looking for them. If we offer you a job, he said, it will be because we think that there is a possibility that you may develop into a man worth $50,000 per year, and such men are hard to find.

It was a conversation that stayed with me. A company does not need good men; it needs men that are constantly improving: it needs men with knowledge.

I finished the work for my degree, thesis and all, in June 1927, though the degree was not awarded till June 1928. The subject of my thesis was "A possible explanation of the packing effect in helium," published in the Physical Review.

Western Electric did indeed offer me a job, and the Bell Laboratories too, and other companies, but I decided to go into the Department of Agriculture.

I entered the Department of Agriculture on 1 August 1927. My work was with the Fixed Nitrogen Research Laboratory, housed in a building rented from the American University in American University Park. This laboratory had been the site of research in the fixation of nitrogen during the war, getting nitrogen from the air, for powder and for fertilizer. The work continued for the benefit of agriculture and general science.

The Deputy Chief at the Fixed Nitrogen Laboratory was a Dr. Charles Kunsman. He had worked at the Bell Laboratories, 463 West Street, New York. Dr. Shewhart and Dr. Kunsman lived in the same apartment house in Brooklyn, and they had become friends, though they did not work together.

Dr. Kunsman was eager for me to meet Dr. Shewhart, somehow feeling that we had a lot of interests in common and that I would learn a lot from Dr. Shewhart. He arranged for me many visits to Dr. Shewhart, the first one in the fall of 1927. In fact, I would claim that I had the privilege to work closer with Dr. Shewhart than any one had in the Bell Laboratories. He kindly spent much time with me as I tried to understand his thoughts.

Somehow, through devious routes that I would have trouble to reconstruct, I found myself in 1936 in charge of courses in mathematics and statistics at the Graduate School in the Department of Agriculture. None of the universities in Washington provided classes for people on the job. The Graduate School in the Department of Agriculture drew students from all over Washington. There was no restriction to people in Agriculture. As a matter of fact, classes were held at various spots in Washington wherever rooms could be had.

One of my activities at the Graduate School at the Department of Agriculture was to invite great men to give lectures. R.A. Fisher was one, J. Neyman was another, J. Wishart another, Frank Yates another. The idea came into my head to invite Dr. Shewhart to give four afternoon lectures. He accepted, and spent a year in the development of these lectures which he gave in March 1938. I remember him pacing the floor in his room at the Hotel Washington before the third lecture. He was explaining to me something. I remarked that these great thoughts should be in his lectures. He said that they were already written up in his third and fourth lectures. I remarked that if he wrote up these lectures as he had just explained them to me, they would be clearer. He said that his writing had to be foolproof. I thereupon let go the comment that he had written his thoughts so damned fool-proof that no one could understand them.

The four lectures were published by the Graduate School, Department of Agriculture under the title *Statistical Method from the Viewpoint of Quality Control* (Graduate School, Department of Agriculture, Washington 1939). I spent the rest of 1938 trying to understand the lectures, and to clarify, with Dr. Shewhart's patience, the manuscript.

We reprinted the book over and over again. It was a great book—a landmark for all industry to listen to. I had long since lost contact with the Graduate School, and the head thereof let the book run out of print in 1982 or thereabouts. Dover Press reprinted it in 1986.

A half century has passed by since Dr. Shewhart's great book of 1931 appeared, and almost half a century since his book of 1939 appeared. Another half century will pass before people in industry and in science begin to appreciate the contents of these great works.

One can say that the content of my seminars held under the auspices of the George Washington University and UCLA, and the content of my books, *Quality, Productivity, and Competitive Position*, and *Out of the Crisis*, are based in large part on my understanding of Dr. Shewhart's teaching. Even if only ten per cent of the listeners absorb part of Dr. Shewhart's teachings, the number may in time bring about change in the style of Western management.

It was my good fortune to spend time at the Bell Laboratories also with Harold F. Dodge. We became fast friends. He furnished the leadership for the development of the *Guides For Quality Control* (now identified as A.S.Q.C. B1 and B2, American National Standards, Institute, 1430 Broadway, New York 10018), first published in 1942 by the American Standards Association. Development of these guides was a great learning experience for me.

Later, Mr. Dodge became Chairman of Committee E-11 of the American Society for Testing and Materials on the quality control of materials. This too was a great privilege. I never missed a meeting during Mr. Dodge's long tenure as chairman.

An anecdote that Mr. Dodge told to me would be lost to society if not recorded. The time came to decide the length of the cord of the new telephone from the cradle to hand-set. (Previous to that, telephones were in the form of a post with a mouthpiece and receiver.) The lot fell to Mr. Dawson and his people, including Mr. Dodge, to test different lengths of the cord. Mr. Dodge and his co-workers would sometimes sneak into Mr. Dawson's office after hours and shorten his cord by a centimeter. This went on for some time cm. by cm.. One day when Mr. Dodge was in Mr. Dawson's office, his telephone rang. The cord was by then only about a foot long. Mr. Dawson had to stoop low or pick up the cradle. He never cracked a smile, Mr. Dodge said. No one ever knew whether he was ever aware of the shortening cord.

It was my honor to write a foreword for the reprinting of Dr. Shewhart's great book, *Economic Control of Quality of Manufactured Product*, put out by the ASQC in June 1980. The foreword is reproduced starting on page 94.

It was my honor also to write a foreword for the reprinting of Dr. Shewhart's book *Statistical Method from the Viewpoint of Quality Control*, Dover, 1986.

Those were good years for me. I was privileged to be around great men who were eager to learn from each other and to share their ideas.

Chapter Fifteen
My Seventh Trip to Japan

This chapter is an exact reprint of a small booklet written by Dr. Deming and printed for a few friends in November, 1965. It is a record of the trip during which he was presented to Emperor Hirohito. In a recent conversation, Dr. Deming was asked why this trip was such an important event. Thinking about it for a moment, he said that by 1965 he could begin to see the results of his work with the Japanese industrialists. He could enjoy their success, and really see the results of his labor with them.

So here is the story, exactly as he told it, complete with his own photographs.

Chapter Fifteen

MY SEVENTH TRIP

TO JAPAN

November 1965

By

W. Edwards Deming

Unexpurgated, unmeditated, unimaginative. Being a candid day-by-day account of the incredible experiences of a weary statistician, working in Japan, in continued admiration and amazement at the ability of the Japanese people to be so charming along with their dazzling attainments. Typed from original notes written on the spot. Illustrated with the author's own snapshots.

Privately printed for a few friends

i.

CONTENTS

182

ii.

Contents cont'd

1.   Sunday 7th

MY SEVENTH TRIP TO JAPAN

(November 1965)

Detour via Anchorage

Sunday 7th November 1965. Off from Seattle on NWAL at 1900, on time. It was a hurried stop. I had to register Lola's pearls with a Customs-officer, which fortunately turned out to be a woman, who knew exactly what to do. She counted them, measured the biggest one, and gave me a piece of paper so that I may bring them back in with no trouble. Mikimoto in Tokyo, where Mr. Koyanagi bought them for me in 1950, will restring and tie them.

It was tough luck that this flight on NWAL, advertised as nonstop Seattle to Tokyo, will deviate from its usual bee-line course to stop in Anchorage to pick up someone (it turned out to be 20 people on a tour), and thus arrive Tokyo 2 hours behind time. I had spent a delightful day with my sister Elizabeth on her fruit farm on Mt. Hood, and had a good rest.

Dinner on board was excellent. I had had the good sense to write to Elizabeth beforehand to tell her positively no dinner at her home, as I couldn't eat twice, nor turn down dinner in flight. Martinis according to my prescription. All kinds of hors d'oeuvres, none fit to eat except the macadamia nuts. The steak was superb. Two and a half hours, Seattle to Anchorage.

Arrived Tokyo

We were at Anchorage 40 minutes, exactly what the note from the travel agency in Washington had told me. It was dark all the way from Seattle to Tokyo, an 8-hour trip. Arrived Tokyo 2330. Mr. Noguchi was at the airport to meet me. It will be different now, Mr. Koyanagi gone. No one can fill his job, I am sure, with anything like his energy, efficiency, and knowledge of Japanese industry and personal acquaintance with top management.

Tokyo was in fog and rain, exactly the kind of weather that covered Portland and Seattle. Anchorage was clear, +15° F, snow on the ground.

Tuesday 9th. It was 0020 Tuesday the 9th when I found myself alone in my room in the Imperial Hotel, New Building, Room 1480 for memory. It is really exquisite.

Up at 6, too tired to sleep. Hungry. Breakfast in my room: best cheese omelet that I've had in a long time. Mr. Noguchi came for me at 11. I must go to lunch at the Skyroom of the Tosho Building, 8th floor, where the conference of top management is being held. The lunch was buffet style, with everything that I could think of to eat. I had to make a bow and a short speech for my lunch. (Picture next page.)

Dinner was at the same place. In the room were several birds and gib fish, carved out of ice, slowly melting.

Life would be more enjoyable if I didn't have to give a public lecture Friday. I understand that it will be held at the new Hibya Park Auditorium, which seats 1800 people. I fear that there will be 1800 disappointed people if they all come. I'd rather sing for them.

2.

TOSHO SKYROOM
/ TOKYO KAIKAN

I was forced to eat here Tuesday the 9th,
lunch and dinner

御 願 い

この方は左記の處へ行かれます、御協力下さい

とみ岡屋
東大病院分院の前
九段を通りニエ戸ニ橋を渡り右折

Directions to Tomioka-ya

The day started off in a fog with rain, and the rain increased to a cloudburst, but I was in a taxicab when it struck. We are on the edge of Typhoon Eva.

First thing this morning what I did was to go to Tomiokaya for my morning coat to wear tomorrow at the Emperor's party at Akasaka Garden. I was at one of the tea-houses in this Garden for dinner, in 1951, with Prince Takamatsu, the Emperor's younger brother. I have no idea what this party will be like.

The girl at the desk on my floor had found the telephone number of **Tomioka-ya**, a most amazing feat, it seems to me; made sure that the people at Tomioka were expecting me, and wrote out directions in Japanese for the taxi-driver (see inset above).

I am continually amazed at the speed and deftness with which men count paper money at a counter--20, 30, 50 bills in a few seconds, and never a mistake.

185

3.

The experience at Tomioka was a repetition of 1960. First, tea, with a piece of delightful cake, which I should not have eaten. I had some small gifts for them: an inexpensive table-cloth with Christmas decorations built in, and a calendar. They had engaged a young man for translation, which was not necessary, and which alone would knock out any possible profit. We eventually took up the matter of the morning coat. I had sent my measurements in advance, and they were well prepared with at least 3 possible outfits, all new. The material was superb, Golden Wealth brand, made in Osaka. Coat, striped pants, straight collar turned down at the edges, grey striped tie.

I can see the bend in the railway below: 8 tracks, 2 being tracks for the new trains to Osaka, the New Tokaido Line, 320 miles in 3 hours. The trains make no noise at all: the hotel is marvelously sound-proofed. It is rare to see the tracks empty: there is almost always one train passing, often 2, sometimes even 3. It is fascinating to watch the new trains come around the bend bound for Osaka. They take off every half hour or oftener from Tokyo Central Station, about a mile away, and pass by here 90 seconds later. A train from Osaka often passes by here in the opposite direction at exactly the same time. Saturday afternoon, I observed the headway between these trains to be only 5 or 10 minutes. Twelve cars to a train. The headlights are 2 balls of white fire; the rear lights 2 balls of red fire.

Mr. Noguchi is a splendid host. He is in charge of the Planning Section of the Union of Japanese Scientists & Engineers, and it falls to his lot to make arrangements for me. He has a good sense of humour and propriety: steers me from one engagement to another without pushing me into impossible schedules.

Many trees in the cities are pruned, wrapped, and tied for snow. I suppose that fruit trees and decorative trees in the villages receive even more care.

I had never before observed so many palm trees in Tokyo. Are there more?

Off for Osaka, 320 miles in 3 hours.
View from my hotel.

186

4.   Wednesday 10th

Mr. Takamatsu, now Managing Director, is breaking himself into his new job with a fine balance of caution and skill.

Girls in school all wear uniforms with blue middy and white collar. In summer, the middies are white. The boys wear a blue cadet uniform.

D. P. E. I see on signs over shops. I know now what it means--Developing, Printing, Enlarging. I was out for a walk in Hakata in 1955 when I finally figured it out.

My speech for the Deming Prize tomorrow night is ready; in fact I sent it here in advance for publication, but besides delivering it, I must pontificate by handing out the two prizes, one for theory, which I understand will go to Mr. Imaizumi, one of my students here in 1951, and the other for application, which will go to the Toyota Motor Company. The hardest part will be to try to remember people's names at the dinner, and to look wise.

Mr. Takamatsu, Managing Director
of the Union of Japanese Scientists & Engineers

My speech for Friday is gradually unfolding, but I've written nothing.

To the Emperor's garden party

Wednesday 10th. This was to be the big day--one of them: the Emperor's party in the afternoon at Akasaka Garden, and the ceremonies for the Deming Prize in the evening. The Emperor's soothsayers, if they selected this date, outdid themselves: it was perfect: never a cloud, no thought of temperature. I hope that he rewarded them suitably. Into my morning coat like a veteran, and I was ready at 1330 for Mr. Noguchi who came in the JUSE automobile. Neither he nor the driver can go to the party. I wonder if they have ever seen the Emperor.

Akasaka Garden is beautiful, hundreds of crysanthemums in cascade. Everything to eat. Musicians playing Japanese instruments. I hope that my photographs will be good. At length came the Emperor into view, with the Empress, chatting with people. All bowed low, of course. A man preceded the Emperor, learning people's names and a few particulars. He spotted the insignia in my lapel, Second Order of the Sacred Treasure, which the invitation had asked me to wear. He introduced me to the Emperor. The Emperor said that he was pleased to see me in Japan, and thankful for what I had done for his country. I met the Empress too, and a fine-looking woman she is.

Wednesday 10th

5.

At the Emperor's party in Akasaka Garden

After I had been introduced to the Emperor,
I stepped back and took this photograph.
This is permissible in Japan.

The Emperor's musicians

6.

The Crown Prince and beautiful Princess followed. I had seen them before, twice, at the meeting of the International Statistical Institute in Tokyo in 1960, when he gave a speech, and we were seated near to them and across the table at a final dinner at the Imperial Hotel. I remember hoping that the Prince's steak was not as tough as mine. The Emperor's younger brother Takamatsu came later, making longer and fewer stops. It was a momentous afternoon, for me, and how I wished that Lola had come. The Emperor looks, of course, just like pictures of him, but he seems not to have aged at all. I was thinking what trials he has been through in his life.

Ceremonies for the Deming Prize

I was almost on time for the ceremonies for the Deming Prize, which started off with a big dinner in the Phoenix Room at the Hotel Imperial. It went off very well, and I saw many friends. Mr. Kano sat next to me at the dinner. I asked him in fun if this was Columbia River Salmon. Excellent steak followed, probably Kobe beef.

There were speeches, one of them being by my good friend Van (Mr. Van Swearingen), representing the American Ambassador. Mine went off well enough. One Japanese man, during dinner, gave a remarkable performance by introducing people in the room, one at a time, about 3 per minute, and giving a brief description of the accomplishments of each one, mid laughter and applause from the audience. I think that most of the applause was appreciation for the man that made the introductions, and knew the accomplishments of everyone.

The English edition of the newspaper Mainichi gave a full account of the Deming Prize; I'll make an appendix of it (page 60).

I remembered today to turn on the radio in my room to the broadcast of news in English. It seemed that there is a tremendous incomprehensible blackout over the eastern part of North America.

Thursday 11th. Some shopping: bought another record with China Night on it, another with Sakura, both favorites of mine. Two record-brushes like the one I took home in 1960: Linda wants one. Small shoe horns, impossible to buy at home. Some stationery. Oh yes, and some of that beautiful soft rice-paper to use for wrapping gifts. A spiral book for this journal. Two tubes of paste: Japanese paste is much better than any other that I know of. A small stapler to carry in my brief-case, if the one that I now carry, bought in Kiel in 1952, ever breaks down.

The event of this day was lunch with Mr. and Mrs. Tatsura Toyoda, son of the motor-magnate, who was in New York one year. He came for me in a Toyota Crown, with all trimmings and accessories. With him was Mr. Mizuno, from the factory at Nagoya. Waiting at the Teahouse Nagoya was Mr. Toyoda's wife, Ayako. I had forgotten that we had sent an ice-pail to them for a wedding gift, but they had not. I guessed the meaning of aya: beautiful. What else could it mean?

Teahouse Nagoya is owned by a Mr. Saito, who owns the Saito restaurant in New York, where I have eaten many times. He and the Toyoda family have apparently been friends for years. Teahouse Nagoya serves only chicken, but there are many ways to cook chicken. We sat on the floor, legs under a beautiful round lacquered table. First, I must have whiskey. Suntory it was, and good. Then sake, and tea. I should have mentioned the beautiful entrance, once inside the gate--stepping-stones and flowers, shoes off, slippers on, up the stairs, every inch polished and clean enough to eat off of.

7.

Ceremonies for the Deming Prize

Mr. Katsuda, Mr. Kano, W. Edwards Deming, Mr. Ichiro Ishikawa

Delivering my speech. Mr. Kano (Ikky) interpreting.

8.   Friday 12th

A woman in kimona took charge. Iron kettle in middle of table, gas burner under.

1st course. In went chicken-fat. Small bits of chicken, onions, ginger, and many herbs. Out came something really delicious.

2d. In went chicken stock, noodles, ground chicken, onions and herbs.

Each of us had a bowl of shredded daikon and ginger, for more condiment. I took pictures of everyone, including the maids, on departure.

I can't be fully conscious that I'm in Tokyo. Here I am, in my room, working on my speeches, when the bright lights of Shimbashi are only a short distance away. I'll be free of this worry after tomorrow, when my public lecture is behind me.

I began at 5 o'clock to write my speech for tomorrow: worked feverishly, 24 pages loosely written.

Around 2300 I took the idea into my head that I was hungry. The Café Terrace was open here, but a little variety would be a good idea, I thought, so out I went into the neon lights. The small restaurants, hundreds of them, with examples of food in the window have always fascinated me. I went cautiously into Indonesia Raya. The interior was tasty, and the hostess and waitress were delightful to look at, but the food was a disappointment. The soup was edible but not a fantasy. The "small fried fishes" turned out to be cold, and I was not sure just what they were. I ate some, but saw no point in continuation. The gohan was excellent. This is certainly not typical Indonesian food.

Friday 12th. At last I've learned to sleep. Had a wonderful night. Maybe I ought to go back to Restaurant Indonesia Raya every night. This was the day for my public lecture. Mr. Noguchi waited for me at 0930 and we walked to the Hibya Park Building. The auditorium was completely full on the lower level, and nearly full in the galleries. The lights nearly blinded me, but I came through as well as the audience.

I had supposed that I'd be clear the rest of the day, but my good friend Mr. Kano who interpreted suggested that we have lunch together. I had thought of going to the Noh plays at the Kanze Kai Kan at 12, but it was 1330 when we finished lunch. I'll go to Kabuki at 1700 today, Noh plays tomorrow.

Any description that I could give to Kabuki plays would do them an injustice and display ignorance, though I have read several books about them. Next to me was a man from Oslo, who was certainly enjoying Japan, in love with the people, admiring their gracious manners, regretting that he has only two more weeks here. He had studied

This Week in Tokyo

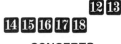

Sun	Mon	Tue	Wed	Thu	Fri	Sat

CONCERTS

Debussy's "Le Martyre de St. Sebastien" by Yomiuri Nippon Symphony Orchestra under the baton of Hiroshi Wakasugi, and Tokyo Philharmonic Chorus. Also, two other numbers. Nov. 15, 7pm. Metropolitan Festival Hall, Ueno Park. Tel. 828-2111 . . . ¶ Finnish conductor Paavo Berglund conducts Japan Philharmonic Symphony Orchestra. Brahms' Symphony No. 2 in D major, Op. 73; and two other numbers. Nov. 16, 7pm. Metropolitan Festival Hall . . . ¶ NHK Chamber Orchestra. Vivaldi's Concerto Grosso in D minor, Op. 3-11; and three other numbers. Nov. 16, 7pm: Little Hall of Metropolitan Festival Hall, Ueno Park. Tel. 828-2111 . . . ¶ Tokyo Bach Ensemble, Eisai Ikemiya conducting. Bach's Cantata No. 8 ("Liebster Gott"), with Oratorio Choir accompanying; and five other numbers. Nov. 18, 7pm. Little Hall of Metropolitan Festival Hall.

RECITALS

Yoko Sato violin recital with Naum Valter at piano. Paganini's Caprices, Op. 16 & 24; Bach's "Unaccompanied Sonata" and several other numbers. Nov. 12, 6:30pm. Kosei Nenkin Kaikan Hall, Shinjuku Banshucho. Tel. 356-1111 . . . ¶ Joseph Molnar harp recital. Nov. 12, 6:30pm. Little Hall of Metropolitan Festival Hall, Ueno Park. Tel. 828-2111 . . . ¶ Tsukuru Oikawa baritone recital. Schubert, Brahms, Verdi and Leoncavallo numbers. Nov. 12, 7pm. Daiichi Seimei Bldg., Yurakucho. Tel. 216-3810 . . . ¶ Noriyoshi Matsuyama tenor recital. Opera arias and lieder. Nov. 16, 6:30pm. Daiichi Seimei Hall . . . ¶ Michi Piano Group. Debussy, Chabrier, Faure, Milhaud and Francaix numbers. Nov. 16, 7pm. Yamaha Hall, 3rd flr., Nihon Gakki Bldg., Ginza. Tel. 572-31111 . . . ¶ Ritsuko Matsuura soprano recital. All Japanese songs. Nov. 17, 6:30pm. Nikkei Hall, 7th flr., Nihon Keizai Shimbun Bldg., Otemachi. Tel. 270-0251 . . . ¶ Prague Quartet from Czechoslovakia. Beethoven's "Rasumovsky Quartet" and two other numbers. Nov. 17, 6:30pm. Asahi Auditorium, 6th flr., Asahi Shimbun Bldg., Yurakucho. Tel. 212-0131 . . . Joint vocal

recital by Kei Kubota, Miyoko Arakawa and 14 other singers. All Kosaku Yamada numbers. Nov. 17 & 18, 6:30pm. Iino Hall, 7th flr., Iino Bldg., Uchisaiwaicho. Tel. 501-2131 . . . ¶ ¶Pianist Hiroshi Ito performs Chopin's "Heroic Polonaise" and five other numbers. Nov. 18, 6:30pm. Daiichi Seimei Hall.

CHORUS

Choir MEG, Megumu Onaka conducting. All Megumu Onaka numbers. Nov. 15, 6:30pm. Iino Hall, 7th flr., Iino Bldg., Uchisaiwaicho. Tel. 501-2131 . . . ¶ Tokyo Philharmonic Chorus under the baton of Hiroyuki Iwaki. All religious chorals by Palestrina. Nov. 16, 7pm. Toranomon Hall, Kokuritsu Kyoiku Kaikan Hall, Toranomon. Tel. 580-1251.

CHINESE OPERA

65-member Chinese Opera Company from Taiwan. Classical and fantasia numbers. Nov. 11, 15, 18 & 19 from 6:30; Nov. 12 from 1; Nov. 13 & 16 from 1 & 6:30. Sankei Hall, 2nd flr., Sankei Kaikan Bldg., Otemachi. Tel. 231-7171.

MISCELLANY

Popular tango concert by Kotaro Hara's Sextet. Nov. 12, 6:30pm. Hibiya Public Hall, Hibiya Park. Tel. 591-6566/7 . . . ¶ American popular singer Peggy March with Elio Maulo Sextet and singer Benny Thomas accompanying. Nov. 12, Sankei Hall, 2nd flr., Sankei Kaikan Bldg., Otemachi. Tel. 231-7171; Nov. 15, Kosei Nenkin Kaikan Hall, Shinjuku Banshucho. Tel. 356-1111 . . . ¶ Waseda University Harmonica Society supported by vocal group, Four Coins. Popular numbers. Nov. 13, 6pm. Toranomon Hall . . . ¶ Japanese koto (Japanese harp) music by Okatoyo Sanagi and other players. Nov. 15, 6:30pm. Nokyo Hall, 8th flr., Nokyo Bldg., Otemachi. Tel. 270-0042 . . . ¶ Popular Latin numbers by Toru Arima's Noche Cubana. Nov. 15, 6:30pm. Hibiya Public Hall.

KABUKI

Grand Kabuki — Starring Utaemon Nakamura, Mitsugoro Bando and Enjaku Jitsukawa. Two plays, "Shin Usuyuki Monogatari," "Sansho Daiyu Gonin Musume" and a dance "Futa-omote Mizu-ni Teru Yuki" in matinee (11am). Two plays, "Ataka-no Seki," "Hosokawa Gracia Fujin" and two dances, "Fujimusume," "Koma" in evening performance (5pm). Nov. 1-25. Kabuki-za Theater, Ginza-Higashi. Tel. 541-3131/9.

NOH DRAMAS

Kanze School — Regular monthly performance of Tessenkai. Two noh dramas, "Semimaru," "Akogi" and a kyogen (comedy). Nov. 12, 5:30pm. Kanze Noh Theater, Shin-Ogawamachi. Tel. 260-7241 . . . ¶ Shomonkai performs popular number "Momijigari" and three other numbers. Also, two comedies. Nov. 13, 12 noon. Kanze Noh Theater . . . ¶ Yamashina Domon-kai performs two noh dramas, "Chikubujima," "Miidera." Also, a kyogen. Nov. 16, 5:30pm. Kanze Noh Theater . . . ¶ Umewaka Kenno-kai. "Seiganji," "Kogo" and a kyogen. Nov. 18, 5pm. Kanze Noh Theater . . . **Hosho School**—Hoshokai's regular monthly performance presenting "Makura Jido" and two comedies. Also, a kyogen "Igui" by Manzo Nomura and others. Nov. 14, 1pm. Suidobashi Noh Theater, Suidobashi. Tel. 811-5753.

SPORTS

HORSE RACING—Nov. 13 & 14, 11am. Fuchu Race Track, Fuchu. Tel. 04236-3141.

PROFESSIONAL BOXING — Manzo Kikuchi vs. Koji Awajima, featherweight, 10R. Nov. 16, 8:30pm. Korakuen Hall, 5th flr., Korakuen Bowling Kaikan Bldg., Suidobashi. Tel. 811-2111 . . . ¶ Takao Sakurai vs. Takeo Bando, Jr. featherweight, 10R. Nov. 18, 9:30pm. Korakuen Hall.

EXHIBITIONS

Kiyoteru Kuroda Exhibition—Some 100 pieces of oil paintings and sketches by the master of Meiji Era, Kiyoteru Kuroda (1866-1924). Also, permanent exhibition of oils, sculptures and other works of art by the world's master artists. Oct. 12-Nov. 14. Bridgestone Gallery, 2nd flr., Bridgestone Bldg., Kyobashi. Tel. 561-6317 . . . ¶ **Paintings in Literary Artist's Style**—370 paintings in literary artists style by Buson Taniguchi, Taiga Ikeno of Edo Era, and other masters. Also permanent exhibition of Japanese work of art. Oct. 21-Nov. 14. Closed Mondays. National Museum, Ueno Park. Tel. 822-1111 . . . ¶ **"Tokyo in Meiji Era" Exhibition**—Some 100 pieces of woodblock and copperplate prints, oil and Japanese paintings, pottery, accessories and other works of art of Meiji era (1868 ~1911). Sept. 25-Nov. 14. Closed Mondays. Suntory Gallery, 9th flr., Palace Bldg., Marunouchi. Tel. 211-6936 . . . ¶ **Rouault Exhibition**—181 pieces of oil, water-color and gauch paintings by the late French master Georges Rouault

The Pacific Traveler

Friday 12th

10.

Snapped en route to the Kabukiza
Friday 12th November 1966

Many restaurants display food and prices.

Dog on bicycle

11.

about Japan for 40 years, and saved, too, I am sure. Meanwhile, Japan has changed several times.

It is amazing how people like me and the professor from Oslo, not understanding a word spoken by the actors or by the narrators, can sit through Kabuki plays for hours, thrilled.

The seats at the Kabukiza are too small for people my size, but I was fortunately on the aisle, and intermissions are frequent and long. A sign at the front shows the length of each intermission. There must be 6 bars and as many tea-rooms in the Kabukiza, but I was not hungry. Opera glasses for rent, but I didn't rent any. I was amused at the professor from Oslo. After every intermission he took the seat exactly in front of where he should have been. The rows are numbered, in hiragana, but he doesn't know hiragana. I learned enough to get back to the right row.

Some American woman remarked about the low numbers on the license plates. She did not seem to know that the first character in hiragana, and the character for the district of registry, take the place of several English letters and numerals.

I cut the Kabuki short at 2030 to take the train to Kamakura, to see the Reverend Michael Yamamoto, a priest in the Holy Catholic Church of Japan. Lola had paid his expenses through the seminary. I had made the arrangement by telephone. He would be clear after 2130, and he would wait for me at the station in Kamakura. I just missed a good train from Shimbashi at 2036. If the guard had seen me coming up the steps, he would have held it, I think. Or, if I had known about this train, and had not said goodbye a second time to the taxi-driver, I might have caught it, or at least got caught in the door. There are timetables posted on all platforms, but I don't know the Chinese characters for Kamakura. The guard looked in his book for me: 16 minutes to wait. I had a 1st class ticket, and I waited in the spot posted "1st class car stops here," but it didn't. I boarded through the nearest open door, not to miss another train. I stood all the way to Kamakura, 50 minutes, but the standing didn't hurt me. Michael was on the platform waiting for me. As the train pulled out and past us, the 1st class car went by, 8 people in it. What I had done was to lose out on a seat that I had paid for, and crowded the 2d class cars besides, just as I did unwittingly in 1951 on my trip to Atami.

The evening with Michael and Elizabeth in their home was delightful: drank tea with them, took the train at 2334. I am sure that I missed a good connexion at Shinagawa by enquiring if it stops at Shimbashi. Off at Yuracachō. The hour was late when I arrived at my hotel, and I was hungry. The Bell Captain said that while many places were open, I'd better go to the Ginza Tokyu Hotel. I had bacon and eggs, returned in a taxi, and crawled into bed at 0200.

I forgot to mention that Pachinko is still a favorite indoor sport: it's all over the city.

Long distance calls are dialed here, about as in the U. S.

12.   Sunday 14th

To a Noh play

Saturday 13th. To the Kanze Kai Kan at 12. Wonderful. Most Japanese
say that they can't understand Noh plays. I can't either, but I appreciate
the skill that goes into them, within the rigid framework. I stayed through:
had coffee and cake during the intermission, in the café upstairs. Went back
to my hotel by train. The stations are so well marked that one can't go
wrong, and anyway, two boys saw that I descended at the right station, after
I enquired whether this train stops at Yuracachō.

I work at odd times at this journal and on instructions for various jobs
at home, most of them pressing.

At about 2300, fancying that I was hungry, or might become so, I betook
myself to the Ginza. I'd like to stop in at one of the hundreds of small
night clubs. Maybe I'm too old; maybe not old enough. Went into the Great
Ginza, Chinese restaurant, had noodles and beer: very good. Several beautiful girls in kimonos came in for food, all very happy. They are hostesses at
various night clubs nearby, the waiter told me, en route home perhaps, or
possibly just enjoying an hour off. There is so much that I wonder about.
I wonder if anyone really knows whether these girls would prefer to be
hostesses, or to work in an office or factory. At any rate, no one could be
happier people than Japanese girls, wherever you see them.

One of the girls at the 4th floor desk told me today that her father
attended my lecture yesterday.

That night, on my bed, was this note:

> Good night, Dr. Deming, sleep well.
> Have a nice time in Japan.
>
> Miyoko

Same girl? (I've changed her name here.) Anyway, it is these alluring
little charms of the Japanese that spin a web around me.

Sunday 14th. Fumiko and brother Kazunari came at 1130 for lunch.
Kazunari remembered the good corn soup at the Café Terrace, from 1960, and
it was good again. I was late at the Noh plays at the Kanze Kai Kan, but
still got my money's worth.

To the Ishikawa estate

Mr. Noguchi came for me at 1700; I am invited to the Ichiro Ishikawas
for dinner. It was delightful. Most of the Ishikawa children were there--
a remarkable family, 8 boys, 8 Ph.Ds.; amongst them my esteemed colleague
Dr. Kaoru Ishikawa: also, I might add, 8 gorgeously beautiful wives: one
daughter, not there. Mr. and Mrs. Ishikawa had recently celebrated their
50th wedding anniversary: he showed me their picture taken that day.

The dinner was served at a regular table, with chairs. Each person
had a little stove, charcoal burning in it, a metal cover. Fry your own
steak, chicken, fish, sweet potato, and bacon. It was much fun.

It was cold today: wore my overcoat.

**Mr. Ichiro Ishikawa is one of Japan's great men, highly respected.
It was his influence and standing amongst executives in Japanese industry,
and the untiring efforts of Kenichi Koyanagi, that made my efforts effective in 1950 and thereafter in the program for the improvement of
quality of Japanese products.**

13.

At the home of Family Ichiro Ishikawa, Sunday, 14 November 1966

Mrs. Ishikawa. The girl is
reflection in the glass. The
model of the ship is made of salt.

W E D with Mr. Takamatsu.
This girl is also reflection.

At Chin.zan.so, Monday, 15 November 1966

Dr. Kurushima
Professor Moriguti   W E D
Mrs. Moriguti

W E D
Dr. Kurushima

14.

Chin.zan.so. Dr. Kurushima
tells me of his Villa Novi Sad

<u>Monday 15th</u>. The symposium on the sampling of bulk materials commenced today. I was to give the opening speech, which had been another one of my worries. I had worked on it seriously since Friday, once Friday's speech was delivered, and I got up at 6 this morning for it. Anyway, it went off much better than I had any reason to predict.

Mei . en	Chin , zan , so
Famous garden	Camellia mountain villa

Reception at Chin.zan.so. Barbecue. I sat next to Dr. Kurushima, host. He designed the camellias on the plates at Chin.zan.so. The camellia (thea japonica), he told me, was carried from Japan to Portugal by Fr. G. J. Kamel, S. J., many years ago, and I perceived for the first time how the flower received its name, from Kamel.

Dr. Kurushima told me of a villa that he has on Mt. Hakone, and that he would be pleased if I would occupy it for the symposium on factor analysis, which will be held Tuesday 23d and Wednesday 24th. I may stay in the villa as long as I wish. (Later: it turned out to be wonderful: see Monday 22d and Tuesday 23d.) He handed to me a picture of his villa, and this description of it, in Croatian, English, and Japanese. For the picture, turn to Monday 22d, page 46.

When I was invited to a chalet located in a forest of the suburb of Novi Sad on the northern bank of the Danube running through Yugoslavia, I was much attracted by that chalet and built a similar one in the garden of Hotel Kowakien, Hakone, and named it "Novi Sad." I always recall, with affections, my good friends in Yugoslavia and the scenery of Frushka Gora beyond the Danube. My "Novi Sad" is a fire-proof house built of concrete block and gypsum board made by Dowa Mining Co., and it was completed with all equipments for electricity, water, steam heating and mineral hot spring bath in 55 days.

I had had in mind these 5 years, if I ever returned to Tokyo, to find the girl Michie with the sweet voice that spoke English so well and showed us in June 1960 the fireflies and the beautiful grounds of Chin.zan.so. She was then expecting to get married, and I wondered if I could find her. A Miss Michiko Sugiyama at the reception desk of Chin.zan.so worked heroically for at least 40 minutes. The manager at the other end of the line remembered her: couldn't think of her married name, at first: then did, Sugii, and he found her: she is on the wire. I explained who I was. She lives near Chin.zan.so:

15.

will come in an hour. We had a good visit. She now has a little boy
3 years old. Her husband is an accountant with a big florist. Fortunately, I had in my hotel a small gift from America that I could send to
her, and I did, on my last day--a calendar for 1966, in the form of a
wall-hanging.

Beautiful warm weather again.

Tuesday 16th. Symposium all day, on sampling of bulk materials.
Lunch at St. Sophia University, arranged by Dr. Saito, who came for me
at 12. We went in a taxi.

Fr. Sagrista   Prof. Koda   Fr. Paus   Fr. T. Ballon

Economics	Statistics	Director of Economics	Director of Finance

Prof. Osawa   W E D   Prof. Saito

Big lunch, fish and steak. Then, I must have a look around St.
Sophia University. Father Ballon sent me back to my hotel in a Crown
de Luxe (Toyo), one of the university's cars.

Dinner at Teahouse Hana.han given by the men that were at our home
in June, and by a few others. The food was sukiyaki, preceded by tea,
accompanied by sake, Kirin beer, and much fun.
I have always liked the transparent noodles
called shirotaki. The men explained where
they come from and how they are made, and we
had much fun as Mr. Kazo Koure, with much
advice, drew a flow chart, from raw material,
the root konniyaku tama, to finished product.
Dr. Aiba refined the chart, also with much
advice. I will show the chart on the next page.

hana
= hill

han
= half

We started toward my hotel, but Mr. Noguchi
thought that I was seeing only a biased sample of
Tokyo. As my host, he must do better. We should
go to the Blue Sky on the revolving roof on the
Hotel Otani, and so we did, 17 stories up, which
is high for Tokyo. This is one of Tokyo's 6 or 7 big new
hotels. Mr. Koure went with us, and his beautiful wife
came later. We sat at a table on the circumference, two
here, two across, and watched the city roll around, once
an hour. It is a great sight--big signs, BROTHER, MAZDA.
Gorgeous garden below. We certainly were neither hungry
nor thirsty, but we had to order something, so we made
off with some beer and some food, including nuts and
smoked salmon. I can't help but marvel at this abundance
of food, ordered now with abandon, and left on the table
with no takers, in comparison with 1946, when things were
in ruins, and one could only get tea. (Pictures page 17.)

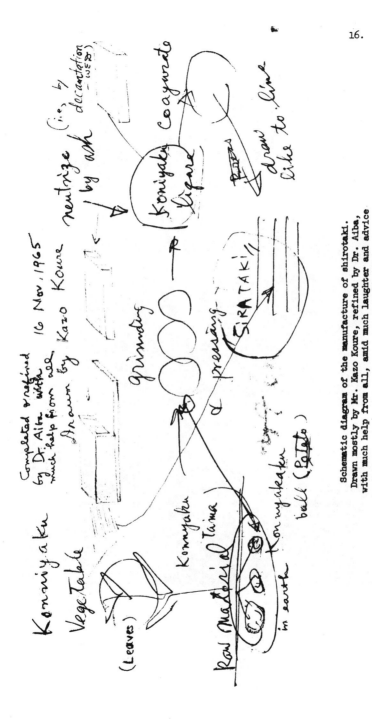

Schematic diagram of the manufacture of shirotaki.
Drawn mostly by Mr. Kazo Koure, refined by Dr. Aiba,
with much help from all, amid much laughter and advice

199

Tuesday 16th

17.

Seating arrangement at Hana.han
Tuesday 16 November 1966

Dr. Ishikawa

Tea
Sukiyaki
  with nonyaku
  and shirotake
Sopporo beer
Kirin beer
Sake
Gohan and pickled
  vegetables

Much fun (see page 16)

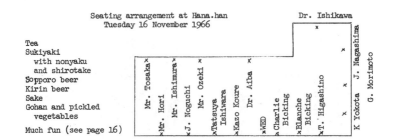

Mr. Tosaka
Mr. Hori
Mr. Ishimura
J. Noguchi
Mr. Ozeki
Tatsuya Ishiwara
Kazo Koure
Dr. Aiba
WED
Charlie Bicking
Blanche Bicking
T. Higashino
K Yokota
J. Nagashima
G. Morimoto

Below, Hotel Otani, revolving roof and other attractions
(from a folder that I picked up)

星空にまわる200坪の客席

■ブルースカイラウンジ
海抜100米1時間1回転、
フロア全体が静かにまわり
居ながらにして東京を一望
のもとにおさめる東洋一の
カクテル・ラウンジです。
ティータイムもございます
ので、ご家族お揃いでお気
軽にご利用ください。

アゼリア

カプリ

■コーヒーショップ
　　"アゼリア"
お気軽にご利用いただける
コーヒーショップ。お客さ
まのお食事にお待ち合せに
是非ご利用ください。
朝定食 ¥300 （コンチネンタル）
　　　 ¥500 （アゼリア）
　　　 ¥500 （和　食）
昼定食 ¥600
夕定食 ¥900
■バー"カプリ"
ロビーの奥、静かに流れる
ピアノソロにゆだねて飲む
ワインの味……。優雅な夜
のひと時をお過し下さい。
ビール(小ビン) ¥150
カクテル　　　 ¥300より

18.   Wednesday 17th

I wished to go to Takashima-ya, and I had resolved to go by subway, but I was not sure which station nor train to take. The girl on the 4th-floor desk told me to go to Shimbashi Station; Ginza station may be a bit closer, she said, but is so big, and with so many trains, that I might become confused. I had never had trouble in the Ginza station, but I nevertheless followed her advice. I knew of course Shimbashi Station on the JNR, but I was not sure how to find the Shimbashi Station on the subway.

SHINBASHI ST

NIHONBASHI
TAKASHIMAYA MAE

新橋の地下鉄駅から
日本橋高島やでおります

IMPERIAL HOTEL MEMO

She wrote out some notes for me in English, and directions in Japanese, so that I could enquire if I needed help. In Shimbashi I asked a boy where the Shimbashi Subway Station is, and he led me into it.

To Nagoya, on the Hikari

Wednesday 17th. Lunch with Mr. Hideo Kato of Nikken Chemicals. His company is doing well, and he has made contributions that have expanded their export-trade in an important way. He declares that he learned it all from me. I think that one explanation of the happiness of Japanese people is their feeling of thankfulness.

This afternoon, the members of the symposium on bulk sampling went to visit the Raw Materials Centre of the great Nippon Kokan KK, Oogashima, where the recipient of the Deming Prize for 1965, John Imaizumi, has introduced a number of important statistical methods. This plant is on a man-made island about 3/4 mile long, and a 1/4 mile wide. (Pictures next page.)

One interesting point (to me) about the trip this afternoon was that I found myself short of film, and was able to replenish my supply in one of the small kiosks in the plant that sells cigarettes, candy, and other small items-- and film.

In contrast, in Turkey one would find film only in a city.

In Japan, one may buy anything, American or Japanese, in hundreds of shops.

Off at 1900 on the Hikari, 2 hours to Nagoya, 240 miles. Mr. Kano is with me, and a man from the Toyota Motor Company, can't be sure of his name. Toyota is footing the bill. It was dark, and I could only see the lights whiz by, but it was a great experience. The speedometer in the buffet car hugged 200 km/hr most of the time, which equals 125 mph. An illuminated horizontal indicator, with the stations marked on it, moves across a scale in the buffet car to indicate where we are.

There are Hikari trains between Tokyo and Osaka, which stop only at Nagoya and Kyoto, and Kodama trains, which make 10 stops. They are all new, 12 cars each--24 Hikari, plus 26 Kodama daily in each direction, with extras Saturday and Sunday.

Wednesday 17th

19.

At Nippon Kokan KK, 17 November 1965

Taking notes in the conference room

Watching ore move on a conveyor

Charlie Bicking   Dr. Kaoru Ishikawa
WED   John Imaizumi

Hikari   Kodama
Light   Sound
         (echo)

To the Hikari at Tokyo Central

Rice straw all over Japan

20.   Thursday 18th

More rice straw

Lunch at Toyota. My place is the vacant chair with napkin

To the Nagoya International Hotel. The bed was excellent. To the roof for dinner. Mr. Kano knows something about martinis, and saw to it that mine was made right, and doubled. Steak. Ice cream. I asked for chocolate sauce on it, and got whipped cream.

Thursday 18th. Up at 7. Put on finishing touches to a rough draft for new procedures in motor freight, to send to Ceil in Washington for typing. It must be in nearly final form by the 6th December, and printed for a meeting in Denver on the 15th. Sending post-cards to friends takes time.

This is the day for a visit to the Toyota Motor Company, the company that won the Deming Prize for application this year. A driver came for us at 0850, but my little clock had gone bad, I discovered afterward, and I was 10 minutes late. We stopped by the main Post Office en route to mail letters, and the big envelope to Ceil. Toyota City is about 30 miles away. Anyway, I enjoyed seeing the country, the rice-straw hanging in bundles to dry, some already stacked, rice stubble. Much farm machinery in use, small in size, to fit the fields.

Toyota Motor Company has magnificent offices. First, tea in a big beautiful conference room. Mr. Ishida had attended my lecture last Friday in Tokyo, and he now rehearsed a lot of it, with plans for application. I knew that they expected me to give a lecture at the plant at 1030. To my astonishment, the auditorium was filled with S. R. O., foremen and managers above foremen, up to Mr. Ishida. Mr. Kano interpreted, and I gave him a vote of thanks.

Lunch at 1205, Western style, in the President's dining room. All magnificent. Automatic sliding doors everywhere.

Tea

Soup, fish and bean cake

Shrimp cocktail

Salad, asparagus no strings, tomato, mayonnaise, and I recalled the

beautiful mayonnaise at Hitosubashi University, in 1950, at a meeting of the Japanese Statistical Society, when they made me an honorary life member: it was made of fish oil and I couldn't eat it.

Steak, which came on a sizzling iron,
about 6 steaks to an iron. A
piece of butter on each steak.
Delightful.

Custard pudding

Melon

Ice cream, vanilla

Coffee in beautiful coffee cups.
I always seem incomprehensible to the Japanese when I
don't put sugar into my
coffee. They love anything
sweet.

Presentation of gift--a tiny transistor radio, vest-pocket size; a
golden cigarette holder, shape of a Crown de Luxe.

Mr. Ishida was talkative and made much fun along with serious business.

Then, in a Toyota Crown de Luxe about 10 miles to several of the
factories for painting, stamping, engine assembly. Tea first, of course.
Photographers busy snapping pictures the while.

Then tea again, but this time with 2 men from the Nippon Keizai Shinbun,
something like the Wall Street Journal, but more influential here. They
wanted my opinion on almost everything except what I am competent to speak
on. I heard afterward from many people that my picture was in the papers
all over Japan, with an account of the interview. The less I know about it,
the better.

To Noritake China, where I saw dishes being made, like the ones that
I have in New York, and of course many other patterns. There must be 20,000
workers in the factory, mostly girls. Tea before and after. At the tea-
table after the tour, they presented me with a gorgeous hand-painted plate,
Okura, and will send it to Washington. We all signed our names on plates,
to fire. I picked out one, and they will send it too.

I was amused to see a truck-load of dishes, in boxes, labeled Quality
for Export to the U. S. A. and Canada.

By then it was nearly 1800. Next, in the Crown de Luxe with Messrs.
Noguchi and the two Toyoda brothers (of Toyota Motor) to a party at Hotel
Kam.mo.me (Sea Gull). Shoes off and up the stairs for tea. This hotel has
mats on the steps, and carpets on the floors, a beautiful Chinese rug at
the entrance. Then down stairs to dinner, 8 men, 5 geisha girls, 3 or 4
beautiful waitresses, and a head waitress. Low lacquered table in a
beautiful new pavilion. Outside, one of the prettiest Japanese gardens
that I have ever seen.

Sake. Next, a tray with handle, in it 7 bits of food, on small
lacquered coasters:

  --Lotus bulb

  --Raw ginger

  --Sushi (rice wrapped in raw fish)

--Egg yolk, boiled, cut like a persimmon,
  a stem and leaf attached

--2 small fishes, cooked

--2 small flat pieces of sweet potato, cut
  like a fan

--potato chips

Scotch

Soup: consomme with shrimp and raw ginger

Soup: consomme with bean cake

Raw blow fish, shredded, and bits of blow fish dipped in hot water

I heard a samisen, and I knew that there would be dances by the
geisha girls.

1st dance, Gomen gaku, 50,000 goku of rice given by
  the shogun to his over-lord

2d dance, Let your wish come true

3d dance, sake mesa, Come board my boat

Soup, thick, with fish, chicken, ginger, herbs

4th dance, The dolphins on Nagoya Castle. One geisha girl
  warped herself at the end into the shape of a dolphin, by
  standing on her head and one hand; much applause.

Much fun. The waitress Mitsuko at my left, well fed, asked me how
old she is and I told her go nana, 17. You make me very happy tonight, she
replied. Mr. Tatsura Toyoda said that he would take Miyako to New York
for me next time he goes. Much discussion on the comparative advantages
and disadvantages of 2d hand automobiles and 2d hand girls.

The geisha girl on my right has a driver's license, which drew much
envy, honor, and applause, as apparently a license is hard to get: the
examinations must be very stiff.

At 2015 the geisha girls disappeared: time up, I suppose. So much
fun they were, yet I'll never see them again. Actually, except for the
dancing that geisha girls do, I often find that the waitresses are more
fun, and are well educated.

Plate of boiled crab. Ginger sauce. I was much relieved when
Mitsuko (waitress on my left) extracted with her chop sticks all the
meat from my crab and put it into a neat pile. Then came (p. 24):

23.   Thursday 18th

Dinner party given by Toyota Motor Company at Hotel Kam.mo.me, Nagoya

Geisha girls dancing.

One girl plays the
    samisen and sings.

Mr. Tatsura Toyoda
    in far corner

Kittens in the
  picture on
  the wall

Gohan and herb-sauce	Tea
Soup	Big orange-colored persimmon, fukugaki

I never cease to marvel that a Japanese woman invariably goes through a door on her knees. Even if the door is open, she still pushes her tray through and then goes through on her knees. If she has no tray, she still goes through on her knees.

On departure, the head waitress introduced us to Mama-san's daughter, beautiful, perhaps 21, probably in college, who will take over the hotel in time and let Mama-san retire bit by bit. Mr. Kano says that the women owners of these fine Japanese hotels are powerful and shrewd in business. They mostly own the businesses outright, husbands in passive seclusion, daughters take over, eventually. They require good financial strength, to extend credit. The restaurant pays for food and help, pays the geisha girls on the spot, yet many customers (mostly big companies) may not settle up till New Year's Day.

I had learned during the day that my room at the hotel would be changed from 902 to 901. I guessed why. One room is not enough: I must have a suite. Mr. Kano and I had had a good talk on the sofa in my new suite, with Scotch and salmon, after our return from dinner.

Why no Maikos? I asked Mr. Kano. We're right in between, he said: too old for maikos, yet not old enough. Wait 20 years and the geisha girls will bring their maikos with them. In Tokyo, the term is not maiko, but han dyoku (half adult, immature girl. Mai = dancing, ko = girl; used in Kyoto for apprentice geisha girl. Each maiko has an older sister in the same district, a geisha-girl, whom the maiko sometimes accompanies at a party, but only by permission of the host.)

Out for a walk, alone, after Mr. Kano left. Night clubs closing. In one spot was a pool with at least 20 men fishing. One caught a fish that weighed, I'd say, $1\frac{1}{2}$ lbs.

Many little odens on the street, as there used to be in all Japanese cities, serving small portions of soup, and morsels of chicken and fish roasting on toothpicks over the coals: room for 1 or 2 people behind the strips of paper or cloth. It smells good and is a temptation.

Looking down out my window in Nagoya

Soothsayers at work, or waiting for a customer, each with his or her little table and lighted candle. This, one sees at night in every Japanese town.

Friday 19th

25.

Chestnuts roasting in hot carmelized sugar, which gives the shells a beautiful glistening sheen.

Then, to my dismay, came my discovery about the hard bed in my beautiful suite. Unfortunately, Room 902 with the good bed was occupied. A boy showed me 801, but it was the same as 901. Every other room was full. A sleepless night ahead; poor preparation for my lecture at Osaka.

<u>Friday 19th</u>, the day for my lecture at Osaka. I had balked at the idea of leaving Nagoya at 8 this morning, for a 3-hour motor trip to Osaka, although I appreciated deeply the generosity of Toyota Motor Company. Better take the train, I thought. So, we will go on the Hikari, leaves at 1102, arrives Shin-Osaka at 1210. I enjoyed the ride, 130 mph: Vibration of course, no sway. The President of Madagascar and his entourage of 20 arrived at Nagoya on Car 7, our car, so the

Ready to depart from Nagoya at 1102

guard on the platform asked us to board Car 8, and pass through. The train came in at 1158½, out at 1102 right on time. Stopped at Kyoto; Kyoto to Shin-Osaka, 25 miles in 18 minutes from a standing start.

The public lecture in Osaka was arranged by the Nihon Kazei Shinbun, whose staff in Osaka took us to lunch at the Imabashi Club. I only had soup and ice cream. The lecture, 1½ hours, went off well enough, Mr. Kano the translator. The auditorium was full, seats for 450 plus 100 standing. I had to wear an enormous bouquet.

Then came the long ride to Kyoto. I'd much rather go on the train. To the Kyoto International Hotel. I have never seen a place so busy. Bed hard. The boy had barely set the luggage down before I decided to keep moving. They all went with me to the Miyako Hotel, where Lola and I were in 1960. It is big and very expensive, covers 16 acres altogether. I found a soft bed there, and was happy. Terribly tired, I lay down a half hour before dinner--soup, cheese omelet, ice cream. To bed early.

Sent a telegram to Lola in regard to certain corrections to make in my report to the Bell Telephone Company of Pennsylvania. I had just discovered some ways to improve clarity on three pages. I was fascinated by the boy at the desk who read my telegram to the main telegraph office. He read it so carefully letter by letter; almost no possibility for error. I don't remember all the letters but he dictated B Boston, E England, K Kyoto, L London, N Nagoya, O Osaka, T Tokyo, "space."

No tips in Japan, though taxi-drivers did reluctantly, twice or thrice, accept 20 extra yen for extra trouble.

26.

Lecture in Osaka

27.

Saturday 20th. The men will come at 10:20. First thing this morning
I set off by taxi for St. Mary's Church. The kindergarten was in session,
and I wish that I had taken a picture of those cute children, especially
when one caught sight of me. A woman showed me to the Reverend John Yamada,
whom we know. We talked a few minutes. I gave him ¥ 5000 for the collection
plate next morning, and he carried me in his car to my hotel. His car is a
1951 Toyo, looks and runs like new.

I had thought that I'd go without breakfast, but gave in--later. The
breakfast-room is beautiful, and I enjoyed it much--juice, eggs and bacon,
gohan, coffee. Mr. Yamada of the great Matsushita Electric Company came
for me at 1015 in a 1962 Fleetwood, with Mr. Noguchi. I was glad that I
had eaten breakfast; it was 1330 when we arrived at Nara Hotel for lunch.

Weather: sloppiest fog that I ever saw. It never did lift. In fact,
I don't think that I ever saw a fog so dense as it was when we went over
the pass from Nara to Osaka that evening. It was dark by 1630. The car
was clear over on the right several times (the wrong side, in this left-
hand traffic). I predicted a clear day for tomorrow. Everyone laughed,
but it came to be.

First thing this morning, Mr. Yamada said, we will go to the Katsura
Imperial Villa. He held up an official document from Tokyo, with red seals,
which gave us permission to enter. It is magnificent. I hope for good
luck on my snaps. I think that I was there in 1946, when all that we had
to do was to show our AGO cards.

As time was slipping, Mr. Yamada thought that we should move on to
Nara. We must have lunch at the Nara Hotel: all arranged. All very fine,
but gohan and coffee at any of the hundreds of little restaurants would
have saved time and given me a new experience.

The first temple was the Daibutsu, established about 750, I think.
I had seen it in 1951, when Dr. Sugiyama and Mr. Niwa of the Nippon Life
Insurance Company showed me around Nara and Kyoto, at the expense of
Nippon Life. The pictures that I look then of the great Buddha show more
than you can see with your eye, because of the darkness.

Second temple, Tōshōdai-ji (Tō = china; shodai means cloisters on all
sides; ji = temple), established 759. I had not seen it before.

Third temple, Yakushi-ji, established 680.

Fourth temple, To-indo. On the altar were flowers, mandarins, apples,
pears, persimmons, for the priests and for the poor.

Droves of hundreds of school children and grown people come. Most
groups are in charge of a girl for escort. I don't know what would become
of Japan without its girls. Rain and fog continued.

All these temples have been destroyed by fire several times, and re-
built.

To the Osaka Royal Hotel, part of the International chain, the biggest
hotel that I've ever seen. Bed hard, so I kept right on moving, everybody

sorry and trying to help. Beds at the Osaka Grand nearby were the same, the desk-clerk said, as they had installed new beds here along with the beds in the new Osaka Royal, same ownership. So, to the Hotel New Osaka, same ownership, but here I was fortunate.

Waiting for me at the Osaka Royal Hotel was an invitation to have dinner tomorrow night with Professor Mizutani of Kobe, and a friendly note from Mrs. Sugiyama.

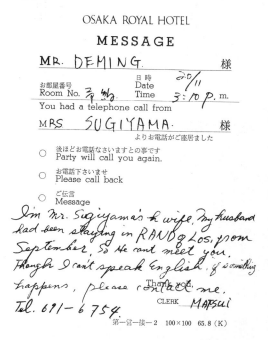

OSAKA ROYAL HOTEL

MESSAGE

MR. DEMING. 様

お部屋番号
Room No. 3 4/3. 日時
Date 20/11
Time 3:10 P. m.

You had a telephone call from

MRS SUGIYAMA. 様

よりお電話がご座居ました

○ 後ほどお電話なさいますとの事です
  Party will call you again.

○ お電話下さいませ
  Please call back

○ ご伝言
  Message

I'm Mr. Sugiyama's k wife, my husband had been staying in RAND of Los, from September, So He can't meet you. Though I can't speak English, if something happens, please contact me. Thank you.
Tel. 691-6754.

CLERK MATSUI

第一営一接一2 100×100 65.8 (K)

I had sent a special delivery letter to Dr. Sugiyama to say that I'd be in Osaka. I had written last June a strong letter of recommendation to RAND in Los Angeles on his behalf, and I was glad to learn from Mrs. Sugiyama's note that RAND had invited him. He will be in Los Angeles about a year. He has the degree M. D., and a Ph.D. in mathematics.

I often recall the first time that I stayed here. It was in 1946, when Margaret Stone and I came here in connexion with the survey on the labor force. The Army had requisitioned the hotel, and rooms went by rank. I drew a beautiful room with bath: Margaret drew a dormitory somewhere. I put up the argument that we had much work to do in a short time: it is necessary that we be together, whereupon, the sergeant gave her a good room here too.

The Hitachi elevators and most others, too, start and stop with no sensation of motion. A lone occupant in an elevator in the hotel in Nagoya, I pressed the button for the 9th floor; the doors closed, and after a while they opened. I supposed for a flash that the elevator was not working, and that a safety device had opened the door, not to encase me. Yet the signal read 9th floor. Could the signal be out of order? No; it's in working order: I'm on the 9th floor. The trains start and stop the same way—no sensation of acceleration nor of deceleration.

Our arrival at Ippoh Tempura Restaurant was a few minutes late, owing to my trouble to find the right kind of bed. We had much fun, once we were all there. I was deeply appreciative of this invitation, and to accentuate manifestation of my feelings, I acted it out as if I had never known of tempura, nor of a tempura bar—certainly not this one.

29. Saturday 20th

In the Emperor's garden, Kyoto

Here is Mr. J. Noguchi,
in charge of arrangements
for me, and Mr. Yamada of
the Matsushita Electric
Company, our hosts for
today through Monday.
In the same garden.

Crysanthemum at entrance to the
Hotel Nara where we had lunch

Nara, tree growing through
a house

Mr. Noguchi and Mr. Yamada
at a temple in Nara

Near Osaka

I snapped this picture to
show the lighted arrow,
which shows the direction
of motion of the train.
Bell ringing. (Monday 22d)

Saturday 20th

31.

1. Tea and mandarin oranges in a beautiful room, with an exquisite
Japanese garden off at my left.

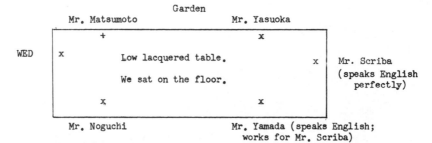

2. Then we moved to one of the many tempura bars in this restaurant.
Ate tempura and gohan till we gave up. One of the men explained that what
distinguishes one tempura bar from another is the various claims for the
best combination of oils. This cook claims to have the best; he uses a lot
of saffron oil. The rest could be cottonseed oil and peanut oil.

Entrance to Ippoh Tempura Restaurant. Note polished
floors. Slippers to put on: leave your shoes here.
(Cut from beautiful folder presented by Ippoh.)

3. Return to the first room
     Codfish soaked in soyu and herbs
     Beer   Tea

Mr. Matsumoto   Mr. Yasuoka
Waitress   WED   Mr. Noguchi

"IPPOH" TEMPURA RESTAURANT

J, Benjiro Seki, Proprietor and Chief of the "Ippoh" Tempura Restaurant in Osaka, have been in the *tempura* business for over 40 years, having succeeded my father and my grandfather, who, since 85 years ago, had been operating the famous "Tentora" Tempura Restaurant in Osaka, whose name is still vivid in the minds of many. At present, it is "Ippoh" that has become conspicuous among the high-class *tempura* restaurants, not only in the Osaka-Kobe-Kyoto area, but throughout the whole of Japan.

History of tempura

It is believed that *tempura* originated among Christian missionaries who came to Japan about the middle of 16th Century following the visit of St. Francis Xavier. Possibly the name of *tempura* derived from Portuguese "tempuras" or the Italian "tempora" (Ember Days in Cartholicism), especially since meat was not eaten on those days. Using the Japanese materials at hand, fish were cooked in the way Jesuits found most palatable, coated in butter and fried in deep oil. Japanese of the Nagasaki area, too, found it good, and its fame was transported to Kobe-Osaka and thence, years later, to Tokyo and the rest of the country, keeping its name as it went.

215

33.

Night life in Osaka

Then to my hotel in the Fleetwood. When all was clear, Mr. Noguchi felt sure that a short excursion into some night life in Osaka would be good for me: there is much to see in Japan besides temples and factories. Of course he was correct, so we ended up in Club New UOS; down an escalator, and into an enormous room, perhaps 50 x 125 feet, orchestra, hundreds of tables it seemed, and hundreds of girls. Three of them were apparently assigned to us. They came from nowhere, like fruit flies. There was Kama Tori (Swallow Bird). Of course, that is not her name, and girls at these places change their names every so often for good luck, usually on advice of a soothsayer. Food and beer came. There was a floor show, 50% clever. Finally, I thought that we ought to go, so we did. The girls went with us up the escalator, and saw us safely into a taxicab, with much waving of hands on parting, and entreaties to return. A very interesting experience.

I marvel at the contrast between the abundance of food these days in Japan, and the scarcity in 1946 and even in 1950. A tearoom in 1946 served tea and not much else.

Sunday 21st. Up at 0640. Took the train at 0723 for Kyoto, as I had determined to attend Mass in English at 8 at St. Mary's Church, and to see more of Kyoto. Bought a packet of Kleenex at one of the small shops in Kyoto Station. Just think; there is no such thing in all of Turkey.

The taxi driver that I picked out at Kyoto Station went all over town to find St. Mary's Church: finally he found a woman that knew exactly where St. Mary's Church is. Stops at a police station and at a police box had elicited little help, even though the ku, chō, and chome were on the card. A Japanese address is really a problem. No wonder the Japanese have so many fires: the fire department can only find a fire when the blaze rises high enough to guide them to it, and then it's too late.

The 8 o'clock Mass is in English: the other services in Japanese. Father Yamada's English is excellent.

A Miss Dortohy D_____ invited, after Mass, to breakfast everyone that wished to come. I volunteered, thinking that some pleasant company would raise my spirits, after the frustration of that taxi-ride. She has lived in Kyoto since 1947: came here to work for the Occupation Forces: never left: as I understand it, is now a Japanese citizen (automatic in 5 years). She had built her house Japanese style, with two beautiful gardens. We sat on the floor, Japanese style--bacon, eggs, Nescafé, rolls, butter. A Mr. Wheeler of the Tokyo Branch of the National City Bank was there, and a woman pediatrician from Los Angeles, who had been attending a meeting in Tokyo; also several others. To the Hotel Miyako with Mr. Wheeler.

Then I set off alone, by taxi. First, to the great Kiyomizu Temple (Kiyo pure; mizu water), which I first visited in 1946. The most interesting thing about it today was the throngs of people coming from everywhere. Most of them come in groups. Girl-escorts assemble a group for instruction; then move onward with a flag in one hand, whistle in the other, to hold the group together. I don't think that a bus could move in Japan without a girl-conductor. I took pictures: am hoping that some will be good.

Walked, bought a small shoe-horn for ¥50 (about 15¢). Further along, I saw it for ¥40. That night in Kobe I got a shine and the same shoe-horn both for ¥50.

34.   Sunday 21st

Came upon a five-story pagoda. The grounds are apparently used for commemorative stones.

Then I came to a big Shinto shrine, perhaps the Fushim Inari Shrine, I don't know. I intended only to snap a photo of the casks of sake, safely protected in boxes or in bundles of rice straw--offerings to the priests. Then I observed that the priests were chanting at one of the altars in one of the temples, and that there was a dancing girl there. A group of about 40 people knelt before the altar, then the whole thing broke up. Amongst the group were a number of little girls,

4 to 8 years old, dressed in white flowered kimonos, complete with obi. I never saw anything cuter--Japanese dolls, the only description that I could give. The mamas and papas thought too that the little girls were cute. Then another group came after a while, and another. The priest chanted, waved a wand over the people, like a feather duster with streamers, and the dancing girls then danced a bit and waved a wand (page 38).

I am fortunate to have seen in my life a far better exhibition of dancing girls before the altar. This was in 1950, at Kashi.ma, on Kyushu, when the superintendent of the Yotuku Inari Shrine called out 6 or 7 dancing girls to come and give me a special exhibition.

I looked at my watch: it's nearly 1400. I must take the train to Osaka, do some writing, send a registered letter with money in it to the Reverend Peter Yamamoto, get a shine, take the train to Kobe, to be there at about 1830.

Lunch in my room--soup and salmon (Columbia River salmon?). Yes, I could get a suit pressed--my one and only suit in Osaka. It would be back in an hour, the boy said, and it was. I was in desperate need of the nap that I snatched. Up; to the Post Office; to the station. Took the train at 1824; arrived Kobe 1848; called Dr. Mizutani.

He took me to the tower on the New Port Hotel (page 40). It revolves, one revolution per hour, like the one in Tokyo. He insisted that I have the full dinner, as I must have Kobe beefsteak, and I agreed with no argument. Everything was delicious--raw oysters, soup, Kobe beef steak, vanilla ice cream, a huge persimmon, coffee. He had hired a car to take me back to my hotel. Except for a short stretch of expressway, one's speed in an automobile between Kobe and Osaka is about the same speed that you can work up passing through Baltimore. How I wished that he would let me take the train at 2100, with a 1st class coach on it. I'd ride in perfect comfort, and beat the automobile by 15 or 20 minutes, but he would not listen to the suggestion, and he came with me. First, he showed me the new Oriental Hotel in Kobe. There wasn't anything wrong with the old one, that I could remember. Anyway, the old one is gone, and a new one there is. Dr. Mizutani has always been extremely kind to me at every visit. He is now retired from the Kobe University of Economics, and is teaching at Aoyama (Green Mountain) University in Nagoya.

Waiting at my hotel were Dr. and Mrs. Asano. To bed at midnight.

35.   Sunday 21st

At Temple Kiyomizu in Kyoto

Here is the pure water, whence the temple took
its name. People reaching for a drink of it
for health and happiness.

Little boy drawing on
grounds of the temple
(father was watching
at left)

Girl-guide is lecturing
to her load of people
before she conducts them
into the temple.

Here a girl-guide
starts her people
off to see the
temple. She
carries a banner
of identification,
and a whistle for
attention.

36.

At Temple Kiyomizu, Kyoto

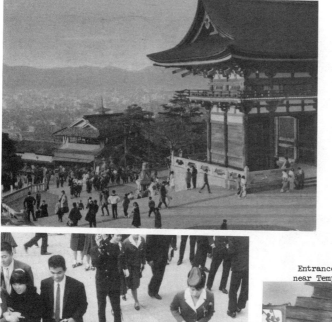

Taken from
the high
ground be-
hind the
temple
(post-card
sent to me
from our
friends the
Beebes).

Girl-guide

Entrance to a shop,
near Temple Kiyomizu

Couple working on the temple-grounds

37.

Shop near
Temple Kiyomizu

Now I started
on a walk and
snapped this
beautiful
entrance to a
home

And this view along
my walk toward the
5-story pagoda

38.   Sunday 21st

Shinto temple in Kyoto with dancing girls

Priest waves wand

but I never understood it.

Girl waves wand

These little girls were in the ceremony somehow,

39.

Sunday 21st

and another

It is easy to find the right train.
Clocks everywhere, with the right time.

Other photos in the Shinto temple

Snapped from the train between Osaka and Kyoto

40.   Sunday 21st

Here we had dinner, Professor Mizutani and I, in the Revolving Roof of the New Port Hotel, Kobe. Lights shone from the boats in the harbor, then lights from the mountain, as we revolved.

⇧ 回転大展望レストラン「鳴門」

Exterior view, the revolving turret on top

Traffic in Osaka, near Central Station

223

I neglected to mention the fabulous mail-service in Japan. A letter that I posted at night in Tokyo was delivered in a suburb early next morning. A letter posted before noon is there in the afternoon. There must be 7 or 8 deliveries per day, and 4 on Sunday.

To the great Matsushita Company

<u>Monday 22d</u>. Up at 0640. Packed. I wish to get a haircut and to be the first customer in the barber shop when it opens at 8, and to be ready at 0840. The barber was a woman, and she did a splendid job. I asked for a round cut, American style. Otherwise, I feared, it might look as if the barber had put a bowl over my head, and cut up to it. That happened to me once when I neglected to specify what I wanted.

Breakfast in the dining room. I ordered hot cakes, and I recalled the beautiful cakes and honey that came to my room in this same hotel in 1950-- beautiful, but stone cold. This time they were equally beautiful but reasonably hot. Messrs. Noguchi and Yamada came for me in the Fleetwood at 0830, as I expected, not at 0840.

To the Matsushita Electronics Division, one of their 13 factories. This one is magnificent. 7000 employees. A girl runs out to open the door to welcome a visitor, escorts him up the steps. I never saw such a pleasing combination of expense, good taste, and beauty all combined. Much glass. Open stairs. A beautiful Japanese garden, about 20 x 50 feet in a court, between buildings. Automatic sliding doors, everywhere. I must have tea first. Mr. Masaharu Matsushita was there. Later his father Mr. K. Matsushita came in a while, the one whose picture was on the front cover of Time about 2 years ago.

I must visit the production line where they make speakers, tiny ones for the smallest transistor radios, on up to woofers. I really enjoyed it, contrary to expectation, as I have been through hundreds of factories. This one was very clear and well-lighted.

Then to the packaging laboratory, to see tests on various ways of packing. There, they subject to terrible tests boxes, closed in various ways, and with contents packed in various ways. They drop the boxes, bounce them, squeeze them, subject them to heat, humidity, vibration. In another place, they try out various new materials for making boxes and for sealing them. The man in charge was very friendly and full of fun, and I wish that I had caught his name. He was very happy when I mentioned, in my lecture, his good work.

Pictures that I missed this morning: a shop labelled

Bar
        ber

which is a common sight. The first thing that pops into my head when I see it is that this is a bar. Second, a 1½ ton truck piled high with cases of eggs, labelled Fresh Eggs in English, with the equivalent in Japanese.

Lunch at 1215, western style. First, a hot towel, my 12th one so far today, I think. It's a wonderful idea. Mr. M. Matsushita was there; Mr. Scriba, and I don't recall who else. (Pictures page 42.)

1. Soup, delicious.

   Beer at this point. Word has gotten around that
I prefer Kirin beer.

   Roll and butter

2. Kuruma ebi, fried, biggest shrimp that I ever saw, bigger
      than Ise ebi

3. Steak, Osaka beef, delicious. A piece of butter on it.

4. Salad

5. Green tea ice cream. It must be vanilla ice cream with
      tea-powder worked into it—tea-powder like that used
      for the Tea Ceremony. (By the way, I've not
      participated in a Tea Ceremony yet on this trip.)

6. Strawberries underneath a beautiful heap of whipped marsh-
      mallow.

7. Coffee.

Then my lecture, 1330-1500. It went off about as usual. A Mr.
Okano from the Shionogi Chemical Company translated it: did well.

   Next, to a conference room. Tea. Here the company presented me
with a magnificent tape-recorder, Panasonic, their best portable: runs
on dry batteries, 9 volts, no charging, but with AC adapter. I think
that I can make good use of it.

   To Shin Osaka station, where the New Tokaido line starts. New stations or enlargements of existing stations were required wherever the new
trains stop. I excused myself at Shin Osaka to snap some photos of the
station. Stations must be 1000 feet long to accommodate the new trains.
This one is on four floors, with escalators, at least 12 restaurants, 12
bars, all kinds of waiting-rooms in some of which (I believe) there is a
charge, especially adaptable to conferences between trains. A shop so
big that I was fearful that I might not be able to find my way out in a
hurry: I must return to the platform in 15 minutes.

   There are no crossings of any kind on the new Tokaido tracks.
Passengers only: no freight.

   Off on a Kodama (Echo), on the new Tokaido line. A Hikari-
train (Light) passed us on the right hell-bent for Tokyo while this
train paused at the station at Shizuoka. It had left Osaka a half
hour behind us. One could only reason by <u>reductio ad absurdum</u> that
it was a train that passed by: it couldn't be anything else. It
was probably doing 120 mph or about 180 feet per second. Our car
took a sudden slight plunge leftward as the compressed air hit us
from the right. The whole 1000 feet of the Hikari passed by in 6
seconds; then this train took a sudden slight list to the right in
the vacuum.

43.   Monday 22d

At Matsushita Electric Company, Osaka

Lunch

Arrival at Matsushita Electric Company

Statistical control of quality

44.   Monday 22d

New Tokaido
line above us

Shin (= new)
Osaka Station

Announcements on the train are in Japanese and in English, and
very clear. Before an announcement, comes a ditty on the xylophone.
I don't know the name of it, but I wrote down the tune.

At every station, about every 50 feet, on every platform, there is
an illuminated clock, and alongside it are posted the time when this train
is due out, and the number of the train. Thus at Atami, there was a clock
showing 1708, train 126 due out at 1710. My watch is obviously 15 seconds
slow. We made sure that we were ready to get off at Odawara at 1721, as
the train barely pauses at a station, like trains in Germany, and I recall
how I failed to make it off the train at Bonn the first time I went there
(1952): went on to Cologne and back to Bonn.

There are on this new Takaido line 28 Hikari trains per day, and
32 Kodamas, plus extras Saturdays and Sundays. Average, 148,000 people
daily.

Into a taxi, and up up 15 kms. to the Hotel Kowaki-en on Mt. Hakone.

箱   根   小   涌   園

Hako   .   ne   Ko   .   waki   .   en
Box or   root   Little   hot gushing   garden
little mountain   spring

227

Chapter Fifteen

45.   Tuesday 23d

                    Hotel Kowaki.en
                 I moved into Novi Sad

        Dr. Kurushima's villa, Novi Sad, is reserved for me. How I wish that
I could describe it, but how can one describe a dream? Dr. Kurushima, at
the dinner at Chin.zan.so Monday 15th, had invited me to occupy it, as long
as I wish. It is a villa on the grounds of the Hotel Kowaki-en, serviced by
the hotel, about 300 feet through the woods from the main building. Mr.
Noguchi thought that I might not like it, as Dr. Kurushima had built it as
a dormitory for his boy scouts. The picture of it that he had showed to
me at Chin.zan.so didn't look like a dormitory, so I had hopes. The bell
boy led us to it in the dark through the trees, over a tortuous path-way,
partly stone, partly gravel, only a dim stone light now and then. Here it
was, cheery, the heat on (chilly outside), the main room octagonal, about
20 feet in diameter. Along 5 of the 8 sides are built-in sofas, for beds.
Any additional number of boys could sleep on the floor. I felt one--soft
enough; I shan't worry. A big TV in the room. Mr. Noguchi had reserved
a room for me in the main hotel, just in case Novi Sad didn't please me.
I can never repay his kindness. (Pictures next page).

        Lola and I were in Novi Sad on Sunday the 19th September, and I thought
that my ears had made a mistake when Dr. Kurushima told me on Monday the 15th
that his villa was Novi Sad. It didn't sound Japanese, but the paragraph
which he handed to me at Chin.zan.so, printed in English, Croatian, and
Japanese cleared that up; see Monday 15th, page 14.

        To dinner in the main dining room with Mr. Noguchi: southern fried
chicken.

        Back through the woods to Novi Sad. Here to my relief in one of the
rooms was a real bed with good mattress, all made up ready to crawl into, a
pretty Japanese lantern on the floor near the head of the bed; radio, kimono,
and slippers. There is another room like it, and a large room with a writing-
table with stationery. A stairway led down to a room below with a door that
opened out to the ground-level at that side, with a huge bath tub, Japanese
style, fed undoubtedly by hot springs; also another lavatory. Also a small
kitchen with gas burners and a refrigerator, the only contents being 8 bottles
of beer and some softer drinks.

        Dr. Kurushima is one of the directors of the Fuji Hakone Kanko Company,
which owns this hotel and several others nearby. The company also owns
Chin.zan.so. He is also a director of International Hotels, Inc., which may
account for our reservations in Nagoya, Osaka, and Kyoto.

        The main hotel is enormous. I thought of exploring it, but gave up.
There are several kinds of pools, hot water from the hot springs, one in a
natural hot spring, another for swimming without suits, several restaurants,
Japanese and western, a Hawaiian room, etc. It reminds me of a place that
grew up a little at a time, with no plan. Yet Japanese always have a plan.

        Tuesday 23d. The early part of this morning was clear, but fog descended,
and rain came, just as Mr. Noguchi hired a car for a sightseeing trip in these
beautiful mountains. The trip was a total loss, except for the beauty of the
fog, intensified by the steam that rises from the hot springs. We may try it
again tomorrow.

46.   Tuesday 23d

One event of the trip was a cup of coffee at a shop that occupied
a beautiful view, except that one could only see fog. The shop had a
concrete floor, small tables with red plastic tops, heated after a fashion
by a kerosene burner. Fortunately, little heat was needed today. I
predicted that tomorrow would be clear.

Dr. Kurushima's post card   Showing entrance to basement

"Novi Sad" u Hotelu Kowakienu, Hakone
箱根小涌園のノヴィサッド
"Novï Sad" at Hotel Kowakien, Hakone.

Beautiful walk through the woods to Novi Sad

47.   Tuesday 23d

Close up
to
Novi Sad

Closer

Inside
looking
out

Beds built in →

Wednesday 24th. Up at 0640 after the best sleep that I had had in
months: over 8 hours. Mr. Noguchi had called on the telephone at about
2300 last night. He was in the Hawaiian Room: said that Mr. Takamatsu
was there, and Dr. Ogawa, and someone else: wished that I would come.
I could hear the steel guitars and other noise, and begged off successfully:
went back to sleep.

This was a perfect day, the air just right, and a real vacation.
Mr. Noguchi was late for breakfast, too much Hawaiian Room I suppose, so
I went ahead and joined Dr. Kitagawa. Dr. Moriguti came soon. As I
predicted, the day was clear except for fog here and there, which the wind
tossed from one mountain to another, and which finally disappeared altogether.
We started off at 9, in a taxi, a Toyo Crown, took the Ashinoko Skyline
Course. Mt. Fuji emerged in all its glory, and stayed out except for inter-
mittent fog. Ashinoko was beautiful, far below (Ashi, reed; ko, lake).

Up the mountain from Hakone.machi, in a cable-car to Komagatake Peak,
2d highest peak in the Hakone range; coffee, photographs at the top.

Upper left: entrance to
Hotel Kowaki-en

Upper right: signs along the
road are easy to follow

Lower: here we are, on our
way up to Komagatake Peak,
the other car making its
descent

49.   Wednesday 24th

In the cable-car.
A girl-conductor, of
course. I wonder if
any vehicle in Japan
could move without one.

Below: Mr. Noguchi on
Komagatake Peak

Above: nikuman in steam
oven. How I'd relish one.
This picture and the one
below I took in the restaurant on Komagatake Peak.

50.

On the Ashinoko Skyline Course

Driver   Mr. Noguchi

Then the descent on the other side in another cable-car, not so long a ride. The driver was waiting, and we arrived at lunch at Kowaki.en at just the right time-- 5 minutes late. I had learned this morning that I had to make a speech at lunch, which I did, briefly.

A sign showed

RESTAU
RANT

At the top of Mt. Komagatake, in a restaurant, were all kinds of food. If lunch at Kowaki.en had not been obligatory, I should have stopped right here to eat some nikuman, buns in a glass oven, in steam, ready to eat, made of gluten rice, meat inside (niku, meat; manju, rice bun). There was a large open ice-skating rink, ice produced by refrigeration.

The car on the ascent had about 15 passengers, and a girl-conductor who explained the scenery, in Japanese.

I didn't know that any vehicle could move in Japan without a girl-conductor, but I learned something--the conductor on the descent was a man.

A sign on **Mt.** Komagatake read RUTE TO CABLE CAR.

Back to Tokyo

The ride on the Train KINTOKI from Yu.moto (Hot Springs) to Shinjuku was a pleasant experience, a repetition of one that we had in 1960. Beautiful coaches, one stop only, a bar on every articulated pair of cars, with every kind of drink and snack, including Coca Cola and Pepsi-Cola, and 4 girls to bring it. First and last, the little hot towel. I wasn't hungry, but must have the experience again--hot tea and piece of cake--excellent. Dr. Ito of Nanzan University, Nagoya, was with us. He helped us with my luggage: the tape-recorder that Matsushita gave to me in Osaka complicates matters. I'll ask Odawara Shoten, Ltd. to pack it, and then I'll put it into the mail, once I get to Tokyo.

Arrived at the Imperial Hotel at 1700, by taxi from Shinjuku, after a perfect day. Many errands to do. Late that night, rain commenced, and it poured all next day, the edge of Typhoon Faye.

Instead of waiting on the platform in Yumoto for train-time, I sneaked away to take a walk and see something of the town, and to take a few photos.

51.   Wednesday 24th

and snapped a few photos ...

Now our train is ready to start

Our train the Kintiki was not ready so I
went out for a walk ...

... in the Village of Yumoto

Thursday 25th

52.

The Reverend Peter Yamamoto, and his wife, and beautiful daughter Margaret, came at 2030 for dinner. I was sure that a fine regular American dinner would be an experience for them to remember, so I took them to the dining room. I should have looked at the prices first: the deal cost me Y 9300, or $26.70, including my double martini, the 10% service charge, and 10% tax. Anyway, it was delicious: Washington soup, baked salmon, Kobe beef steak, chocolate sundae.

I wished that I could find a piano here for Margaret, so that I could hear her play tonight, but I was unsuccessful. She apparently has an enviable job, though she works long hours--private secretary to a wealthy industrialist in Kamakura, and private tutor to his talented 7-year-old daughter. She will make a tape with her piano, and send it. I helped her financially in her musical education, but had never seen her nor heard her play.

Thursday 25th. This was Thanksgiving Day at home, but I never thought of it till next day. Rain came down by the barrel, in the edge of Typhoon Faye. Many errands: I can't understand how anyone could accumulate so many papers and packages and such a huge inventory of errands yet undone.

I almost saw another Noh play

The joke was on me. Had a most exasperating hunt for Noh plays at noon today. The girl at City Information in the hotel had told me that there would be an amateur production, free, to begin at 10; it would run on for hours, one play after another, at the Kanze Kai Kan she said. I thought, though, that she said Kanda Kai Kan, which came into my head in memory of 1946, when Virginia used to invite me there for steak. But apparently there is no Kanda Kai Kan any more. The driver, assisted by police, his radio, and several hundred citizens, could find no trace of it. It was a big building on the main street along the moat, I was sure. How stupid not to know where it is, I thought. I was sure that I could find it, if I could ever get back to the point where we started from.

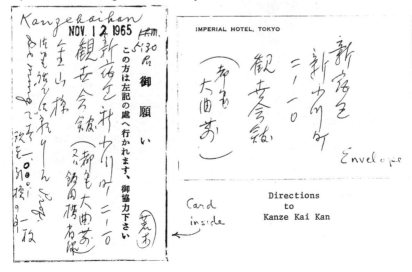

Card inside

Directions to Kanze Kai Kan

Envelope

53.

The man at the YMCA was sure that I should be headed for the Kanze
Kai Kan. How stupid of me: the Kanze Kai Kan is the place where I've
been a number of times before for Noh plays, but I really never knew the
name of it. At the hotel, afterward, the girl declared that she had said
Kanze Kai Kan (what else could she have said?) and that I repeated it after
her. Oh well, there will be more Noh plays tonight, and maybe I'll try
it again.

The story is a carnival of errors. I'll never know why the driver
didn't use the directions that the girl wrote out (he had them in his hand);
and why I never looked at them, nor showed them to the scores of people
that tried to help. My only explanation is that the flood of rain and the
noise of Tokyo traffic washed all my brains away.

I really did see another Noh play today

More trouble with Noh plays! The driver took me to the Kanze Kai Kan.
Dark! This he did in spite of the directions to Suidobashi Noh-Gakudo that
the girl had written out. He must have supposed that he knew without looking at her directions. We took counsel together in the cab in the pouring
rain. I said Suidobashi. He disappeared, then reappeared. Then up and down
he drove in those narrow streets in the downpour. No one seemed to know
where we should be. It's already after 1830, but it won't matter much: the
first hour will be a Kyogen which I'll not understand anyway (not written in
English).

Directions to
Suidobashi Nohgakudo

Finally, the driver drew up alongside a woman that seemed to know something about Noh plays and Suidobashi Noh-
Gakudo, but gave up trying to tell him
how to find it: folded her umbrella in
the flood, climbed in, and directed him.
At last, here we were. I thanked the
woman profusely; paid off the driver,
with at least ¥100 extra to take the
woman home.

This is the Suidobashi Noh-Gakudo.
I had not been here before. It is large,
unheated except for odorless kerosene
stoves here and there. Seats about 800,
I estimated. Practically full. The Kyogen
was still playing when I arrived. Intermission. No food; only hot tea. I was
much amused. People lined up for tea.
Three women trying to serve tea to so many
people. One made tea, one poured, one
washed cups in a tiny sink. Bought at the
stand a book in English A Guide to Noh.

The play was Shari, and I enjoyed it
much.

54.

Postcard purchased in the Suidobashi
Noh-Gakudo shows view inside

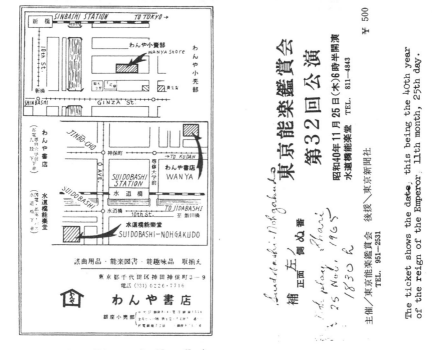

東京能楽鑑賞会

第32回公演

補 正面左側必番

昭和40年11月25日(木)6時半開演

水道橋能楽堂 TEL. 811—4843

主催／東京能楽鑑賞会 後援／東京新聞社

TEL. 951—2531

¥ 500

Suidobashi-Nohgakudo

5th play Phani

25 Nov, 1965

1830 K

The ticket shows the date, this being the 40th year
of the reign of the Emperor. 11th month, 25th day.

I picked up this map inside. Next
time I'll know how to find the place.

55.

SHARI, The Bones of the Buddha

By Zeami

Fifth group

All schools

Characters

Act I: Waki . . . . a travelling priest

Kyōgen . . . . a servant

Shite . . . . . . a villager

Act II: Nochi-shite . . . . . the devil Sokushikki

Nochi-tsure . . . . . the god Idaten

A priest visiting the capital goes to the Sennyu-ji to worship the holy bones kept in the temple, and there he is joined by a villager who tells him the story of the relics. Suddnely, however, the skies darken and the innocent-looking villager, who is in reality the devil Sokushikki, seizes the bones and makes off with them. Much alarmed, the priest calls a temple official and in answer to their prayers the god Idaten comes and retrieves the sacred relics from the devil, who has reappeared in his true form.

The Noh theatre at the Kanze Kai Kan had all kinds of food upstairs, but not this one.

All Noh Gakudo have the same stage, with the cedar tree, and the grand entrance on the left. The Noh plays and the acting are highly stylized, and what amazes me is the tone and message that the actors convey within the rigid framework. The cedar tree holds over from the days when the Noh plays were held outside. The actors are all men, as in the Kabuki plays.

Back to the hotel in a taxicab in the deluge; arrived there about 2200. Suntory (Japanese Scotch whisky), soup, salmon meinière in the Café Terrace.

I forgot to mention my interview this morning with Mr. Stuart Griffin, writer for the London Observer, Oriental Economist, and several other papers. He had called Mr. Noguchi every day about seeing me. I had fixed this day

56.

at 10. He called at 0800, wondered if we could meet at the Hotel Okura, because of the rain. Well why not? One of us must go out into the rain, I thought, and he presented the feeble excuse about having a photographer at the Hotel Okura (an enormous new hotel). Anyway, we met there. He wished to write up a story on how statistical methods had helped Japanese industry. We talked two hours. I wonder how badly garbled the stories will be.

Friday 26th. Again, I'll never understand how anyone could be so busy doing nothing. It was a race all day, purchasing items, taking them to Odawara Shoten in the Arcade to wrap them, or wrapping them myself. Mr. Noguchi came at 10 with yen. Professor Asahi also came: wished to guide me through the day. It turned out that he saved the day. To Maruzen Department Store, where I bought Japanese blackboard erasers for my study at home, a small punch (to use in case the one that I carry ever breaks down or goes into disrepute). Oh yes, Japanese dictionaries, two, which was the main purpose of the trip to Maruzen.

I had decided to purchase a tape recorder just like the one that the Matsushita Company had given to me. Professor Asahi seemed to know just where to go, but it was all wrong: none of this model in stock. Lunch at the Cafe Terrace. I ate only soup. Professor Asahi took my advice and ordered almost everything, and I became fidgety waiting for him to finish his lunch: in fact, I didn't: went to the Arcade on a short errand. He is so kind and helpful: attributes to me all good that has happened to him and to Japan.

Finally, a call to the Tokyo office of Matsushita was successful. My tape recorder is not yet in production, but there is one in Tokyo, and they will recall it: they will have it at 1500, and they did, but meanwhile Seinosuke came. He is now Chief of the Technical Section, Kawasaki Steel Company, a long climb from the time when he and Toyoko worked for me in the Osaka Shosen Building in 1950.

It turned out that the man at Matsushita that Professor Asahi had talked to by telephone was Mr. Aranogi, who had visited our home in Washington in June. I was in much fear the while that they would try to give the tape recorder to me, but there was no problem: he took the money, but with an 18% discount. They had to call in several experts to find out just what all the levers and buttons do, as meanwhile I was counting the minutes: I'll be late for my farewell party.

One day, some weeks ago, I had stopped to look at a big signboard in the Ginza which flashed numbers--79, 81, 78, 83, etc. It couldn't be temperature: it's not that warm, and temperature does not change so rapidly. I asked a man who tried to explain it, but I understood him not. Today, Professor Asahi explained it--noise-level. Apparently even the Japanese are trying to do something about noise. I used to think that they loved it.

Picked up lenses and camera at Suga Photo for Mr. Brousseau in New York. I had meanwhile paid for them, and had the proper paper in my passport for no tax.

Arrangements for departure seem to occupy time. Japan Air Lines must be doing good business. Two weeks ago when I asked for a reservation to San Francisco on flight 812 for some date (I've forgotten what), she could give me JAL only to Honolulu, whence I would take UAL to San Francisco. Now, however, for Saturday, I can have JAL all the way, with no change.

57.   Friday 26th

Farewell party at Hap.po.en

I can't count now how many packages Odawara Shoten wrapped for shipment by post, nor how many I wrapped myself. Anyway, I was ready about 1800, just 40 minutes late. The party was at Hap.po.en, the biggest tea house in Tokyo. One of the girls recognized me during the evening, so I had to admit that I'd been there before (1960). I prefer to let each host think that all his entertainment is new to me.

About 20 men were there, and two women, Sueko and another girl. These are all employees of the Union of Japanese Scientists and Engineers.

1. Tea.

    Sake, much

2. Small triangular tray. On it (a) herbs, (b) raw squid, (c) soy-bean cake.

    Here I switched to beer, as the girls pour sake too fast,

and sake is not a dry wine.

3. Sukiyaki, and I successfully avoided the raw egg on the side. Ingredients: beef (Kobe?), shirataki (shiro, white; take, waterfall; see page 16), onions, bean cake, several kinds of mushrooms, Chinese cabbage. Very good.

4. Two dances by geisha girls

    Yoshiki museum

    Otemogen, with masks, one mask with Okame, face-mask for a girl, changed to Hyottoko, face-mask for a young man.

5. Solo by a geisha girl on the okoto. She was obviously a master of this very difficult instrument.

Mr. Sooma sang a Japanese folksong.

Mr. Sazaki sang in Japanese a folksong by Stephen Foster; then in English My Darling Clementine.

Mr. Morie sang something from an American movie. Everyone knew it but me.

We all sang China Night in Japanese.

I sang Jolly Fat Friar.

Messrs. Soona and Shirai sang a duet.

58.   Saturday 27th

Mr. Kokada sang Kuroda Bushi (Thief of Kuroda;
passed down for ages).

6. Gohan with pungent herbs   8. Mandarin orange

7. Tea   9. Tea

Whereupon we adjourned with many exchanges of good wishes and hopes to
see you again.

Messrs. Noguchi and Kokada and Hiromi thought that we should not go
straight to my hotel. It is essential to see some other parts of Tokyo. Did
I know anything about Shinjuku-ku? Well, Bar Mexico from 1960. We passed
by hundreds of night clubs, one of them being <u>Passe Temps</u>.

Club Night Train

In we went to Club Night Train. It was lots of fun. As usual, you don't
order, you just pay the bill. On comes beer and wine, and platters of Japanese
hors d'oeuvres, the nuts being the only thing worth reaching for. Four girls
for the four of us, cozily situated, chairs each side of the table. One of the
girls said that she is smarter than Mr. Noguchi. Mr. Kokada asked one of the
girls to marry him, but she said that she could do better. Next time I come, I
said, I'll live in some hotel in Shinjuku, and we'll hold all our evening conferences at Club Night Train.

A man played an electric organ once in a while for dancing. The dance
floor measured all of 5 x 10 feet. There was some discussion about the pictures
on the wall, some in modern art. They all knew more than I about it. At length
we departed. I think that Japanese people really appreciate the beauty in their
beautiful girls.

Packed and wrapped till 0115, my last night, what is left of it.

Professor Moriguti and Kimiko

She is 21 and has a driver's
license now. She drove the
family car one day to bring
her father to see me at the
Imperial Hotel.

<u>Saturday 27th</u>. Up at 7. I was
ready at 8, in spite of the necessity
to unpack and repack my big valise to
find the screw that I just discovered
had slipped out of the handle. The
boy at the 4th floor desk had a screw-
driver, and the operation required
only 15 minutes.

I had wished to go to Haneda Airport on the monorail, and we did,
though it was some bother to shift
from the taxi to the monorail train.
It was nevertheless an experience
not to miss. To Haneda in 15 minutes.
It was built by Hitachi-Alweg, I observed. It runs on rubber tires in
the middle of the car. The track is
an inverted U, the top being concrete
for the rubber tires, the sides for
flanges and pick-up of power.

59.

A number of people came to see me off at the airport. Professor Moriguti was there, with daughter Kimiko, and I suppose that Family Moriguti will soon see why every family should have two automobiles. Kimiko came one day two weeks ago to see me (photo preceding page). It was in 1951 and 1952 that I visited their home and took dresses and other things that make little girls happy, to her and to her sister Michiko, now 17.

JAL Flight 812 was due to leave at 10. At 10 o'clock, within 5 seconds, it began to move, and we were soon off for Honolulu, at 37,000 feet, ground speed 740 mph, 5 hours to Honolulu. The pilot is American. He told me that about half the pilots on JAL are American. They were all American a few years ago. UAL still reconditions and repairs the aeroplanes of JAL at the airport at San Francisco.

Rain, fog, heat, and oppressive humidity at Honolulu. We'll be off for San Francisco in an hour. I'll visit my sister Elizabeth near Portland, on the west side of Mt. Hood. Then, off Monday 29th at 0800 for Chicago. I'll attend the dinner Monday night in Chicago for Mr. Coxe's retirement from the Illinois Bell Telephone Company; then work Tuesday in Chicago with the CNW Railway: home Tuesday night, and thus will end my 7th trip to Japan.

Asian Productivity
MONTHLY BULLETIN

Vol. V   No. 12   **December 31, 1965**

• • •

Published by
**ASIAN
PRODUCTIVITY
ORGANIZATION**
Aoyama Daiichi Mansions
No. 11, 4-chome
Akasaka Omote-machi
Minato-ku, Tokyo, Japan
Tel : (408) 4251, 9284
Cable : APOOFFICE TOKYO

JAPAN

Deming Prizes Awarded for Quality Improvement

The Deming Prizes attesting excellence in personal and corporate endeavors for quality improvement were awarded to an engineer of Nippon Steel Pipe Co. and the Toyota Motor Co. in solemn ceremonies held at the Imperial Hotel, Tokyo, on November 10 under the auspices of the Japan Scientists' and Engineers' Union.

Mr. Edwards Deming, Professor at New York University, in whose honor the eponymous prizes had been established, was present at the site.

The recipient for the 1965-66 year of the Deming Prize for excellence in personal endeavors was Mr. Masumasa Imaizumi, Chief, Standards Section, Technological Dept., Nippon Steel Pipe Co. He has contributed much toward raising the general level of quality consciousness in Japan. He succeeded, for example, in applying quality control techniques to process analysis in the company. He often served as instructor in the quality control courses and seminars sponsored by the union, JPC and other organizations.

The Deming Prize for excellence in corporate endeavors for the same year was conferred on the Toyota Motor Co. in recognition of its many years' services rendered for quality improvement and cost reduction. The company ranks first in Japan and 11th in the world in the production of automobiles. Ten percent of its products are exported to foreign countries.

61.

The Mainichi
Daily News

No. 15357　TOKYO　(C)　日　刊　(大正11年4月10日第3種郵便物認可)

(昭和35年5月4日国鉄特別扱承認)　© The Mainichi Daily News, 1965　　15 Yen

WEDNESDAY, NOVEMBER 10, 1965

— • —

Deming Prize Contributes
To Japanese Industry

● For many years Japanese manufacturers have made a daring attempt to wipe out the reputation of inferior quality and cheap price which their products had built up before World War II. Today they emerge victorious. Japanese merchandise is tremendously p o p u l a r around the world not because it is cheap but superior and dependable.

Behind this success are the fatherly guidance and devotion by a leading American statistician, Dr. W. Edwards Deming, now professor of New York University. In the early postwar years, he opened the eyes of Japanese manufacturers to the modern approach to the quality problem and taught them how to make their products attractive among the world consumers.

Dr. Deming is now in Tokyo on his eighth visit to Japan. This afternoon, he and Mrs. Deming will be distinguished guests in a grand ceremony at the Imperial Hotel, Tokyo, to fete the 15th anniversary of the establishment of the Deming Prize—the nation's most coveted award given every year to the outstanding contributors to the research and application of statistical quality control which the U.S. scholar had introduced to Japan.

A highlight of the gala function will be the presentation of the 1965 prizes. This year's winners are Masumasa Imaizumi, chief of the Standards Section, Technical Department, Nippon Kokan K.K., and Toyota Motor Co.

The Deming Prize was created in 1951 by the Union of Japanese Scientists & Engineers (JUSE) to commemorate the friendship and contribution of Dr. Deming to the whole spectrum of Japanese industry. The prize has played a significant role to give an impetus to industry in its dazzling growth.

Dr. Deming

Dr. Deming has been an unequalled teacher and consultant to Japanese industry. He has worked together with thousands of Japanese corporate executives, engineers and scholars for the past 15 years. He set the guideline to bring prosperity to this island country burdened with scarce natural resources. What the U.S. scholar showed his Japanese students was the scientific way to turn out more products that have greater uniformity, dependability and marketability all over the world.

He told the Japanese industrialists that the conventional process of designing the product, manufacturing it and trying to sell it is already obsolete. The statistics scholar emphasized the importance of taking to statistic thinking in all manufacturing stages which should be extended as far as consumer-research. He told of the need to redesign the product according to findings of surveys of users and non-users.

Dr. Deming's theory of statistical quality control was rapidly brought into practice by a growing number of Japanese industrialists. Its effect has

been tremendous. Quality Japanese goods are being exported at record proportions.

It is noted that the prize was instituted with gratitude to his friendship as well as in commemoration of his tremendous contribution. Originally with the Allied Occupation Forces as an advisor in sampling techniques, Dr. Deming never rode the high horse as others did, but loved and fraternized the Japanese people. He was cordial and exchanged frank opinions with everybody. The Japanese Government thanked him for his friendly devotion by investing him with the Second Order of the Sacred Treasure in 1960.

The scholastic contact between Japan and Dr. Deming dated back to April 1950 when Ken-ichi Koyanagi, managing director of the JUSE, wrote to Dr. Deming, then in the U.S., asking for lectures on statistical quality control when he visited Japan later in the year. He readily accepted the plea.

At that time, few Japanese realized the significance of quality control. In the prewar years, there were, indeed, some Japanese scholars and engineers who were engaged in the study of quality control, and some of them attempted to put it into practice. But no company dared to carry out the wholesale introduction of the revolutionary idea.

After the war, the nation's industry was quick to rise again, but the quality of its products were all but inferior. Faced with enormous demand, manufacturers were all busy in turning out as many products as possible, and no one cared about quality. →

The concept of quality control made inroads into the Japanese industries in the form of an Occupation Forces order to communication equipment manufacturers. When they started to employ the modern production formula, some private organizations paid a deep concern. Soon they stepped into the field and started dissemination activities.

Independent from these organizations, the JUSE also launched an educational service of quality control in 1948. A series of lectures was sponsored on the subject of statistical analysis of small samples. Several Japanese experts gathered to form a research group, primarily aimed at collecting necessary literature. But these activities had a discouraging result: there was little experience and material available. Still under occupation, Japan was in no position to obtain enough literature and material related to quality control.

Then came the offer from Dr. Deming to the joy and surprise of all the people concerned. In his first lecture meeting in Tokyo in mid-1950, 230 scholars and statisticians gathered, impressed by the exciting concept of statistical quality control uttered by the U.S. scholar. In another lecture meeting in Fukuoka, 110 were present.

Dr. Deming called on the students to come out of their studies and, with courage and confidence, go into factories, to keep contact with, and teach, business managers and engineers, and to promote their theoretical research on the application of statistical methods. Also among the students in his following lecture meetings were some 100 top-level business leaders. Since then, Dr. Deming has been a frequent visitor to Japan, each time bringing a raft of new exciting ideas to the Japanese students.

Year after year, the wave of quality control application spread fast. It has extended over the length and breadth of the industry. Today approximately 1,000 companies are in close contact with the JUSE, eager to employ new methods. A growing number of smaller firms are looking for the introduction of quality control in their management.

The research work designed to further improve the quality control theory has been progressing at an amazing tempo. Some of their findings have been exported to the world. Many books by Japanese statisticians have been written. Some of these books, as Dr. Deming has put it, extend to the frontiers of statistical theory.

The funds for the Deming Prize come mainly from the royalities of Dr. Deming's work, "Elementary Principle of the Statistical Control of Quality," which he used as the textbook in his first lecture in Japan in 1950. This book enjoyed a big circulation (the first printing 2,000 copies, the second 2,000 and the third 1,700) and the royalities ran up to a substantial amount. Dr. Deming donated them to Ken-ichi Koyanagi, managing director of the JUSE, who eventually took lead to create the Deming Prize in 1950.

The Deming Prize is a silver medal. Designed by Prof. Kiyoshi Unno of Tokyo University of Fine Arts and some other artists, the medal bears an engraved profile of Dr. Deming.

The Deming Prize is divided into three categories. The prize for research and education is awarded to those who made excellent researches in theory and application of quality control. Another prize for application is given to corporations or plants which attained outstanding results in practicing quality control. The third prize is provided for smaller enterprises.

The prize has been awarded annually ever since 1951. The Deming Prize Committee is responsible for the selection of the winners from among a number of candidates. Parallel with the progress in Japan in the concept of quality control, the selection standard has been rising year after year, and the race for the laurels has become keen. It is said that most corporate candidates are spending years in streamlining and reinforcing their quality control setup under the guidance of specially invited experts before they apply for the prize.

History

Deming Prize For Research, Education

1951 Dr. Motosaburo Masuyama
1952 Dr. Shigeru Mizuno and his group for their well-coordinated activities for education and research in statistical quality control, including
Dr. Tetsuichi Asaka
Masao Goto
Hidehiko Higashi
Dr. Kaoru Ishikawa
Dr. Masao Kogure
Shin Miura
Eizo Watanabe
1953 Dr. Toshio Kitagawa
1954 Dr. Eizaburo Nishibori
1955 Dr. Shigeichi Moriguchi
1956 Yasushi Ishida
1957 Dr. Jiro Yamanouchi
1958 Takeshi Kayano
1959-60 Ken-ichi Koyanagi
Dr. Gen-ichi Taguchi
1961 Takeo Kato
1962 Dr. Ikuro Kusaba
1963 Jo Yamaguchi
1964 Dr. Teikichi Shimizu
1965 Masumasa Imaizumi

Deming Prize For Application

1951 Fuji Iron & Steel Co.
Tanabe Seiyaku Co.
Showa Denko K.K.
Yawata Iron & Steel Co.
1952 Asahi Chemical Industry Co.
Furukawa Electric Co.
Nihon Electric Co.
Shionogi Pharmaceutical Co.

Takeda Pharmaceutical Co.
Toyo Spinning Co.
1953 Kawasaki Steel Corp.
Shin-etsu Chemical Industry Co.
Sumitomo Metal Industries
Tokyo-Shibaura Electric Co.
1954 Nihon Soda Co.
Toyo Bearing Mfg. Co.
Toyo Rayon Co.
1955 Hitachi
Asahi Glass Co.
Honshu Paper Mfg. Co.
1956 Fuji Photo Film Co.
Konishiroku Photo Industry Co.
Mitsubishi Electric Mfg. Co.
Tohoku Works
1957 None
1958 Kanegafuchi Chemical Industry Co.
Kureha Chemical Industry Co.
Matsushita Electric Corp.
Nippon Kokan K.K.
1959-60 Asahi Special Glass Co.
Kurake Spinning Co.
Nissan Motor Co.
1961 Nippon Denso Co.
Teijin
1962 Sumitomo Electric Industries
1963 Nippon Kayaku K.K.
1964 Komatsu Mfg. Co.
1965 Toyota Motor Co.

Deming Prize For Application In Smaller Enterprises

1958 Nakayo Tsushinki Co.
1959-60 Towa Industry Co.
1961 Nippon Radiator K.K.

MESSAGE

By Dr. W. Edwards Deming
Professor Of New York University

It is a privilege to congratulate winners of the Deming Prize. Every manufacturer that has competed for the Deming Prize, this year and in previous years, has contributed to the advancement of quality of Japanese product.

It was in Japan in 1950 that I defined the statistical control of quality in the following way:

The statistical control of quality is the application of statistical principles and techniques in all stages of production, directed toward the economic manufacture of a product that is useful and has a market.

Translated into action, this meant use of statistical methods for the following activities:

1. Conducting tests to determine minimum requirements on raw materials and piece-parts.

2. Constructing meaningful specifications of raw materials and piece-parts. A specification must be operational. There is a specification for a unit, and the acceptance procedure for lots.

3. Constructing meaningful specifications for performance of product.

4. Meaningful and economical procedures for conducting tests of performance.

5. Assistance to vendors to help them to improve the quality of their product that they deliver to you.

6. Tests of machines and of processes to determine:
— capability of the process in respect to precision and output.
— improvement of process.

7. Process control:
— To detect the existence of specific causes of variability, which the operator can correct.
— To discover what part of the variability in dimensions, weight, color, etc., or wrong average level, is attributable to common causes, which only management can correct.

8. Acceptance sampling for a guaranteed level of quality of incoming or outgoing product.

9. Consumer - research to discover faults in the product, reasons for the consumer's satisfaction or dissatisfaction with the product.

10. Continual re-design of product, and introduction of new products, for greater satisfaction of the consumer, and for improved sales. Results:

More output of salable product per pound of incoming raw material.
More output of salable product per man-hour.
More output of salable product per machine.
Greater uniformity.
Greater dependability.
Lower price.
Quality suited to the market.
Better competitive position.
More exports: more satisfaction at home.

I made the prediction in 1950 that if Japanese management would take heart and give statisticians and statistically-trained engineers a chance to work, many Japanese products would be definitely competitive by 1955, and that Japanese products would invade and capture the market in many parts of the world by 1960. You know that these predictions turned out to be true.

The advancement of quality and the strong competitive position of many Japanese products is known and admired all over the world.

It might be well to enquire what can be done to hold the lead. In my opinion, it is the responsibility of Japanese management to look ahead, with the best statistical and mathematical assistance possible:

To forecast what products will be in demand five years hence.

To decide what re-design and new design would be desirable.

To decide which products will be profitable in consideration of the manpower, raw materials, machinery, and new processes to be available.

To support statistical research in their plants and in courses, and in universities, and to continue to encourage statisticians and statistically-trained engineers to find ways to improve quality and to reduce costs.

Management has obligation to focus attention on common causes of variability and wrong average level. Some common causes are in the following list:

Poor light.
Inept management.
Humidity not suited to the process.
Procedures not suited to the requirements.
Vibration.
Machines and raw materials not suited to the requirements.
Poor instruction and poor supervision.
Mixing product from streams of production, at different levels.
Raw materials unsuited to the requirements.
Lack of a proper quality program.
Poor food in the cafeteria.
Poor training of operators.

Once a common cause is identified, management must decide whether it be economically feasible to change it. Would better raw materials be worth the extra cost? Would new machinery be worth the cost? better lighting? air conditioning?

Common causes of variability are often as important as specific causes. Common causes affect all machines and all operators. Only management can change a common cause; the worker can not. No matter how well an operator or a foreman does his work, his efforts may be ineffective if he is handicapped by poor light, raw material that is too variable or otherwise unsuitable, or by any other common cause, such as those listed above. This is why management must continually accept the responsibility to find common causes, and to eliminate them if economically feasible.

A very important contribution of statistical methods in production is that they determine the level of responsibilities for the removal of causes of variability. Statistical methods such as Shewhart charts, run charts, tests of significance, detect the existence of specific causes, which the operator or foreman can correct. When all specific causes have been removed, there remain common causes. Statistical experimentation is often helpful in the identification of a common cause.

65.

Imaizumi, Toyota Motor Awarded '65 Deming Prize

Masumasa Imaizumi

This year's Deming Prize for research and education will go to a 43-year-old engineer, Masumasa Imaizumi, of Nippon Kokan K.K. (Japan Steel & Tube Corp.) for his many years of devotion to the study and dissemination of quality control throughout Japan.

A graduate of Tokyo University, Imaizumi started studying the introduction of statistical methods into factories as a student of the applied chemistry course of the university's graduate school. In 1949, he participated in the first basic class on quality control sponsored by the Union of Japanese Scientists & Engineers (JUSE). He has been an active member of the quality control research group of the JUSE ever since.

In the second JUSE class, he joined the ranks of lecturers. Since then he has made an immense contribution to the dissemination of quality control in Japan. He has taught a myriad of people not only in the JUSE seminars but also in many other lecture meetings sponsored by such organizations as the Agency of Industrial Science and Technology, the Japanese Standards Association and the Japan Productivity Center.

In one of his notable achievements, Imaizumi discovered the importance of popularizing the quality control concept among the foremen at manufacturing plants. As chairman of the preparation committee for the first foremen's conference in 1962, he made the meeting a stunning success.

The success of the conference eventually led to the nationwide formation of the quality control circles. Imaizumi is now the caretaker of the circles, which number 4,700 with a total membership of 70,000. In addition, he is busy as associate editor of the "Workshop and Quality Control" magazine, committee member of the Foremen's Quality Control Conference, editorial committee member of the Foremen's Quality Control Conference, editorial committee member of the "Quality Control" magazine and others.

Imaizumi joined Nippon Kokan K.K. in 1951, and has been the chief of the Standards Section of the Technical Department of the firm since 1961. Much credit for the progress of the company in quality control belongs to his aggressive work.

Among his contributions to Nippon Kokan were the introduction and application of quality control, establishment of industrial standards within his company, promotion of the quality guarantee system and quality control guidance for users. He has been cited for his outstanding work in the programing for electronic computers. His company was awarded the Deming Prize for application in 1958.

Toyota Motor Co.

Toyota Motor Co. will be awarded with the 1965 Deming Prize today for its years of thorough application of quality control through close coordination with its multitude of related industries, including distributors and subcontractors.

The nation's leading automaker introduced the total quality control concept in 1961 in an attempt to weather the coming impact of the import liberalization of foreign automobiles. In setting off the drive, the company management came up with three basic targets. They were:

1. To direct all the efforts toward growth into a leading automaker in the world.

2. To elevate the reputation for quality through a constant awareness of better products and better ideas.

3. To contribute to Japan's economic growth through mass production and reduced prices.

Toyota's campaign to carry out quality control is pyramided on the teachings of the late Sakichi Toyota, founder of the firm, that quality comes first.

Another feature of its drive was the concerted efforts to improve quality by all the Toyota group companies. Mutual understanding among top-management of the automaker, suppliers of parts and components and distributors served as a significant prop to the aggressive enforcement of the drive.

It is also noted that the drive was carried out under the three clear-cut principles. Not only top-management but also administrators of individual sections took adequate, workable steps to keep the campaign rolling ahead smoothly.

Emphasis was on the guarantee of quality and cost control. To attain these goals, a unique administrative setup was formed through streamlining and beefing up individual sections.

Toyota Motor pioneered the automobile industry in extending the service period for its clients. It also succeeded in cutting down the number of claims, and realized the quick and stabilized supply of new models.

All these efforts have been rewarded. Toyota's automobile production is the biggest in Japan, and 11th in the world. Toyota Motor has made an impressive contribution to the advance of Japanese vehicles on the world market. At present, 10 per cent of its products are being shipped to foreign markets.

Chapter Sixteen
My Boss

Other people have written books about Dr. Deming. I chose not to write a standard biography. Instead, recognizing the many facets of this remarkable man, I am bringing to the reader essentially two things: one, some personal recollections from more than thirty-eight years as his secretary. Two, with his specific permission, a selection of papers from his voluminous personal files. Together, they are intended to provide some insight to his character and personality, as opposed to an analysis of his work.

The 25th of July 1954 was for most people an uneventful date. For me, it was memorable because it was my first day as Dr. Deming's secretary. The job was at first part-time. As a statistical consultant, he was usually visiting clients worldwide during their normal business hours, leaving Saturdays, Sundays, and holidays, plus evenings (when he was in Washington) for work in his office. His practice increased rapidly, and my position soon became a full-time job, and then some.

At Work

On the very last street in Washington, right off Westmoreland Circle, is Butterworth Place, the lovely Deming home. Dr. Deming's study is four rooms in the basement, with washer, dryer, refrigerator, and furnace-room competing for wall space. Many prestigious journals from all over the world, to which he is sometimes a valued contributor, line every available inch of the walls. The Indian journal *Sankya* dates back from 1900. Our office equipment ranges from the old 10-row adding machine to the modern word processor and facsimile—all the staples of a busy, modern office.

Small wonder the Japanese look up to all 6'1" of Dr. Deming: he towers above them. Towering also are his cannas. Feet taller that he, these salmon-colored beauties peek through the picture window of his study as much as to say, "Have a productive day," and we do. And his Jet Star tomatoes are the envy of any farmer.

The very first week that I worked with him I realized what a prodigious worker he really was. Soon a definite pattern emerged. As I expended increasing time and effort, he generated additional requirements. Work turned into pleasure, with the result that I developed a tremendous capacity to handle his high volume of work with short deadlines.

To this day, Dr. Deming and I chuckle about the so-called part-time status, because of the horrendous, almost insurmountable, never-ending workload. Work begot more work. There was never *nothing to do*—just do it!

It is difficult to keep his office tidy. Letters of appreciation come from all over the world; likewise letters of enquiry. They come in faster than he can turn out notes of thanks and answers to questions. Another difficulty is that every week brings a new framed certificate of some new honour, or a piece of art inscribed to him. We can't find space for all of them. The mantel, 15 feet long, is over-full. We have to put some of them in boxes for storage. Recently, this problem was remedied to some extent when the American Statistical Association dedicated the W. Edwards Deming room in their Alexandria, Virginia headquarters. We were able to contribute a great deal of memorabilia and many awards to that endeavor.

Diamonds may be a girl's best friend, but all I wanted at that time was a brand new IBM typewriter, and this came from Dr. Deming at Christmas, for use in my home in the suburbs. One of the highlights of my life was to be home when Railway Express rolled up my driveway, with a brand new IBM! Merci!

Almost immediately, my husband Jack converted a seldom-used screened porch into a pine-panelled picture-windowed study for that IBM, and added filing cabinets, a wall unit with a desk, loads of shelves, and an extension to our telephone.

The study and the IBM typewriter gave a whole new dimension to my work. In those early years Dr. Deming was in Washington much more than in the 80's, so that any work that I could not finish in his study, I took home to finish, first by the armful, then enough to fill a brief case, then a boxful to be delivered to him the next morning.

The nucleus of his work-week—and mine, too—up until the 70's was Friday night, after he returned from visiting a client, Saturdays, Sundays, and most holidays. In those days he retired at midnight, so it was not uncommon to work till 9, 10, or even 11 p.m. One night after 7 p.m., he suggested that I "take the afternoon off, have dinner with your boys, but if you get a chance, maybe transcribe my dictation, and bring it to me tonight," which I dutifully did. There he was at midnight, with the help of a recorder, studying Japanese.

One solution to a heavy workload is to apply more time to it. (Maybe I too could become famous by inventing an eight-day week!) It was therefore not unusual for me to arise at 4 a.m., type for over an hour, then after an invigorating swim and walk, go to Dr. Deming's office for a day's work with him. So much for a part-time job!

This will sound like Point 12 of Dr. Deming's 14 Points, but I really take pride in my shorthand and typing, and did I ever put it to good use here. Just look at the bibliography (pages 345–356). The faster I typed, the more he dictated in his study or over the telephone from cities throughout the world. What an outlet for my shorthand!

For every sampling plan, for every testimony, for every chapter of his books, there were several in the wings waiting. Hurry.

We invented four levels of priority:

    1)   for top priority (do it today, no matter what)

    2)   to work on if I finished priority 1.

    3 and 4) fill-ins to await him on his next return to Washington.

Believe me, in between I set my own priorities, just to pave the way. Pride of workmanship! 10 and 15 hour days seemed to fly like 10 or 15 minutes.

Katie, long time house-keeper to the Demings, was in seventh heaven when Dr. Deming went marketing: he bought six of everything: cereal, raisin tea loaf, cookies, and especially ice cream. (I might add parenthetically that his trips to the market brought to me two boxes of fresh strawberries, no matter the season.) His own recipe for lemon ice cream brought him great relaxation not only to make, but to serve. His martinis are world famous.

All the inter-city motor freight in the U.S. and Canada is studied by statistical procedures prescribed and monitored by Dr. Deming. For his clients in the telephone and railroad industries, he needed six- and seven-digit random numbers. I plunged into a sea of random numbers. For one telephone company alone, there were hundreds of pages of these monstrous numbers, no duplicates allowed, of course. This was an ongoing project lasting for years. First, I would select a number from a book of random permutations within certain boundaries that Dr. Deming had calculated, to which he instructed me to add, with the help of a wonderful but old ten-row Monroe adding machine, a certain zoning interval. A number like (say) 876,301 would tell the inspector at a telephone company to inspect Manhole No. 876,301 in a certain city, or it might lead him to a certain relay in a definite switch in some wire-center.

Have you ever tried to proof-read a book consisting only of pages of numbers? No words, no characters, no plot—just numbers. Go to the last page of the book, and start all over again. I must have been blessed with stick-to-it-ive-ness! Shades of "Mom, what's for dinner tonight—random numbers?"

Table of Random Sampling Numbers

Eighty-seventh Thousand

	1-4	5-8	9-12	13-16	17-20	21-24	25-28	29-32	33-36	37-40
1	8780	0250	2089	6833	3167	2133	4375	7986	7270	0783
2	4694	7282	1381	2531	6268	5587	8980	7954	1973	2041
3	3277	8068	3605	1000	2869	9716	3198	2993	3365	2538
4	7613	0716	1866	3362	3042	4105	3038	5574	6092	9000
5	1701	3346	6614	5001	4863	6012	1123	6103	7882	1336
6	2583	0295	9167	1703	2008	0729	3323	4706	4052	7002
7	6037	0446	3033	0992	1148	5512	9273	1249	7792	1904
8	8765	7964	5131	8640	1613	3727	4972	2925	1773	1134
9	9702	9228	9087	9008	7211	4467	5054	8605	4960	5440
10	8804	3987	9903	2773	1558	4644	1312	5625	4150	6315
11	5127	5340	6666	6017	5291	8467	5023	8833	1477	7102
12	5157	3250	5430	8784	5146	6033	9779	6585	5711	1051
13	0919	7076	4029	5386	1835	9774	9811	0179	3620	3895
14	7835	3638	4314	2175	4861	2495	2738	5792	0216	9027
15	9728	1742	3385	0985	0881	5772	6342	5867	7821	4619
16	5276	3085	8134	4911	0649	4498	9909	2248	5379	2702
17	6130	2852	7916	5252	4688	5307	0359	0953	5166	7852
18	5013	9335	7795	9727	4836	3953	4834	4682	0520	3112
19	8220	8721	9431	5984	2340	5716	6582	6472	4224	6591
20	9651	1975	9283	5254	2223	5167	4731	1406	9321	3743
21	4248	9524	2054	5631	0227	8393	0675	6206	1062	9056
22	9366	8256	1814	2667	3426	7221	9573	4583	6177	2393
23	1750	7368	6891	0013	0207	6609	4937	6003	1497	2659
24	3271	5949	0294	5196	2464	1109	9452	8853	2972	5154
25	3213	0192	7791	7673	8830	0853	2253	4598	3444	7695

Eighty-eighth Thousand

1	0423	5999	9096	4684	9488	1487	4423	8238	6479	7330
2	8517	5811	7968	2620	1028	5614	7693	7766	0295	3547
3	5625	8423	1257	2131	4701	9732	2508	3271	7449	7865
4	4842	3562	7390	9955	4075	2191	7724	7788	5473	2759
5	2264	9173	5244	9648	3839	2626	4926	6328	9685	5380
6	8594	5936	3458	2289	9112	0598	6896	2667	8443	6755
7	5052	0587	4234	9329	8559	5357	5283	9396	0626	9514
8	7080	0488	1875	5391	6553	4432	2915	4779	6569	9384
9	1810	4021	3757	3705	6549	4033	4144	9166	8230	6068
10	7967	6150	4105	4846	5232	5902	7216	6156	8403	4675

Working for Dr. Deming the Author

Writing a book is a labor of love for Dr. Deming, involving years of revisions, certainly not a draft or two. After many revisions, just when I was about to send his manuscript to the publisher, came even more drastic revisions: plural. The reader will perceive the patience, the effort, the time, the expertise, and the love that he puts into a book. Passages or even chapters that he had dictated (say) in 1983, then redone on scraps of paper on an aeroplane or in the Red Carpet Room—passages that he had dictated to me from all over the world, were revised and revised. How could they not be perfect? How could some of them be eliminated? An articulate student of the English language, a change suggested by a client, conversation with production workers. And change we did. I should say changes. He was never satisfied with his own words.

But the finished products are beautiful. How proud I am of the Japanese edition of *Sample Design in Business Research* (Wiley, 1960). This was a mathematical book, and more than once he would say to me, "Wait'll I get in a mathematical trance." I felt like an army private at attention! And a flurry of happy memories with *Quality, Productivity, and Competitive Position* (Center for Advanced Engineering Study, Massachusetts Institute of Technology, 1982), now superseded by *Out of the Crisis* (also MIT, 1986). Dr. Deming says that anyone with a job is entitled to pride of workmanship, and I agree. I have it. *Out of the Crisis* has been published in several languages.

My family and I like to travel abroad, but just about our favorite haunt is the posh Greenbrier in White Sulphur Springs, West Virginia. It's only four hours from Washington, now all interstate. For some 20 years we have savored the groaning board there at Thanksgiving, but in November 1983 Dr. Deming told a colleague over the loudspeaker telephone that "what is not in *Out of the Crisis* this week, will not go in it. This is it!" Music! That evening I convinced my boys that in view of the impending publication, maybe we should cancel the Greenbrier for just this one Thanksgiving, and that I would stuff the turkey for a change. Finally, *Out of the Crisis* appeared three Thanksgivings later!

Dr. Deming's writings are in a continual state of revision, owing to additional experience accumulated almost daily, also from reading, and from association with his students and clients, as well as with people in his four-day seminars, many of whom are scholars in one field or another.

Acapulco was cancelled because of complex legal testimony, and more than one performance at the Kennedy Center for the Performing Arts. From that time onward, season tickets were out of the question.

Life After the NBC White Paper

Just about the only way for me to keep in touch with the world was to turn on the morning television news after an early swim and walk, armed with a cup of hot tea with lots of lemon. This was June 1980. There on my favorite program, The Today Show, was NBC promoting its White Paper entitled, *If Japan Can ... Why Can't We?* with a screen image, larger than life, of my Boss saying, "Work smarter, not harder." Somehow I was working harder!

Lights, cameras, action. Five cameramen, with more cameras, spotlights, recording machines, plus Clare Crawford-Mason and her producer, Lloyd Dobyns, put all of their equipment on my desk, the inference being that I was in the way.

Clare warned us that our lives would never be the same, and so right she was. The program was a huge success. Our phones rang off the hook. Another person should have been hired just to answer the telephone. Dr. Deming's mail quadrupled, and beyond.

On reflection, I wish now that I had kept at least a partial diary of my Deming life: no two days alike in over three decades. But we were too busy to realize that his fame was lurking in the shadows.

His commitments were at once astonishing and overwhelming, absorbing his calendar well into years ahead. The reader will perceive his Napoleonic calendar for the latter half of 1985:

17–21 June	London
23–29	Home, sweating on page-proof of new book
1–5 July	Pretoria, South Africa

9–10 July	Nashua Corporation (Boston area)
11–12	Ford Company (Detroit)
15–18	Monterey, California
22–25	General Motors (Windsor, Michigan)
26–27	Detroit: Seminar for Consultants
30 July-2 August	San Diego
7	General Motors (Lansing, Michigan)
8	Ford, (Kansas City)
10–23	New Zealand
27–30	Washington, 4-day Seminar
2–4 September	Lake of the Ozarks with client
5–6	Nashua (Boston area)
9	New York
10–13	Philadelphia
16	New York
17–18	General Motors (Detroit)
19–20	Ford (Detroit)
23	New York
24–27	St. Catherine's, Ontario
1–4 October	San Diego
9–11	General Motors (Detroit)
12 October	Detroit: Dedication of school
15–18	Sea Crest, Cape Cod AT&T Network
6–20 November	Japan
26–27	General Motors (Detroit)
3–6 December	Washington, 4-day Seminar
10–13	San Diego, 4-day Seminar
17–18	Ford (Detroit)
19–20	General Motors (Detroit)

There were eye-openers all along the route. I would, for example, deliver Dr. Deming to the airport at dusk, after a day's work in his study.

In his briefcase he was carrying work that he had dictated earlier that day and which he wished to look at one more time. Next morning—just about 12 hours later—came a special delivery envelope to my home with (say) corrections to a sampling plan for a client, which he authorized me to mail, once re-typed; or a chapter with yet another revision, which I might in turn send special delivery to his further destination (Detroit, San Diego, Osaka). Some days I would receive several envelopes from him. Man, there were days that I felt even busier than he!

After the program appeared in June 1980, we really needed call forwarding, so from that day forward, whenever I leave Dr. Deming's study, I transfer his telephone to my home in Arlington, to miss no important calls. Busy, busy, busy. This is Dr. Deming's office.

To handle the volume of mail, Dr. Deming had 100 pigeon-holes and more shelves installed in one of the rooms of his study. Katie, the maid, said that soon her washer and drier would land on the TV antenna! But even the new shelves could not accommodate all of the medals, plaques, photographs, and certificates from universities, conferring eight honorary degrees on Dr. Deming. On the wall overlooking this long shelf is a 2x3 foot replica of the Deming Prize, carried to Washington in 1952 by Mr. Kenichi Koyanagi (deceased), then Managing Director of the Union of Japanese Scientists and Engineers: the work of artists at the University of Tokyo.

Most telephone enquiries appear to assume that Dr. Deming is at his desk in Washington awaiting the call. Not so! Just look at his Herculian schedule for a week in 1991:

22 September	Address to the International Association of Fire Chiefs, Toronto. 10,000 present (see next page)
23 September	Class at New York University
24–25 September	Nashua Corporation, San Francisco
26 September	General Motors, Detroit
27 September	A.C. Rochester, Rochester
28 September	Washington

When he addressed the International Association of Fire Chiefs in Toronto, he used an example which has become a favourite with audiences and students. It is irresistible to reproduce it for you!

We know how to optimize pieces, but optimization of a larger system is difficult. A system must be managed.

Here is a tiger. Without an aim in life, he is only a tiger. Once he had an aim, then there will be a system. The tiger will be an important part of the system, but he alone does not make a system. What might be his aim? Here are some possibilities (with apologies to Mr. Stafford Beer of Toronto):

Aim of a tiger

1. To become a great hearth rug;
2. to stabilize the number of deer in the forest;
3. to stabilize the number of people in the village.

He will conduct in 1992, twenty public 4-day seminars and seven private seminars for his clients. Foreign travel, acceptance of honours and awards, testimonial events, and keynote speeches require much travel and time.

During the academic year, he usually departs Washington on Sunday afternoon to be on hand Monday morning in New York for Columbia University where he is a Distinguished Lecturer, and at New York University in the afternoon, where he has taught for almost 50 years and is now Professor Emeritus of Statistics. He has overseen the doctoral theses of many graduate students. Later, he is whisked to LaGuardia Airport or JFK to enplane at 5:30 to his next destination.

Thus, the reader will perceive that Saturdays and part of Sunday are the nucleus of his workweek. He and I are on the telephone morning, noon, and night during the week days in order to keep the work flowing and to map strategy.

He is dictating telegrams, sampling plans, passages for his books from all over the world. There have been days that he would call me from four different states. So this was a good time for me to add yet another telephone extension in my home. I was always within arm's length with a notebook, for dictation from him from any part of the world. I think that perhaps that, in my own way, I was installing quality control.

Nothing tickles me more than when he tells just about everyone: "Call Ceil, she's on duty 24 hours a day." Not quite, Doctor—23 is more like it, because I'm in transit almost an hour coming and going to your study—which could be easily solved with a cellular phone.

In French

Ma Secretairé (Ceil) répondera au téléphone 24 heures par jour.

In Japanese

私の秘書のセイルは一日
24時間 電話に出ます。

A Week-end with Dr. Deming (October 1991)

Saturday:

Catch up on correspondence and telephone calls, especially International: London, Tokyo, Caracas, Melbourne, Nigeria

Speech at a Washington hotel

Camera crew of PBS sets up equipment for an hour-shoot

Short walk in the yard; pick up twigs

B-12 shot

Work on book

Rest

Be sure that necessary papers are in briefcase for following week, especially the Red Beads.

Pick flowers in the yard; put them on Lola's grave

Sign 42 letters

More telephone calls

To the Mason home: lobster dinner, followed by taping for the Deming Library

Return home at 9

Gin at the fireplace

Retire

Sunday

Church on Sunday morning

Work on book

Off to New York by 3 o'clock

Dr. Deming says that Saturdays are slave days, his only chance for connected hours; telegrams, mountains of correspondence, notarized testimony, manuscripts, books, and telephone calls! One Saturday, after slaving for at least twelve hours, word came from upstairs that "Dinner will be ready in two minutes." Actually, dinner was not quite on the table when he got upstairs, so to the Steinway he went for that minute to add another note to the Mass that he was composing—making every second count.

This is a true story. Three days before Thanksgiving 1985, Al Forlenzo drove both of us to the Washington Hospital Center, across town, for removal of a cataract from Dr. Deming's right eye. The operation, 100 percent successful, took only about two hours. I looked for him all over ICU, thinking that he would be completely knocked out, and there he was in the recovery room, eating a cracker and sipping a cup of hot tea. On the return trip from the hospital, I hoped that he might stay in bed the rest of the day. No way. He worked with the bandaged eye till 8:30 that night. I'm pleased to report that a gadget on his desk which he had perceived for decades to be transparent like water, turned out in fact to be yellow. Music! An equally successful removal of a cataract from his left eye was accomplished two days before Thanksgiving 1986. Truly, two Thanksgivings to be thankful for. Now the blues are blue, and the greens are green.

On the second day of his 4-day seminar in Newport Beach in July 1990, Dr. Deming collapsed. He was rushed to the hospital, where a pacemaker was implanted. The pacemaker had to be replaced in Washington. He had four operations in three weeks (his observations of hospital care, found in Chapter 10, result from this experience), was in and out of the hospital for three weeks, and then recuperated at home. Round-the-clock nurses allowed him to come down one flight of stairs. Recovery was slow but his faith sustained him.

It was customary during his convalescence for me to accompany him and the nurse upstairs when he retired for the evening, usually about 7:30 p.m. One evening in September as he, his nurse, and I went up four (of twelve) steps, he suddenly collapsed, but we somehow managed to carry him the rest of the way.

Friends and colleagues ask me, "How does he do it?" Answer: sweat. He is not putting on airs at a country club, nor playing games, nor watching ball on television, nor in fact watching television at all. He is looking for problems all around the world, and trying to help solve them. Two feet of snow in a blizzard will not keep him home. You would only see him trudging along in the storm, which has paralyzed the East Coast, and kept most people inside their own houses!

Finally, "And, Ceil, how do you do it?" Same answer: sweat, though if you got up early enough, you would see me walking around in Arlington and enjoying a swim. The rest of the day went unflinchingly to Dr. Deming. That's how we do it.

Traveling Around the World

By mid-sixties I had heard a lot about Japan and the Deming Prize, so my family and I went to see Japan for ourselves: unbelievable! The polite Japanese people, the bullet train, the Noh-play, the Ginza, the cleanliness, and of course my Mikimoto pearls (which have appreciated tenfold). This was an inexpensive chartered university trip, preceded by an unbelievable trip to Hong Kong. We had to be at Haneda Airport at 6 a.m., for our return to the U.S. Our hotel was the charming Okura Hotel in Tokyo, across the street from the American Embassy. Would you believe that the manager of the hotel rose at 4 a.m. to supervise breakfast on white table-clothed tables? And at 5 a.m., he and the entire hotel staff came to our chartered bus to wave bon-voyage—only in Japan.

The generosity of Mary Ann Gould, then President of Janbridge of Philadelphia, made my third trip to Japan possible in November 1985 for the 35th Anniversary of the Deming Prize, the celebration of which can only be described as stupendous! We stayed at the lovely Imperial Hotel.

Twelve times to London, and so much that I have not seen. While shopping at Harrod's, a client waves to Dr. Deming: small world. A flurry of memories of the Abbey, St. Paul's Church, music and dancers at Queen Elizabeth Hall, the London Coliseum, Ashridge.

Many people at his seminars in London graciously invited him and me to go sightseeing and to dinners in special places. It was not possible for him to accept all of them, but one night in London, we had a very special dinner. The only female at the table, I selected Dover sole and fresh raspberries with cream. One by one, everyone at the table, including Dr. Deming himself, selected the same dinner menu, which simplified life for the waiter.

Now we all know that flying is strictly for the birds. Crossing the Atlantic and Pacific Oceans several times yearly, Dr. Deming makes good connexions out of the country—Japan, New Zealand, Australia, Europe—but some of the domestic trips boggle the mind. On a recent one-hour Washington to Boston trip, he waited in the plane seven hours for takeoff. No turbulence in Washington, nor in Boston, but loads in between. And in Boston was Chris, who also waited 7 hours, ready to haul Dr. Deming to Nashua, New Hampshire.

On the other hand, the Concorde to London is the ultimate experience in flying. At 10.4 miles above the earth and at supersonic speeds of over 1500 miles per hour, it whisks you from Heathrow to Dulles in 3 1/2 hours. Lunch in London, and another in Washington. The way to go! The Mach meter on the front cabin wall of the Concorde shows passengers when they reach the speed of sound (Mach 1) and twice the speed of sound (Mach 2).

Tokyo or Toronto, New York or New Zealand, Brisbane or Buffalo, I am Dr. Deming's wake-up call at 7 a.m. his time, wherever he is. I had no trouble with time zones out of the U.S., but I remember one sleepy morning when he told me that it was only 5 a.m. in Portland! I was only "doing my best."

Fame and Its Consequences!

In my experience, most newspaper and television reporters think only of their own deadlines, and write only what they want to be read. "We need to see Dr. Deming tomorrow—to go on the air by the end of next week." Pleasant dreams. End of the week of what year, I would think to myself, as I looked over his over-committed calendar. After much re-arrangement, exchange of air tickets, it became possible in some instances to have a reporter interview him on the plane, in action at a seminar, or observe at a client, or all of the above. This is no easy matter to arrange. Months later, comes a telephone call from the same reporter, on the pretext of thanking me for all of this rearrangement, but to ask for just one more appointment, to come to his study. "Why? You have all the meat of the story, right from the guru himself?" "But we've heard so much about his cluttered study." Cluttered it may be, but it's a gold mine for the printed and spoken word. (How would he know?)

First-time callers, hoping to see him soon, are polite with "... and how old is he?" "Ageless in wisdom and young in spirit," is my response. "Furthermore, you'd need roller skates to keep up with him, no matter what your age."

Dr. Deming is a walking office in perpetual motion. What doesn't fit in his brief case bulges the pockets of his custom-made suits: calculator, airline tickets, calendar, pencils, pens, a pocket flashlight, rubber bands, clips, index cards, and (are you ready?) dog-eared slips of paper, on which he jots down names and addresses of people, further ideas for his books. He will say over long distance, "You know, that clause that I wrote about..." On a recent trip from San Diego, he returned with over fifty calling cards, each of whom wants the name of a good consultant to hire on a long-term basis, or some literature, or whatever. His briefcase contains air tickets for use months hence, plus 10 shuttle tickets, Washington to La Guardia, and onward to Boston; and 3200 white and 800 red beads for his famous bead experiment.

Periodically, I count the wooden beads to make sure that Dr. Deming is using 4000 (3200 white and 800 red) beads. Mix the beads thoroughly. One scoop with a paddle containing 50 beveled depressions pulls up 50 beads—some red, to show the fault in the system, but not with the worker. White beads are good—red beads prove that even the best worker can not beat a bad system.

He carries in a 6-hole notebook for instant reference hundreds of names and addresses of almost everyone that he knows. He's a target of the postal card people. Every Tom, Dick, and Harry—Mary, too—gets a postcard from some exotic place.

Once I called in Osaka to ask for one word for a telegram that he had dictated to me. By that time he had thought of a synonym for that word.

Significant Birthdays

Dr. Deming was born at the turn of the century, 14 October 1900, making it easy for all his friends and colleagues to remember his age each year. Birthday celebrations have become legendary!

In 1983, he was surprised six times by as many clients in as many cities! Miss Massachusetts joined one of the parties. Various hosts included Bob King, then of Western Electric; Jim Olson, then President of A.T.&T.; William Hoglund of Pontiac; Bill Scherkenbach, then at Ford Motor Company; and Mr. Jim Henry of Eastern Motor Carriers Association. Then in 1986, colleagues and friends helped him celebrate his 86th birthday in style in five cities: Dayton, Detroit, Los Angeles, Philadelphia, and Washington.

After four operations in three weeks, and several weeks of confinement, on 12 October 1990, it was possible for him to attend a birthday party, his 90th, at the lovely home of Clare and Bob Mason. Over 100 people came, including Jean-Marie Gogue of Versailles. I brought my son John and his wife Ann.

On 11 October, as a special birthday tribute, Peter Jennings of ABC Nightly News had named Dr. Deming as Person of the Week. For those not able to see him on television, the Masons replayed the program in their specially equipped video set-up (CCM Productions). As always, many gifts and greetings poured in from all over the world!

For his 91st birthday he received, among other things, at least seven birthday cakes (3 alone in Detroit), 5 homemade apple pies, a year's supply of Schrafft's vanilla ice cream, a framed three-by-six foot birthday card from the House of Representatives depicting Dr. Deming's initial visit on Capitol Hill on 22 July 1991, at the request of Congressman Newt Gingrich (R-Georgia); 91 exquisite baby orchids (for each one of Dr. Deming's tender 91 years) from Honolulu. Books, baskets of fruit, caviar. No less spectacular were the homemade bread, European style cookies, jams, jellies, Godiva.

Just to be sure, his grand-niece Linnea Erickson (of Oregon, but living in Dr. Deming's home at that time) baked a cake for him on his return to Washington.

On 14 October 1991, Dr. Deming's actual birthdate, Dr. Aaron Tenenbein of the Stern School of Business of New York University arranged for his 130 students to share a huge birthday cake. No matter where you slice it, it's Happy Birthday!

Birthday Card from General Motors

Awards and More...

Japan Broadcasting videotaped his lecture at New York University on 23 September 1985. TeleJapan came to Washington to do a story for showing throughout Japan on the program, "Japan Today," on the Deming Prize and the Japanese companies that received the Deming Prize.

There are three portraits on the walls in the main lobby of the Toyota building in Tokyo: one of the founder, one of the chairman, but looming larger than either of them is the portrait of Dr. Deming.

He was enshrined into the Engineering and Science Hall of Fame in November 1986.

Columbia University has established the W. Edwards Deming Center for Quality Management. It will encompass a chair in management of quality, a visiting professorship by an internationally respected scholar, doctoral and MBA fellowships and faculty field studies.

Deming Day has been celebrated by the Stern School of Business of New York University, Fordham University, and the University of Colorado at Boulder. Similar programs of appreciation and scholarships are planned at several other universities.

The Deming Room in the new Headquarters Building of the American Statistical Association in Alexandria, Virginia was dedicated in 1991.

In recognition of Dr. Deming's contributions to American industry, the Philadelphia Area Council for Excellence (PACE) has established a one-year fund to restore the 100-year-old Japanese Glen in Fairmount Park.

The Sioux City Chamber of Commerce, in cooperation with the W. Edwards Deming Business Center presents small businesses in the Siouxland area with the W. Edwards Deming Entrepreneurial Award.

He received the Cosmos Club Award on 11 April 1992.

All over the country, Deming Study Groups are forming to study and help businesses put Dr. Deming's knowledge into practice.

The honours, awards, and tokens of appreciation are endless. He is modest, never making a fuss over them; is always a gracious recipient. And he always seems to have plenty of time for anyone he is talking with. His love of and interest in people always shines through.

THE NATIONAL MEDAL OF TECHNOLOGY

is awarded by

THE PRESIDENT OF
THE UNITED STATES OF AMERICA

to

W. Edwards Deming

For his forceful promotion of statistical methodology, for his contributions to sampling theory and for his advocacy to corporations and nations of a general management philosophy that has resulted in improved product quality with consequent betterment of products available to users as well as efficient corporate performance.

1987

Ronald Reagan

**The Lovely Geisha Doll,
gift from the President of Pentel.**

Dr. Deming, the Man at Home

The lovely home of the Demings has overtones of Japan: a huge Geisha doll encased in a glass enclosure, which arrived unscathed from Tokyo, a gift from the President of Pentel, takes up the entire corner of the dining room. Many Japanese paintings and screens are evident. Both Dr. and Mrs. Deming loved to collect beautiful remembrances from their travels, and these memories are in evidence.

Dr. Deming is a perennial student of English grammar and of the theory of music. His mother was a musician, and he took piano and voice lessons from her. He studied theory under Dr. James Dickinson of Washington, beginning about 1930. Dr. Dickinson came from London, and was in fact a choir boy under John Stainer, later Sir John. Dr. Deming, after Dr. Dickinson's death, found teachers in theory at the Cathedral in Washington, and later took lessons in theory from Mr. Russell Woollen of Washington.

In his studies of theory, Dr. Deming has put forth a number of compositions, all liturgical, plus the Star Spangled Banner. Copies of his compositions are in Chapter 19 of this book.

Dr. Deming has sung in choirs from childhood. He studied music under Roger C. Frisbie, organist at the Cathedral in Laramie, the seat of the University of Wyoming. While at Yale, he sang in the choir of Christ Church, thankful (he says) for the stipend of $10.00 per month. (Those were gold dollars, he reminds me.) He reluctantly gave up this diversion years ago, as he is away most week days, unable to attend rehearsal.

In the 38+ years that I have worked for him, I have seen him watch television only about four times. I remember his fascination with the television reports of the space program. He saw on television the visit of the Pope to this country. He of course saw the NBC White Paper, *If Japan Can ... Why Can't We?* He takes a quick look at the *Washington Post* the mornings that he is home, but he never looks at the stock market, preferring to leave these disappointments to the Riggs Trust Company. To the best of his memory, the last movie that he saw was decades ago, *A Doctor in the House.* By contrast, he enjoys music at churches or at the Kennedy Center for the Performing Arts. He is fond of ballet.

Actually, I would say that his hobbies are work, teaching, writing, conversation over dinner with colleagues and music—and cats! Early one morning when I was alone with more international than domestic telephone calls, couriers delivering documents like mad, mail galore—so much to do, and so little time to do it—I spot in this academic atmosphere not one, but four boxes of *Tender Vittles*. But we have no cat! Mystery solved: days later, as I rolled up in my car, there was Dr. Deming in the front yard feeding Tiger, the neighbor's cat.

Now in statistical parlance, one uses with extreme care such adverbs as *above* and *below* average, but I'm here to tell you that Tiger is an above average cat. He beats Dr. Deming to the front steps of his home most Friday nights when he alights from a taxicab.

Dr. Deming gives one-day seminars every year in Cleveland to benefit the Cystic Fibrosis Foundation. This charity began years ago when he became aware that the child of a colleague suffered from the disease. His contribution of time and effort has provided a significant source of funding for this worthwhile cause.

You might ask, what is the difference between his schedule in the 1960s and 1990s? The difference is entirely one of orientation, not of effort expended, and the result is that he was equally as busy in 1960 as he is now. For example, in the 60s and 70s he was able to spend a few more hours a week at home: let's say an occasional weekday, which is almost unheard of nowadays. In the earlier years, it was possible for him, upon request, to address a group of students at a local university, or to attend a seminar "next week." Now, with his appointments lined up for a year or more in advance, such a request would be well nigh out of the question.

Time that he used to spend directly on work is now diluted by extensive travel. Several times a year he must even take a private plane where no commercial connexion is available.

And he is always working on a book. *Some Theory of Sampling* and *Sample Design in Business Research*, both mathematical books, were published in the 1960s. In those days he was home on an occasional week day, and we would work till 11 p.m., or even midnight. *Out of the Crisis*, published in 1985, is used as a text in his seminars, and you read earlier about the years of work that went into it! Now he is desperately at work on *The New Economics for Industry, Education, Government* which will also be used in his seminars in 1992. (A book is never finished—the author merely puts it aside!)

So who is this Dr. W. Edwards Deming? Allow me. He is a perennial student and teacher (he enters a class or a seminar to learn as well as to teach), a scholar, a legend, a prophet of his time, with a keen sense of humor. He is kind, considerate, industrious, a humanitarian, with a heart as big as his brain—and he's my Boss! He loves all people, and he especially loves Japan and the Japanese people. The Japanese manufacturers created in 1951, in his honor, the annual Deming Prize. The Emperor of Japan decorated him in May 1960 with the Second Order Medal of the Sacred Treasure. Those who know him best agree with me when I describe him as being pure gold!

Professor M.V. Jambunathan of the University of Mysore sent the following letter under date of 14 November 1956.

> The pamphlet describing the Deming Prize was interesting to read as it was inspiring, and I can not refrain from congratulating myself on my good fortune in being able to come under the tutelage of so eminent and noble personality as yourself. I do not want to embarrass you, but I should say that you have conquered, as it were, a whole nation by kindness, love and human sympathy, which the might of arms have failed to achieve. My earnest prayer is that God may shower his choicest blessings on you and your family, and long life in the service for the cause of international peace and goodwill.

In 1960 Diana Deming Cahill asked me to be Godmother to her son, John Vincent Cahill. His daughters maintain close relationships with Dr.

Deming, as do nieces, nephews, and grandchildren. Daughter Linda crew-cuts her father's hair in all of three minutes.

Throughout his seminars and in his literature, Dr. Deming stresses the *arms-around relationship* that Japanese companies enjoy with their vendors. That relationship I found right here in his charming wife, Lola, who until she died, literally welcomed me with open arms every day of my Deming life.

Most of the contents in this book came my way via dictation from Dr. Deming. He has kindly permitted me to share it with the world.

Chapter Seventeen
Dorothy Deming Baker

Dorothy Deming Baker
Born in Washington 26 Jan. 1928
Died in Ft. Lauderdale 22 Feb. 1984

It was on Sunday the 12th of February 1984 that Dorothy's friend Kathy called me by telephone to say that she had taken Dorothy to the hospital with severe angina pains. I wonder how many times Kathy had taken her to the hospital for this very same complaint. I called Dorothy by telephone later that day, Holy Cross Hospital, Room 259, our last conversation. We talked about her house, her recently renovated bathroom, "I feel like a princess to think of it," she had said, and so happy she was also with her new kitchen, installed three years ago by the same company in Ft. Lauderdale. I assured her that I would talk to the superintendent to ask for a change of rules so that her little dog could come to see her. I tried to keep the conversation light, and so did she, but we were both hiding our thoughts. She must have tests the next two days.

Dorothy Deming Baker
7 July 1931

I must be in New York next day (Monday), in Detroit the next, in Los Angeles the next, Portland the next. No change of plan seemed possible nor was there any reason to change. This could only be a replay of previous visits to the hospital, I supposed. Her ailments seemed to diminish in duration and in frequency as the years went by, it seemed to me.

Ceil, my secretary, called me Wednesday morning in Los Angeles to say that the report was grave: Dorothy must have a coronary by-pass. The operation would take place the next day. Dorothy had written to me two months before to remark that her physician had asked her if she would be willing to undergo this operation. I never replied: I was not in favor of it.

Kathy called me in Portland next day to say that Dorothy was in a coma. The surgeon found serious emphysema and could not finish the operation. Dorothy never regained consciousness. She was declared dead on the 22d, six days after the operation. I was in Worcester holding a four-day seminar, Tuesday through Friday, the hardest week that I have ever had. I dared say nothing about my worry and anxiety. I took a nonstop flight Boston to Ft. Lauderdale Friday the 24th as soon as possible after the close of the seminar.

Dorothy's funeral was held next day at 1 o'clock, and she was buried alongside her late husband Pete, so good he was, who died 14 October 1967 of a heart attack.

Dorothy's boys, Billy 32 had come from Toronto, and Andrew 29 had come from Chattanooga, and had made arrangements for the funeral. Diana had come from Los Angeles. Dorothy had been for many years a faithful member of the N.E. Baptist Church, and had a host of friends.

Dorothy had been home for Christmas, and we had good times together. I was home the eight or nine days when she was here. She found the Christmas trappings in the attic, stockings for Dorothy and Linda. I had bought tiny lights for the Korean holly trees at our front door. Candles in the windows. We went to the Cosmos Club twice, and had a feast each time. We went to the Chinese restaurant several times. I made pancakes and corn soup. Dorothy said wassles for waffles when she was little, so we had wassles, with hot buttered maple syrup (real). We did about everything that could make us happy together. We talked about her childhood days, for example, the yoyo paddle that Lola kept in the closet and only had to mention to Dorothy and Diana for improvement of behaviour. Dorothy and Diana were mortally afraid of that paddle. Whether Lola ever had such a paddle I was never sure. She certainly never used it.

Dorothy had been home in the spring of 1983 and had helped me to plant cannas, white begonias, and tomatoes. We had set dates for her visit home in the spring of 1984.

Dorothy loved our tomatoes. I sent four tomatoes to her last summer, big ones, picked a bit green, sent them off in a box by priority mail. They were exactly perfect on arrival, Dorothy said, as she declared that she had never tasted anything so good.

It was my custom to write to her twice a week, though there were failures, and I called her often by telephone. I would ask, "Is this daddy's Chincapin?," or "Is this daddy's girl?" My letters began with "My dear little Chincapin."

Chincapin she was to Lola and me, our little Chincapin. Lola gave her that name and taught her to answer, "Because I'm a little nut," when we'd ask why we call her Chincapin.

She learned a lot about dogs. She had taken a job in a kennel with a Mrs. Rich in Mt. Vernon, New York, and went along when Mrs. Rich moved her business to Palm Beach. They were great friends. Her marriage to Pete took place at Mrs. Rich's home in Palm Beach. I was there, and gave her away. "Daddy, I could wish for nothing more in this world so much as for you to come and give me away." And so I did.

She was 14 months old when Agnes and I adopted her. We lived then at 3100 Wisconsin Avenue, Apartment 304, I remember well. No one could love a baby more than Agnes loved her. Then Agnes died 30 November 1930, and I was alone with Dorothy. I put her in St. Ann's Infant Asylum, and would go every evening to play with her. She did not eat well. Sister Rose told me that Dorothy, instead of eating her food, would put some of it under her plate. Later, I moved Dorothy to the Children's Country Home, out toward Hyattsville, and I still can't remember why. After some months, I found a place for Dorothy with a Mrs. Tigh on Porter Street, not far from 3100 Wisconsin Avenue. Mrs. Tigh took care also of two boys, Jimmie and Freddie, a bit older than Dorothy. Jimmie and Shreddie, Dorothy called them. "My home, Daddy, my home," she said one evening, as we rode past 3100 Wisconsin Avenue.

Lola and I were married on 2 April 1932, and moved into 2712 Wisconsin Avenue. We would bring Dorothy every evening to our apartment. Lola's mother came for a long visit, and wished to have Dorothy with us all the time. We were easily persuaded, and Dorothy too.

Later, we moved into a large apartment at 2844 Wisconsin Avenue, 4th floor. Diana had meanwhile come along, and at 18 months was far too lively for an apartment. We went out one evening to look for some other place to live in, we knew not what; saw this house for sale, bought it next day, and moved into it on 1 August 1936, and here we are. This is the only home that Dorothy remembered.

All my life the words haunted me in the letter that released her for adoption by us. "The child is indigent, neglected, destitute, and homeless, and in danger of impairment." Never more would those adjectives describe her.

I think that a father and daughter were never closer than we were. She loved us beyond words, and we were growing closer with time. It is all so incredible that she is not here. She will dwell in our thoughts forever.

Her papers (will, cheque book, insurance policies, etc.) were in a box in good order. She must have known that any day could be her last.

She was frugal with money, and never lost her head for having money in the bank. It was simpler for me to send at the first of the year her allowance for the entire year, and save paper-work. I had sent to her bank in January 1984 $10,000 for her regular expenses, plus $4500 to pay for enlargement of her living room to absorb the car port, never used as a car port. The money was all intact in her account.

Her home was nearly paid for, four more years to go, on a 30-year 5-1/4% FHA loan. She left a letter with her will to explain why she left everything to me. I had provided everything for her, she explained, so it should be mine.

Some years ago when she came for a visit she brought from her bank a card for me to sign to make her account joint with me. I had forgotten that, but my secretary was positive that she remembered it, and it was so.

Added 24 March 1984

My heart is now further touched. She left $500 to me by an insurance policy. Her gift to me: something that she could do for me. I had already asked my secretary to write a cheque to Dorothy's church for $500. Now I will make it $1000 and ask her pastor to think of some kind of useful item that $1000 could buy, and designate it as a memorial to her. Later on I sent a much larger cheque, in her name.

I had marked my calendar to have dinner with her Friday evening the 23d, as I would be in Key Biscayne Thursday and Friday. I had also marked my calendar, "Dorothy" 20–27 April. She would have to miss participation in the Easter cantata at her church, but I had little choice, as I shall depart on the 28th for New Zealand. We were going to plant begonias and cannas and tomatoes. She had returned to Fort Lauderdale after Christmas in time to take part in the Christmas cantata.

We were pleased when she bought a second-hand bicycle for $60 a few months ago. That indicated that she felt free to spend a little money on herself. Moreover, she could get exercise that way. Walking for exercise was not possible for her, because of her swollen leg. I gave her bicycle to Kathy.

Kathy was with her all the time in the hospital.

Dr. Deming loved each of his three daughters with the love only a father can give. Dorothy was as much his child as if she had been born to him. Even now, when in Florida, he visits her grave.

Chapter Eighteen
The Last Chapter

It was something like nine or ten years earlier that I observed that Lola's memory was failing. When she left her camera (a gift from the President of Konica Company) on the platform at Nagoya Station in Japan, I suspected that something was wrong. This event resembled the mixup on luggage on arrival at Marita, when she did not know whether she had all her luggage. The stress of the trip to Japan may have accelerated the beginning of her trouble. One event seems to recall another.

There is no clear beginning. We used to have season tickets to a series of concerts at the Kennedy Center. Parking our car, and getting out, began to worry her. We had to give up Kennedy Center. As I look back, it must have been ten years since she began to fail.

She could no longer go with me on a trip. She wished that Ceil would go with me. She became shy about going to the Cosmos Club for dinner with anyone but a friend of long standing. Anyone that she did not know well caused stress. She was afraid that she would say silly things from loss of memory, and embarrass me. Entertainment at home, one of my joys, ceased.

Lola Shupe Deming

Born 31 May 1906
Died 25 June 1986

She would come to the door to let me in and greet me when I would arrive from a trip. In recent years, she would forget to turn on the porch lights. She would sometimes greet me unaware that I had been away. Also, sometimes when I had merely been out of the house on business in Washington for a few hours, she would greet me as if I had been away a long time.

She would come down to my study once in a while to ask if there was anything that she could do for me, recalling the years at the Fixed Nitrogen Research Laboratory when she helped in every possible way, and good she was. I could sometimes find some simple calculations for her to make on her Calculet in her study upstairs, but in time this kind of work frightened her. Surely I could have discovered other work that she could do, but I was not imaginative. She had been my helper for many years at the Fixed Nitrogen Research Laboratory, and at home. She made some difficult calculations for me by least squares in a legal case years ago, after she retired from the National Bureau of Standards.

Lola asked frequently about my book, how was I doing on it. I would explain that I was struggling with revision of parts of it; that the end was near; that it would be published before long, maybe in July, or September. She wondered if she could help me in any way. She helped me in earlier books with calculations and proof reading. No one could be better help. The book has come out, and she will not see it.

Another indicator of trouble, which has come back to my mind time and again, was her difficulty, years ago—how many I can not fix—to balance her cheque book. She was about to go to pieces. I helped her. She had accounts in two banks. Her trouble turned out to be that she had entered two cheques on the stub for one bank, but written the cheques on the other bank.

I took her several years ago to Dr. Marshall Folstein at the Johns Hopkins University Medical School. I was able to make the appointment through the help of Dr. John D. Rainer, whom I worked with at the New York State Psychiatric Institute of the Columbia University Medical School on West 168th Street, along the Hudson River. Dr. Folstein had no encouragement to offer, but could include her in one or more experimental groups, with medicines not yet approved. Such a plan was totally out of the question, as she could not make the trip to Baltimore again. She talked to Bessie for days about that awful trip to New York that Ed took her on. Dr. Folstein might put me in touch with some group in Washington that she could join. This too was beyond her limit. I took her to Dr. Nick Lau, in Washington, Dr. Nancy Thomas's husband. He prescribed lecithin and vitamins four times a day. Horse capsules, we called the lecithin. Lola had a hard time with those horse capsules. It was all useless.

She could do simple kinds of household work, in which she felt occupied and useful. She would wipe our beautiful kitchen floor with a mop. She would sweep the front steps and walk. She would dust the furniture, and wash dishes, put them in odd places. She was forever running the vacuum cleaner, especially, it seemed, if I had a client in my study below. She would sometimes help me in the garden. Together as late as 1985 we cleaned out the dirt that had accumulated and pushed out of shape the bottom of the wire fence where I plant tomatoes. It was hard work. She did her share and more.

She had a calendar in the kitchen; wished me to show on it when I would be away, and when I would be at home: also anything else of importance such as a visit from Diana. The calendar made a lot of trouble for Lola. She would study it, not sure what month we were in, nor what day. She would sometimes declare that I had given her no advance notice that Diana would come, when Diana's arrival was plainly marked on her calendar.

We would go for short walks in the neighborhood after dinner. I was sometimes so tired and uncertain that I had to hold on to her to keep from reeling.

Needlepoint provided diversion. She spent a large portion of her recent years in a chair by the fireplace, making needlepoint. She was expert at it. She made pillow tops for Diana and Linda and Diana's children, and for friends. I was thankful that she had such a useful hobby. A chair that she made needlepoint for many years ago was put on display in the window by the owner of the shop that fitted it to the chair.

On my return from a trip, she would be in the chair by the fireplace, working on needlepoint, waiting for the doorbell, overjoyed to see me. If not too late, we would have wine together. Of recent years, she consistently forgot to turn on the front lights. I would hand to her the little pieces of chocolate that the maid had left on the nightstand at the hotel, or peanuts from the aeroplane. She would eat them in her chair by the fireplace, as she continued her needlepoint. Bessie, Lola's dear sister, would be on the sofa, helping with the peanuts. And then I'd serve wine.

We (Bessie and Lola and I) had our supper on a folding table at the fireplace one night in January 1986, as we had done with much pleasure now and then in past years. We had Campbell's mushroom soup, with additional frills in it, such as cheese—tampering that I enjoy. We were never again around the fire for supper.

She one time expressed the thought that I should be home more, and so did I. The fact is that I arranged my time in 1987 to be home several consecutive days or even a whole week, twice a month. But I must go on with 1986 as promised and planned. Cancellation of a seminar would be difficult and costly for a sponsor. Now it is too late.

When Lola and I were alone for dinner, I would sometimes make corn soup, or mushroom soup with my special infusions of cheese, as Lola sat in her chair in the kitchen and watched. I made spoon bread several times (from a package), served it with melted butter and honey and hot maple syrup. We were both happy to have some good simple food. Lola could not recall that she used to make spoon bread ground up, nor that she used to make baked apple in a crust, with orange.

There was a wild cherry tree in the thicket that the builder left for us between the garage and the patio, twisted around another tree, the name of which I can not say. It delivered a harvest of cherries, to be removed every few days from the fountain. Lola was on the patio one day, as a raccoon on a branch high up, filled himself up with cherries and went to sleep. The tree developed a crack about fifteen feet up, and it was only a matter of time till it would break off. It did, in a deluge of rain, as a gust of wind broke it off. Lola happened to be watching it from the kitchen window. She talked about

W. Edwards Deming and Lola S. Deming, 1932

Their Children:
Dorothy, born 26 Jan. 1928, died 22 Feb. 1984
Diana, born 28 Dec. 1934
Linda, born 27 June 1942

it for days. It came down without harm to the garage or to anything else, and furnished much firewood. The remaining tree now 40 feet high, is dying, and I have arranged for its removal. Even trees have their life-span.

She was, up till 7 or 8 years ago, very active, hard working, strong, and limber as a kitten. A precious photo of her shows her prone on the front lawn, pulling weeds. She could sit by the hour on the floor though a Japanese dinner with her legs folded under her, just as well as Japanese could. She was pretty and dapper. She could wear anything and look good in it. She made any clothes look better, as I often told her.

She liked much her 4-door 1975 Maverick, but had to give up use of it. She would lose her way on the return trip from Linda's house. She could not possibly pass the test in 1983 for renewal of her license. I convinced her that the trouble to go down town and take the examination, and the driver's test, was not worth a license. I tried to be ready to haul her to any place that she wished to go to. She enjoyed a ride in anybody's car. We went out on short trips that spring to see the Judas trees with their red blossoms in the woods before the leaves came out; later, several times, to see the dogwood and azaleas that beautify Washington in the springs.

She was my life, my reason to live and to work. We had 54 years and 84 days together.

It is easy to forget how active and strong she was before she started downward. She stopped work at the Fixed Nitrogen Research Laboratory before Linda came, 27 January 1942. One day after Linda came, our friend Dr. Alfred N. Watson, then a Major in the Army, persuaded her to come to work in Selective Service. After a few years there, our friend Dr. John Curtiss persuaded her to come and work with his group at the National Bureau of Standards. She worked there for years; retired 1960. She would do half a day's work at home before she would leave home for her job. I marvelled at her stamina.

We had many enjoyable trips together. She went to Japan with me six or seven times, and to Europe as many.

We enjoyed having friends at dinner. I would help Lola all the way through. We had much laughter when I would put on the chef's hat and apron that Diana gave to me, and appear in them at the door as people came as if I were chief cook. It was not funny to Lola. Everything had to be planned with care. Pot luck always gave her stress, as when around 1941, I worked late at the Census and brought Monica home with me to take pot luck. I never did anything like that again.

She came from La Junta in 1928 to work for me at the Fixed Nitrogen Research Laboratory, in the Ohio Building, rented from American University. She remembered where she lived when she first came to Washington, 1020 16th Street, later at the Lee Mark, or maybe the reverse. She often remarked how good Agnes was to her on arrival in 1928 and after till Agnes died in November 1930, leaving me in sorrow and with little Dorothy, the baby that we had adopted in 1928 at 14 months. I remember that I put Dorothy in St. Ann's Infant Asylum, then on Washington Circle. I would go every evening to play with her, and to take her to my apartment, Apartment 304 at 3100 Wisconsin Avenue. I wished her to know that she had a home, even if there was no mother in it. "My home, Daddy, my home," she said to me as we went by it one time in my Model A Ford. She knew that she had a home and a daddy. In later life, when she lived in Fort Lauderdale, she remarked to her friend Kathy that she could not understand how anyone could love anyone as much as I loved her.

Lola and I published a number of papers together at the Fixed Nitrogen Research Laboratory on physical properties of compressed gases. Some people that used the papers observed that Lola's name on the authorship changed from Lola E. Shupe to Lola S. Deming, an announcement of our marriage.

3.　The equation of state of a mixture determined from the equations of state of its constituents, by W. Edwards Deming and Lola E. Shupe, J. Franklin Inst., vol. 208, 1928: pp. 389–395

8.　The constants of the Beattie-Bridgeman equation of state with Bartlett's p, v, T data on nitrogen, W. Edwards Deming and Lola E. Shupe, J. Amer. Chem, Soc., vol. 52, 1930: pp. 1382–1389

9.   The constants of the Beattie-Bridgeman equation of state with Barlett's p, v, T data on hydrogen, W. Edwards Deming and Lola E. Shupe, J. Amer. Chem. Soc., vol 53, 1931: pp. 843–849

10.   The Beattie-Bridgeman equation of state and Bartlett's p, v, T data on a 3:1 hydrogen nitrogen mixture, by W. Edwards Deming and Lola E. Shupe, J. Amer. Chem. Soc., vol. 53, 1931: pp. 860–869

14.   Note on the heat capacity of gases at low pressure, by W. Edwards Deming and Lola E. Shupe, Phys. Rev., vol. 37, 1931: pp. 220

15.   Some physical properties of compressed gases, I. Nitrogen, by W. Edwards Deming and Lola E. Shupe. Phys. Rev., vol. 37, 1931: pp. 638–654

16.   Some physical properties of compressed gases, II. Carbon Monoxide, by W. Edwards Deming and Lola E. Shupe, Phys. Rev., vol. 38, 1931: pp. 2245–2264

17.   Some physical properties of compressed gases, III. Hydrogen, by W. Edwards Deming and Lola E. Shupe, Phys. Rev., vol 40, 1932: pp. 848–859

21.   Some physical properties of compressed gases, IV. The entropies of nitrogen, hydrogen, and carbon monoxide, by W. Edwards Deming and Lola S. Deming, Phys. Rev., vol. 45, 1934: pp. 109–113

29.   Some physical properties of compressed gases, V. The Joule-Thomson coefficient for nitrogen, by W. Edwards Deming and Lola S. Deming, Phys. Rev., vol. 48, 1935: pp. 448–449

36.   Some physical properties of compressed gases, VI. The fugacity of carbon dioxide, Phys. Rev., vol. 56, 1939: pp. 108–112

38.   Theory of the van der Waals adsorption of gases, by Stephen Brunauer, Lola S. Deming, W. Edwards Deming, and Edward Teller, J. Amer. Chem. Soc., vol. 62, 1940: pp. 1723–1732

United States Department of Commerce
AWARD FOR MERITORIOUS SERVICE
Lola S. Deming
is hereby highly commended for
Meritorious Service

CITATION:
FOR EXTREMELY COMPETENT PERFORMANCE OF OFFICIAL DUTIES, AN OUTSTANDING RECORD OF DEPENDABILITY AND RESOURCEFULNESS, AND VERY VALUABLE CONTRIBUTIONS TO SCIENCE, TECHNOLOGY, AND PROGRAMS OF COOPERATION WITH INDUSTRY.

February 15, 1960

SECRETARY OF COMMERCE

She was awarded on 18 February 1960 the U.S. Department of Commerce Meritorious Service Award for her work. The medal is in my study, on the mantel.

U.S. Department of Commerce
National Bureau of Standards
Washington   July 1960

MRS. DEMING RECEIVES COMMERCE
DEPARTMENT SILVER MEDAL

Lola S. Deming of the Statistical Engineering Laboratory, National Bureau of Standards, has received a U.S. Department of Commerce Silver Medal for Meritorious Service. She was cited for "extremely competent performance of official duties, and outstanding record of dependability and resourcefulness, and very valuable contributions to science, technology, and programs of cooperation with industry."

Mrs. Deming is primarily concerned with the mathematical publication activities of the section of which she is a member. This includes assistance in the writing and preparation of manuscripts for publication, both in outside technical journals and in the Bureau's series of publications.

Born in Columbus, Kansas, Mrs. Deming received her A.B. in mathematics and chemistry from the College of Emporia, Kansas, in 1928, and her A.M. in mathematics from George Washington University in 1932. Prior to joining the Bureau in 1943, she was chief of the Periodic Reports Section, Selective Service System, and scientific aide with the U.S. Department of Agriculture.

Diana Deming, age 2, with her mother

Linda Deming, age 2

She could step into any automobile and drive it. We rented a car in Florida a number of times, and she was the driver. The long monotonous trip across Florida on Alligator Alley gave stress to her the last time we were there, which may be as far back as 1975. I did not at the time recognize this stress as the beginning of her long ordeal.

She was always ready to haul me to the airport, or to meet me on arrival there. She did the banking. She loved to tidy up the garden. She years ago took a liking to ferns, and I successfully transplanted a number of roots. Our garden became a garden of ferns. She had some special day lilies, a gift from Marian Carson. We enjoyed sitting on the patio evenings, sipping wine, listening to the tinkle of the fountain, marveling at the fireflies. The stars and the moon would come visible, maybe peeking through the branches of our holly tree. She watched for aeroplanes as they came in or went out over the river. A tall tree (120 feet?) on an adjoining lot was a source of wonder as the branches swayed in beautiful patterns, depending on the wind. We sat on the patio every night when I was home up until a few weeks before she died.

The patio, the size of it, was her idea. I had thought that it should be smaller. I am thankful now that she stubbornly stood her ground when the Italian artist came to lay the stones—blue, red, and grey slate, in irregular shapes.

Diana and Linda called her Momie. Dorothy called her Momie or Lolo. Diana's children in their attempt to say Lola said Wowo, and so she was with them ever after. I also sometimes called her Wowo, but usually we were to each other Big Boy and Little Girl. I reminded her once in a while that she was my Littlest girl, as Dorothy, Diana, and Linda were all "taller than Momie." Dorothy was sometimes, to us, Chincapin or Little Chincapin.

She loved brownies—anything in fact that is heavy with chocolate. I would buy for her at Wagshal's, whenever I went there, several Brownies. Then Diana on one of her visits made them out of a package, so I would usually make a batch when I was home. Then she had to reduce her weight, so brownies were less frequent.

Bessie (Lola's sister) was always Annie to Diana and Linda and Dorothy, and to Diana's children. Diana, when she was little, in her attempt to say Aunt Bessie, said Annie, and so Bessie has been Annie ever after.

Kevin said Dandy for grand-daddy, and so I have been ever after to Diana's children. An envelope came from one of Diana's girls, after her family moved to Palos Verdes (Los Angeles) addressed to

> Wowo and Dandy and Annie
> 4924 Butterworth Place
> Washington 20016

I saved the envelope, but more came, addressed the same way.

One of our joys is a hand-written bound book, written by Diana's girls, entitled the Wowo and Dandy Book. It could only be described as precious. It came for Christmas five years ago. In it were fragments of re-membrances, such as this: "Will you have a round cracker or a square cracker?" as Lola would ask the twins Kimberly and Courtney meaning a Ritz cracker or a Waverly cracker.

Lola enjoyed this book over and over. Every reading was new to her, with only dim recollection of seeing it before.

What brought on her trouble in the first place? No one will ever know. She had used for 40 years for asthma Isuprel (isoproponol) in a nebulizer—the only relief that she had ever found, obtainable only on pre-scription. It was an oculist that told her about it, and wrote out her first pre-scription for it. Could it have induced damage to brain cells?

I somehow supposed that our life together would continue for many years. I had no idea that it was about to end.

It was some months before, maybe in January 1986, maybe earlier, when she complained of severe pain in her back. She would sometimes double up and nearly fall with sudden screaming pain. It was necessary to get sitters for her day and night. I could not be home on a week day, but Melanie and later Patsy took her to Dr. Sloan. He must have known what the trouble was, and that nothing could be done. Pain killers like Tylenol did no good. Tylenol with codeine was worse than the disease. Finally, he directed a scan. He must have had a pretty good idea beforehand what it would show. Dr. Lawrence Fink wrote to her that her symptoms, as shown by the scan, were of caudal stenosis with consequent narrowing of the spinal cord. Surgery was not advisable, he said, because of her advanced age. He prescribed Indocin-SR after breakfast, hoping that it would allay somewhat the pain, along with sparing use of Percocet, only when absolutely necessary. Nothing helped. She screamed now and then with pain; could no longer do needlepoint.

"Can't anything be done?" she would ask me. I would rub her back gently, apply cold or heat. She said that it helped. "Put your arm around me." Nothing else mattered: nothing else helped.

It was time for me to leave home in a taxicab for the airport, to go to Detroit or somewhere. She was in bed, in pain. She looked to me in hope, as if trusting me to do something to help her, but I must go. I never felt so helpless, so useless, so guilty of neglect.

I asked Dr. Sloan for a narcotic. No one can live forever in pain. Something had to be done. He did, but it gave her little relief. Every hour of every day and of every night was an hour of pain, sometimes shrieking. With her loss of memory, every attack of pain was new, a new experience, not pain after pain repeated. The pain grew worse, and more persistent.

Diana came from Los Angeles the 8th May, supposedly for five days. I was away. The second morning of Diana's visit, at about 5 o'clock, Lola came short of breath. Diana supposed that the trouble was asthma, and indeed Isuprel in the nebulizer for asthma helped. Next morning came the same trouble, at about the same time. Nothing helped. Diana called Dr. Lovina who directed Diana to take her mother straightaway to Sibley Hospital. Diagnosis: congestive heart failure. She was in the hospital two weeks. She had no idea where she was, nor why. Diana rented a hospital bed when Lola came home, and a wheel chair, which Lola never sat in.

Dr. Lovina put Lola on a salt-free diet. A dietician at the hospital came in to Lola's room to give lessons to Linda and me on diet for Lola.

The salt-free food in the hospital was terrible. Lola could not eat it. She had always had a good appetite. It seemed to me that she was suffering enough without enduring tasteless food.

The dreadful experience that I lived through Monday evening and night the 23d June taught me first hand how Lola must feel, overwhelmed by pain and hunger. My plan was to leave Washington at 1715 hours via NWAL 367 for Detroit. The man at the counter of NWAL informed me that this flight had been cancelled (mechanical trouble, I suppose) but that he had reserved for me a seat on U.S. Air to leave at 1755 hours. U.S. Air started off late for removal of gasoline to decrease the total weight to the allowable maximum, because of 45 passengers transferred from Northwest. Then came other problems. Ready for takeoff, the pilot did not like the thumping noise in one of the engines. Back we went to sit and sit in that crowded waiting room. We were informed of various possibilities. Repairs may be finished by 2030 hours. Or, an incoming flight, due to terminate at Washington, may be put into service to Detroit. I was several times on the verge of going home, to try my luck next morning.

At last we were off. Meanwhile, the pain in my stomach increased. I had taken faithfully the antibiotic that Dr. Lovina prescribed for me that morning, on my complaint of a bad cold and cough as a result of riding in the front seat with somebody in a blast of cold air, two weeks earlier. The antibiotic, taken without food, caused the pain. Dr. Lovina had warned me. I could not bear the thought of touching that wretched food on board, and could only take a sip of apple juice.

I could not, I thought, on arrival at Detroit, with my luggage walk to the spot where I could call the Airport Hilton for the wagon. I explained this to the girl at the U.S. Air on arrival. She tried to get someone to wheel me; failed, wheeled me herself.

The wagon came. I struggled on board, and off at the hotel. The manager carried my luggage to my room; then had to run back for a key before my card would open the door. The dining room was still open, but I had no interest in food; I could only flop on the bed, lucky to have a spot to flop on to. The pain grew worse, and then the cough. I was sure that the hernia that Dr. Burchell in New York had warned me about had become a reality. The cough had torn everything lose, I thought. I could care about nothing; nothing matters; this is the way Lola must feel, so I thought. I eventually went to sleep, maybe around 4 or 5 o'clock. I awakened in time to meet Mr. William Scherkenbach for breakfast at 7:30, feeling fit. The antibiotic must have helped, but I took no more of it.

Diana came again from Los Angeles late Monday night, 23d June. I had gone to Detroit, as I just said. Next morning Lola was stricken again with what Diana would have thought was asthma, but for the previous experience. She called Dr. Lovina. Put her in an ambulance at once for Sibley Hospital, were her instructions. This time it was a massive coronary failure, plus congestive heart failure.

I was working with Mr. Scherkenbach at Ford on Detroit Tuesday 24th when Ceil called me at 2 o'clock about Lola. He insisted that I leave at once. He hauled me first to the Airport Hilton Hotel to pick up my luggage and to check out; then to airport: on board NWAL Flight 362 for departure at 3:15. Home at 6, and to the hospital. Lola knew me, I think. I could only tell her that I loved her, and I think that she heard me. She was at peace, no pain, I think, under a narcotic. She was so pretty. Diana stayed with her all Tuesday night, came home at 9; went back to the hospital. I too would have stayed with Lola had I known that Dr. Lovina had thought that she might live only 24 hours. I did not learn this till afterward.

Dr. Lovina had agreed with me on Monday the 23d June to let Lola have regular food. She (Dr. Lovina) must have been pretty sure that Lola had only a short time to live, salt or no salt.

Her heart stopped at one o'clock Wednesday 25 June 1986. Linda and Diana were there. I had just returned from Dr. Principato's office because of that stubborn cold and cough, and loss of hearing.

Her sweetness and goodness were so obvious in her last hours.

We (Lola and I) had agreed that it was wrong to keep someone alive in a pump. She was so pretty in death, her beautiful white hair, pretty eye brows, in her pretty blue nightie. She had slipped away, her lips almost with a smile, in a pose of serenity and peace.

Diana's children came Friday 27th May from Palos Verdes (Los Angeles). Vincent was already here, as he lives and works in Washington. Lola called him Kevin Tuesday night the 24th June when he went to see her, but that was an easy mistake to make.

Her brow was cool, her fingers cool. Later, still cooler. Dr. Lovina thought that for my own good I should not stay longer. My last look. So beautiful. Her beautiful body will soon be ashes.

She often remarked during the past few years about the happy life that we had had together—never a word of complaint to one another; no ill feeling against each other; only love and approval, so she thought; so much to be thankful for—our lovely girls, our home; she had forgiven me all my impatience. She remembered only what was good.

One of us had to go first. I had often thought of the pitiful state that she would be in if I were to die first. She would be expecting me daily. Eventually she might put me out of mind most of the time. She could not manage the house. The burden of the house would be too much for Bessie. What would happen?

I remembered that years ago, Lola, after consulting me, sent a cheque for $900 for space for our ashes in St. Columba's garden. I agreed, but with as little discussion as possible, such an unpleasant subject. Why bring it up ahead of time?

I got only a recorded announcement when I tried to call the Reverend Mr. Harry Harper, Church of Redeemer at Glen Echo, the Church that Lola loved. Father Daughtry came from St. Paul's to help me. He would say the Burial Service Saturday at 10 at the Church of the Redeemer if the Reverend Mr. Harper was away. Actually, Father Harper was out making calls. He came to our home Wednesday night. He would have it all as Lola would have wished to have it.

We thought that we understood that on Friday at 5 we all (whole family) would go to St. Columba's garden to see the space for her ashes; that they would be committed there Saturday after the Burial Service at the Church of the Redeemer. Instead, a woman priest was ready at St. Columba's Church Friday at 5 o'clock, expecting us. She committed Lola's ashes to rest, all according to the Prayer Book. A mason sealed the stone. It took us a while to come to our senses. Yet how sensible it was. The committal was finished. It was better that way.

Many friends came to the funeral Saturday at 10 at the Church of the Redeemer, Glen Echo. The Tangs came; Janet and Bill, Sam and Selma Greenhouse, Ben and Ruth Tepping, Ruth Dedrick, Betty Gibson, Joe Cameron, Gilbert and Leal Barnhart, Staunton Calvert. J. W. Perkins and Al Forlenzo came; Jim Henry, Hank Hudson and Eileen from Akron; John McFadden, General Counsel for the Rate Bureau in Akron. Clare Crawford came, and Dr. Lovina. The church was full. Dr. Harold Haller came from Cleveland, but went to the wrong Church of the Redeemer. The organist played some hymns that Lola liked. The priest closed with Lola's prayer, which I did not know about. Linda or Diana found it in her night stand.

My Daily Prayer

*May my mind be clear —
— my hand steady —
my words kind
my smile ever ready.
And may I never fail
to see your face
in all humanity.
Amen*

Lola S. Deming

Then everyone—nearly everyone—went to the garden of St. Columba's Church, for a prayer and the blessing. Then to our home where the Baggots had prepared food. Everybody was gone by 2 o'clock.

I must face life by myself, lonely. But she had been even lonelier. Bewildered, she needed me more than ever. She knew that her mind was deteriorating. I tried to assure her that it was not; that we all forgot this and that.

She said to me on the last Saturday night when we went out for a short walk that she remembered the evening when we went for a walk on Macomb Street, before I had asked her to marry me. How lovely she was, and so she was all her life and in death, beautiful. I will keep her with me, telling her about little events that would be of interest to her.

The Angel of Death came and carried her away. The song Death and the Maiden, Der Tod und das Madchen, filling my ears, the words by poet Goethe, the music by Franz Schubert. I used to sing it when the music club gathered here.

Das Madchen	The Maiden
Geh lieber, geh lieber,	Hasten away,
Du wilder knochen Mann.	You savage man of bones.
Ich bin moch jung.	I am still young
Geh lieber,	Hasten away.
Und ruher mich nicht an.	Don't touch me.

Der Tod	Death
Gib deine Hand	Give me your hand.
Du Schön und zark Gebild,	You beautiful, slender child,
Bin Frend, und Komme nicht	I come as a friend
zu strafen	And not to hurt you.
Sei gutes Muths	Be of good cheer,
Ich bin nicht wild,	I am not a savage,
Sollst sanft in meinen	You will sleep safely in
Armen schlafen	these arms.

Also in my ears is my favorite chant, De Profundis, composed by Henry Purcell (1659-1695) for Psalm 130, used in the Burial Service.

697

J. TURLE, from H. PURCELL

Out of the deep have I called unto thee O Lord;
    Lord hear my voice.
2 O let thine ears consider well
    the voice of my complaint.
3 If thou LORD wilt be extreme to mark what is done amiss,
    O Lord, who may abide it?
4 For there is mercy with thee;
    therefore shalt thou be feared.
5 I look for the LORD; my soul doth wait for him;
    in his word is my trust.
6 My soul fleeth unto the Lord before the morning watch;
    I say before the morning watch.
7 O Israel trust in the LORD, for with the LORD there is mercy,
    and with him is plenteous redemption.
8 And he shall redeem Israel
    from all his sins.
    Glory be to the Father and to the Son,
      and to the Holy Ghost;
    As it was in the beginning, is now and ever shall be
      world without end.
Amen.

To Lola

A mighty gulf it is
That separates me from Heaven.
Too deep it is to wade across,
Too wide to swim;
Only God can carry me over it.
But I can see across;
I can see her.
She waves to me.
She loves me.
No pain there, nor sorrow,
Nor sighing.
She prays to God for me,
Asking him in His mercy
To forgive my sins
And to carry me across the gulf
Where I may embrace her,
For I adore her. I miss her,
And she loves me.

W.E.D.

Chapter Nineteen
The Music of Dr. Deming

Dr. Deming has been a student of music for nearly all of his life. His mother, a fine musician, encouraged his experimentation with music at an early age. He began piano lessons with her. Throughout his life, he has studied music, played the piano and other instruments, and sang in a wide variety of choirs. During these latter years, his busy schedule has made it impossible for him to participate in choir rehearsals. However, he has continued to study and has composed a number of pieces.

Believing, along with many Americans, that the national anthem is impossible for the average person to sing, he has written a new arrangement of The Star Spangled Banner. He has also composed a baritone solo, and a number of religious pieces.

Compositions

Benedicite, Omnia Opera
> (The Song of the Three Holy Children)

Benedictus Es, Domine

Missa Reginae Caeli
> (In his own handwriting)
>> *Kyrie Eleison*
>> *Gloria in Excelsis Deo*
>> *Gloria Tibi*
>> *Sanctus & Benedictus Qui Venit*
>> *Agnus Dei*

Look Thou Upon Me
> (Words from Psalm 25)
> (In his own handwriting)

Missa Spiritui Sancto (Mass to the Holy Ghost)
>> *Kyrie Eleison*
>> *Gloria in Excelsis Deo*
>> *Sanctus*
>> *Benedictis Qui Venit*
>> *Agnus Dei*

The Star Spangled Banner

To my friend Dr. Ralph Edward Gibson

BENEDICITE, OMNIA OPERA
or
The Song of the Three Holy Children

The words from the Apocrypha

The music by
W. EDWARDS DEMING, Ph. D.

May be sung in unison if desired

Published by W. EDWARDS DEMING
4924 Butterworth Place, Washington 20016

Printed in the U. S. A.

To the Reverend Charles T. Warner, D. D.,
Rector of S. Alban's Parish, Washington

BENEDICTUS ES, DOMINE

The words from the Apocrypha

The music by
W. EDWARDS DEMING, Ph. D.

Published by W. EDWARDS DEMING
4924 Butterworth Place, Washington

Prices, post paid: {*Single copies* **15¢**
{*Thirty copies* **$3.50**

Printed in the U. S. A.

Copyright **1938** by W. Edwards Deming

*There is no C nor C♯ in this chord; open fifth.
Benedictus 4

ZIMMERMAN PRINT,
CINCINNATI

Missa Reginae Caeli

by

W. Edwards Deming

Price: 50 cent per copy
Dr. W. Edwards Deming
4924 Butterworth Place
WASHINGTON 20016

1976

315

KYRIE ELEISON

W. Edwards Deming

GLORIA IN EXCELSIS DEO

4

SANCTUS and BENEDICTUS QUI VENIT

5

AGNUS DEI

L O O K   T H O U   U P O N   M E

Sacred solo for baritone

In mode iii

By

W. Edwards Deming

Words from Psalm 25

Dr. W. Edwards Deming

4924 Butterworth Place

Washington 20016

Telephone: (202) 363.8552

4

MISSA SPIRITUI SANCTO

(Mass to the Holy Ghost)

Voices in unison

For choir or for congregational singing

by

W. Edwards Deming

KYRIE ELEISON

W. Edwards Deming

W. EDWARDS DEMING
4924 Butterworth Place
Washington 20016
(202) 363-8552

17 March 1989

GLORIA IN EXCELSIS DEO

Gra - ti - as ag - i - mus ti - - bi prop - ter mag - num glo - ri - am

tu - am. Do - mi - ne De - - us, Rex coe - les - tis. De - us

Pa - ter om - ni - po-tens. Do - mi - ne Fi - li u - ni - ge - ni - te

6

SANCTUS

BENEDICTUS QUI VENIT

san – na   in ex – cel – sie.   Be – ne – dic-tus qui ve –nit in

no – mi – ne do – mi – ni.   Ho – san – na   in ex – cel – sis.

AGNUS DEI

A – gnus De – i, Qui tol – lis pec-ca – ta   mun – di,

The Star Spangled Banner

Music by

W. Edwards Deming

The Star Spangled Banner

Key Bridge

Words by Francis Scott Key

W. Edwards Deming

Appendix A
W. Edwards Deming

W. Edwards Deming
Tokyo, August 1951

W. Edwards Deming, Ph.D.

Academic and Honorary Degrees

B.S., University of Wyoming		1921
M.S., University of Colorado		1924
Ph.D., Yale University		1928
LL.D. *(honoris causa)* University of Wyoming		1958
Sc.D. *(honoris causa)* Rivier College		1981
Sc.D. *(honoris causa)* The Ohio State University		1982
Sc.D. *(honoris causa)* Maryland University		1983
Sc.D. *(honoris causa)* Clarkson College		1983
Dr. Engineering *(honoris causa)* University of Miami		1985
Dr. Public Service *(honoris causa)* The George Washington University		1986
Sc.D. *(honoris causa)* University of Colorado		1987
Sc.D. *(honoris causa)* Fordham University		1988
Sc.D. *(honoris causa)* Oregon State University		1989
Dr. of Laws *(honoris causa)* The American University		1991
Dr. of Business Administration University of South Carolina		1991
Sc.D. *(honoris causa)* University of Alabama		1991
Dr. of Laws *(honoris causa)* Yale University		1991
Dr. of Humanities *(honoris causa)* Muhlenberg College		1992

Past Positions

Instructor in engineering, University of Wyoming	1921–22
Assistant professor of physics, Colorado School of Mines	1922–24
Assistant professor of physics, University of Colorado	1924–25
Instructor in physics, Yale University	1925–27
Mathematical physicist, Department of Agriculture	1927–39
Adviser in sampling, Bureau of the Census	1939–46
Professor of statistics, Graduate School of Business Administration, New York University	1946–

Consultant in research and in industry	1946–
Distinguished Professor, Columbia University	1985–
Seminars, four days, for improvement and productivity,	1981–

Seminars, four days, for improvement and productivity, based largely on statistically stable and unstable sys-t ems, supported by The George Washington University and by the Quality Enhancement Seminars, Los Angeles. About 20,000 people in annual attendance.

International Activities

Statistician, Allied Mission to Observe the Greek Elections,
January-April 1946; July-October 1946
Consultant in sampling to the Government of India,
January and February 1947; December 1951; March 1971
Delegate from the A.A.A.S. to the Indian Science Congress,
New Delhi, January 1947
Adviser in sampling techniques to the Supreme Command of
the Allied Powers, Tokyo, 1947 and 1950
Teacher and consultant to Japanese industry, through the
Union of Japanese Scientists and Engineers, 1950,
1951, 1952, 1955, 1960, 1965, and onward
Adviser in sampling techniques to the High Commission for Germany,
1952 and 1953
Exchange scholar to Germany, 1952 and 1953
Lecturer Universität Kiel; Institut für Sozialforschung Universität Frankfurt;
Technische Akadmie, Wuppertal-Elberfeld; Technische Hochschule,
Nürnberg; Osterreichesches Institut für Wirtschaftsforschung,
Wien; 1953
Member of the United Nations Sub-Commission on Statistical
Sampling, 1947-52
Consultant to the Census of Mexico, to the Bank of Mexico,
and to the Ministry of Economy, 1954, 1955
Consultant, Statistisches Bundesamt, Wiesbaden, 1953

Consultant to the Central Statistical Office of Turkey, 1959–62
Lecturer, London School of Economics, March 1964
Lecturer, Institut de Statistique de' Université de Paris,
    March 1964
Consultant to the China Productivity Center, Taiwan,
    1970, 1971
Lecturer in Santiago, Córdoba (Argentina), and Buenos Aires,
    under the auspices of the Inter American Statistical
    Institute, 1971

Honours

Taylor Key Award, American Management Association, 1983

The Deming Prize was instituted by the Union of Japanese Scientists and Engineers and is awarded each year in Japan to a Japanese statistician for contributions to statistical theory. The Deming Prize for application is awarded to a Japanese company for improved use of statistical theory in organization, consumer research, design of product, and production.

Recipient of the Second Order Medal of the Sacred Treasure, from the Emperor of Japan, 1960, for improvement of quality and of Japanese economy, through the statistical control of quality.

Recipient of the Shewhart Medal for 1955, from the American Society for Quality Control.

Elected in 1972 most distinguished graduate from the University of Wyoming.

Elected in 1983 to the National Academy of Engineering.

Enshrined into the Science and Technology Hall of Fame, Dayton, November 1986.

Recipient of the National Medal of Technology from President Ronald Reagan at the White House, June 1987.

Inducted into the Automotive Hall of Fame, 1991.

Recipient of Madeleine of Jesus Award, Rivier College.

Recipient of Wilbur Lucius Cross Medal, Yale University.

Societies

American Statistical Association (Fellow)

Royal Statistical Society (Honorary Fellow)

Institute of Mathematical Statistics (Fellow)

American Society for Quality Control (Honorary Life Member)

International Statistical Institute

Philosophical Society of Washington

World Association for Public Opionion Research

Market Research Council

Biometric Society (Honorary Life Member)

American Society for Testing and Materials (Honorary Member)

Union of Japanese Scientists and Engineers (Honorary Life Member)

Japanese Statistical Association (Honorary Life Member)

Deutsche Statistische Gesellschaft (Honorary Life Member)

Operations Research Society of America

American Institute of Industrial Engineers (Honorary Life Member)

Committees

Various committees, national and international, on statistical techniques in standards of safety and for research and industrial use, and on standards of professional statistical practice.

Books and Brochures

On the Statistical Theory of Errors, by W. Edwards Deming and Raymond T. Birge (The Graduate School, Department of Agriculture, Washington. This is a reprint of paper number 24 with additional notes added in 1937 and 1938.)

Least Squares (The Graduate School, Department of Agriculture, Washington, 1938)

Facsimiles of Two Papers by Bayes, with commentaries by E. C. Molina and W. Edwards Deming (The Graduate School, Department of Agriculture, Washington, 1940; Stechert-Hafner, 1963)

Statistical Adjustment of Data (John Wiley and Sons, 1943; Dover 1964)

A Chapter in Population Sampling, by W. Edwards Deming, Morris Hansen, William Hurwitz, and Benjamin J. Tepping (Bureau of the Census, 1947)

Some Theory of Sampling (John Wiley and Sons, 1950)

Elementary Principles of the Statistical Control of Quality (Nippon Kagaku Gijutsu Renmei, Tokyo, 1950; 1952; in English). Out of print.

Sample Design in Business Research (John Wiley and Sons, 1960)

Out of the Crisis (MIT and the Cambridge University Press, 1985)

The New Economics for Industry, Education, Government (MIT and the Cambridge University Press, 1993)

Principal Papers

(The authorship is W. Edwards Deming alone unless otherwise indicated.)

1. Equipotential surface electrons as an explanation of the packing effect, Phys. Rev., vol. 31, 1928: pp. 453–465

3. The equation of state of a mixture determined from the equations of state of its constituents, by W. Edwards Deming and Lola E. Shupe, J. Franklin Inst., vol. 208, 1928: pp. 389–395

4. Chart of the electromagnetic energy relations, J. Optical Soc., vol. 18, 1929: pp. 50–51

6. On the determination of the parameters in an empirical formula, Proc. London Physical Soc., vol. 42, 1930: pp. 97–107

7. The application of least squares, Phil. Mag., vol. 11, 1931: pp. 146–158. Read at the New York meeting of the American Physical Society, 22 Feb. 1930

8. The constants of the Beattie-Bridgeman equation of state with Bartlett's p, v, T data on nitrogen, W. Edwards Deming and Lola E. Shupe, J. Amer. Chem. Soc., vol. 52, 1930: pp. 1382–1389

9. The constants of the Beattie-Bridgeman equation of state with Bartlett's p, v, T data on hydrogen, by W. Edwards Deming and Lola E. Shupe, J. Amer. Chem. Soc., vol. 53, 1931: pp. 843–849

10. The Beattie-Bridgeman equation of state and Bartlett's p, v, T data on a 3:1 hydrogen nitrogen mixture, by W. Edwards Deming and Lola E. Shupe, J. Amer. Chem. Soc., vol. 53, 1931: pp. 860–869

14. Note on the heat capacity of gases at low pressure, by W. Edwards Deming and Lola E. Shupe, Phys. Rev., vol. 37, 1931: p. 220

15. Some physical properties of compressed gases, I. Nitrogen, by W. Edwards Deming and Lola E. Shupe, Phys. Rev., vol. 37, 1931: pp. 638–654

16. Some physical properties of compressed gases, II. Carbon Monoxide, by W. Edwards Deming and Lola E. Shupe, Phys. Rev., vol. 38, 1931: pp. 2245–2264

17. Some physical properties of compressed gases, III. Hydrogen, by W. Edwards Deming and Lola E. Shupe, Phys. Rev., vol. 40, 1932: pp. 848–859

19. Chart of electromagnetic relations, by W. Edwards Deming and F. G. Cottrell, Rev. Sci. Instruments, vol. 3, June 1932

21. Some physical properties of compressed gases, IV. The entropies of nitrogen, hydrogen, and carbon monoxide, by W. Edwards Deming and Lola S. Deming, Phys. Rev., vol. 45, 1934: pp. 109–113

22. The dissociation constant of nitrogen-nitrogonase in azotobacter, by Hans Lineweaver, Dean Burk, W. Edwards Deming, J. Amer. Chem. Soc., vol. 56, 1934: pp. 225–230

23. On the application of least squares, II. Phil. Mag., vol. 17, 1934: pp. 804–829

24. On the statistical theory of errors, by W. Edwards Deming and Raymond T. Birge, Reviews of Modern Physics, vol. 6, 1934: pp. 119–161. Reprinted, with additions, by the Graduate School, Department of Agriculture, 1937.

25. On the chi-test and curve fitting, J. Amer. Stat. Assoc., vol. 29, 1934: pp. 372–382

26. On the application of least squares, III. A new property of least squares. Phil. Mag., vol. 19, 1935: pp. 389–402

27. On the optical anisotropy of molecular crystals, by Zeitschrift für Kristallographie (A), vol. 91, 1935: pp. 290–301

29. Some physical properties of compressed gases, V. The Joule-Thomson Coefficient for nitrogen, by W. Edwards Deming and Lola S. Deming, Phys. Rev., vol. 48, 1935: pp. 448–449

35. On the frequency interpretation of inverse probability, Nature, vol. 143, 1939: p. 202

36. Some physical properties of compressed gases, VI. The fugacity of carbon dioxide, Phys. Rev., vol. 56, 1939: pp. 108–112

38. Theory of the van der Waals adsorption of gases, by Stephen Brunauer, Lola S. Deming, W. Edwards Deming, and Edward Teller, J. Amer. Chem. Soc., vol. 62, 1940: pp. 1723–1732

39. On the sampling problems of the 1940 population census, by F.F. Stephan, W. Edwards Deming, and Morris H. Hansen, J. Amer. Stat. Assoc., vol. 35, 1940: pp.615–630. An abstract of this paper appeared under the same title by W. Edwards Deming, in the Cowles Commission report of the 6th Annual Conference on Economics and Statistics at Colorado Springs, July 1940.

40. On a least squares adjustment of a sampled frequency table when the expected marginal totals are known, by W. Edwards Deming and F.F. Stephan, Annals of Math. Stat., vol. XI, 1940: pp. 427–444

41. On the sampling methods of the 1940 population census, by F. F. Stephan and W. Edwards Deming, Bulletin issued by the Bureau of the Census, Feb. 1941

42. On the interpretation of censuses as samples, by W. Edwards Deming and F. F. Stephan, J. Amer. Stat. Assoc., vol. 36, 1941: pp. 45–49

44. On the elimination of unknown ages in the 1940 population census; bulletin issued by the Bureau of the Census, Jan. 1942

45. On sample inspection in the processing of census returns, by W. Edwards Deming and Leon Geoffrey, J. Amer. Stat. Assoc., vol. 36, 1941: pp. 351–360

48. Errors in card punching, by W. Edwards Deming, Benjamin J. Tepping, and Leon Geoffrey, J. Amer. Stat. Assoc., vol. 37, 1942: pp. 525–536

51. On some census aids to sampling, by Morris H. Hansen and W. Edwards Deming, J. Amer. Stat. Assoc., vol. 38, 1943: pp. 353–357

52. Some principles of the Shewhart methods of quality control, Mechanical Engineering, vol. 66, 1944: pp. 173–177.

54. On errors in surveys, American Sociological Review, vol. 9, August 1944: pp. 359–369

55. On training in sampling, J. Amer. Stat. Assoc., vol. 40, Sept. 1945: pp. 307–316

57. On a population sample for Greece, by Raymond J. Jessen, Richard

H. Blythe, Jr., Oscar Kempthorne, and W. Edwards Deming, J. Amer. Stat. Assoc., vol. 42, 1942: pp. 357–384

58. Some criteria for judging the quality of surveys, J. of Marketing, vol. 12, 1947: pp. 145–147

60. A brief statement on the uses of sampling in censuses of population, agriculture and in public health and commerce, United Nations, Sub-Commission on Statistical Sampling, 1948 (International Documents Service, Columbia University Press, New York 27)

63. Observations on the 1946 elections in Greece, by Deming, Jessen Kempthorne, Daly, Amer. Sociological Rev., vol. 14, 1949: pp. 11–16

65. On a method of estimating birth and death rates and extent of registration, by C. Chandrasekar and W. Edwards Deming, J. Amer. Stat. Assoc., vol. 44, 1949: pp. 101–115

66. Some problems in the sampling of bulk materials, by Louis Tanner and W. Edwards Deming, Proceedings of the A.S.T.M., vol. 49, 1949: pp. 1–6

68. On the sampling of physical materials, Revue Internationale de Statistique, vol. 18, 1950: pp. 1–20

70. On an important limitation to the use of data from samples, by Morris H. Hansen and W. Edwards Deming, Bulletin de l'Institut International de Statistique, Bern 1950: pp. 214–219

78. Statistical techniques as a national resource, Bulletin of the Indian Society for Quality Control., vol. 1, 1953: pp. 29–37

79. Sampling in a government statistical system, Grundfragen der Vorbereitungsarbeit eines Deutschen Mikrozensus, Statistiches Budesant, Wiesbaden, July 1953

80. A statistical test of significance applied to a sociological problem: variation in accident rates from motor vehicles, by W. Edwards Deming, Josephine D. Cunningham, and A.D. Battey, Amer. Sociological Rev., vol. 17, No. 6, Dec. 1952: pp. 755–761

81. On the distinction between enumerative and analytic surveys, J. Amer. Stat. Assoc., vol. 48, 1953: pp. 244–255

82. Statistical techniques and international trade, J. of Marketing, vol. xvii, 1953: pp. 428–433

82a. Techniques statistiques et commerce international, Courier de la Normalization, No. 109, Jan.-Feb. 1953: pp. 41–44

83. Management's responsibility for the use of statistical techniques in industry, Advanced Management, vol. xviii, No. 1953: pp. 8–12

84. On the presentation of the results of sample surveys as legal evidence, J. Amer. Stat. Assoc., vol. 49, 1954: pp. 814–825

87. On a probability mechanism to attain an economic balance between the error of response and the bias of nonresponse, J. Amer. Stat. Assoc., vol. 48, 1953: pp. 743–772

88. On the teaching of statistical techniques to people in industry, Proceedings of the International Statistical Institute (The Hague), 1953.

89. Die Verantwortung der Betriebsführung für die Anwendung Statistischer Methoden in der deutschen Industrie, Weltwirtschaftliches Archiv (Kiel), vol. 71, 1953: pp. 234–250

91. On simplifications of sampling design through replication with equal probabilities and without stages, J. Amer. Stat. Assoc., vol. 51. Mar. 1956: pp. 24–53

93. On the contribution of statistical standards to law and accounting, Current Business Studies, Graduate School of Business Administration, New York University, No. 19, Oct. 1954: pp. 14–32

94. On the use of theory, Industrial Quality Control, vol. xiii, No. 1, July 1956, being as address delivered upon receipt of the Shewhart Medal, at the 10th annual meeting of the American Society for Quality Control, Montreal, 7 June 1956

96. On statistical standards for legal evidence, Transactions of the American Society for Quality Control, Philadelphia, Feb. 1957: pp. 107–116

102. On the problem of matching lists by samples, by W. Edwards Deming and Gerald J. Glasser, J. Amer. Stat. Assoc., vol. 54, 1959: pp. 403–415

103. Standards of probability sampling for legal evidence, American Statistician, vol. 12, Feb. 1958: pp. 25–26

104. Principles of professional statistical practice, Annals of Mathematical Statistics, vol. 36, 1965: pp. 1883–1900

105. On some new methods of concepts in sampling, Science in Management, American Society for Quality Control, Washington, 5 Mar. 1959, pp. 89–96

106. Replicated sampling design in a problem in accounting of an inventory, Proceedings of the American Society for Quality Control, New York, 26 Feb. 1960

107. Uncertainties in statistical data, and their relation to the design and management of statistical surveys and experiments, Proceedings of the International Statistical Institute, Tokyo, June 1960

108. Some stratified sampling plans in replicated design, Estadística, 1960

109. Design of a replicated sample to measure the change in value of an inventory, Proceedings of the International Statistical Institute, Tokyo, June 1960

111. Some statistical principles for efficient design of surveys and experiments, being Chapter 5 in Kallmann's GENETICS IN PSYCHIATRY (Grune and Stratton, New York, 1962).

112. On the correction of mathematical bias by use of replicated designs, an invited paper for Festschrift an Herrn Professor Dr. Hans Kellerer, Sonderband Metrika, 1962, pp. 37–42

113. On some of the contributions of interpenetrating networks of samples, an invited paper in honor of P.C. Mahalanobis's 70th birthday, Sankhya, vol. 24, 1963

116. Sampling procedures: methodology of a survey of the deaf population of the State of New York, being Chapter 1 in Kallmann, Rainer, Deming, FAMILY AND MENTAL HEALTH PROBLEMS IN A DEAF POPULATION (Department of Medical Genetics, New York State Psychiatric Institute, New York 32, 1963): pp. 3–12.

117. Demographic aspects of the deaf: number, distribution, marriage,

and fertility statistics, by John D. Rainer and W. Edwards Deming, being Chapter 2 in Kallmann, Rainer, Deming, FAMILY AND MENTAL HEALTH PROBLEMS IN A DEAF POPULATION (Dept. of Medical Genetics, N. Y. State Psyc. Inst., N. Y. 32, 1963): pp. 13–27.

118. On the use of sampling in management and research, I.C.C. Practitioners Journal, vol. xxxi, No. 2, 1963: pp. 135–147

120. Some responsibilities of a statistician, Industrial Quality Control, vol. xx, No. 9, March 1964.

121. Recent advances in the statistical control of quality in Japan, Proceedings of the American Society for Quality Control, San Francisco, September 1964. To appear in Sankhya, Calcutta

122. Theory of surveys to estimate a roving population, by W. Edwards Deming and Nathan Keyfitz, World Population Congress, Belgrade, 30 Aug. 1965

124. A review of regression estimators, by W. Edwards Deming and Morris H. Hansen, FESTSCHRIFT AN HERRN PROFESSOR WAGENFÜHR, Universität Tübingen, 1966

125. Code of professional conduct, Sankhya, Series B. Volume 28, 1966, Pages 11–18

126. Some remarks on the statistical control of quality in Japan, Sankhya, Series B, vol. 28, 1966, pages 19–30

127. What happened in Japan? Industrial Quality Control, vol. 24, No. 2, August 1967, pages 89–93

128. On a recursion formula for the proportion of persons having a first admission as schizophrenic, Behavioral Science, vol. 13, Number 6, Nov. 1968: pp. 467–476

129. A Markovian analysis of the life of newspaper subscriptions, by W. Edwards Deming and Gerald J. Glasser, Management Science, vol. 14, 1968: pp. B283–293

130. Interaction measurements in psychiatric patients with early total deafness, by Kenneth Z. Altshuler and W. Edwards Deming, Archives of General Psychiatry, vol. 17, Sept. 1967

131. Sample surveys, International Encyclopedia of the Social Sciences (The Macmillan Company and The Free Press), Vol. 13, 1968: pp. 594–612

132. Influence of interviewers and questions on precision of results, a paper read at the Market Research Council, New York, 15 March 1968.

133. Boundaries of statistical inference, being chapter 31 in the book by Norman L. Johnson and Harry Smith, NEW DEVELOPMENTS IN SURVEY SAMPLING (Wiley-Inter-Science, 1969), pp. 652–670.

134. On a statistical procedure for study of accounts receivable in motor freight, by W. Edwards Deming and T. Nelson Grice, read at a meeting of the American Statistical Association in Pittsburgh, August 1968: Management Accounting, vol. 51, March 1970: pp. 17–21

135. Changes in fertility rates of schizophrenic patients in New York State, by L. Erlenmeyer-Kimling, Susan Nicol, John D. Rainer, and W. Edwards Deming, Am. J. of Psyc., vol. 125, Jan. 1969: pp. 916–927

136. On statistical techniques as aids to management, Proceedings of the American Society for Quality Control, Stanford meeting, Oct. 1969.

137. Statistical control of quality in Japan, Proceedings of the International Congress on the Control of Quality, Tokyo, Oct. 1969.

138. A further account of the idiots savants, experts with the calendar, by William A. Horwitz, W. Edwards Deming, and Robert F. Winter, Am. J. of Psychiatry, vol. 126, 3, Sept. 1969: pp. 160–163

139. A reappraisal of the contribution of statistical methods to quality-assurance, by Charles A. Bicking and W. Edwards Deming, an address given at a meeting of the International Statistical Institute, Washington, 10–20 Aug. 1971: to be published in the Bulletin of the International Statistical Institute.

140. Some statistical logic in the management of quality, Keynote speech at the All India Congress on Quality Control, New Dehli, March 1971

140a. Sur une certaine logique statistique dans la gestion de la qualité, Bulletin de l'Association Française pour le Contrôle Industriel de Qualité, vol. viii, Sept. 1972: pp. 3–15 (This is paper 140 in French.)

140b. Cierta lógica estadística en el tratamiento de la calidad, Instituto Argentino de Control de Calidad, Buenos Aires, vol. 2, no. 11: pp. 188–203 (This is paper 140 in Spanish.)

141. On variances of estimators of a total population under several procedures of sampling, reprinted from CONTRIBUTIONS TO APPLIED STATISTICS, 1976: pp. 73–80

142. Making things right, a chapter in the book by Judith Tanur, Fred Mosteller, William Kruskal, STATISTICS, GUIDE TO THE UNKNOWN (Holden-Day, 1972), pp. 229–236.

143. Some theory for the influence of the inspector and environmental conditions, with an example, by W. Edwards Deming and Morris H. Hansen, Statistica Neerlandica, vol. 26, 1972: pp. 101–112.

144. Study of psychiatric symptoms of systematic lupus erythematosis, by Vivian Hoff, Barry J. Gurland, W. Edwards Deming, and Bernice Fisher, Journal of Psychosomatic Medicine, vol. xxxiv, 1972: pp. 207–220

145. On probability as a basis for action, an address delivered at the American Statistical Association, vol. 29, 1975: pp. 146–152

146. Code of professional conduct (paper 125 revised), International Statistical Review, vol. 40, Aug. 1972: pp. 215–219

147. Statistician's report to management, Quality Progress, July 1972, vol. v, No. 7. (In Dutch in the journal Sigma, Amsterdam; in French, in the journal Qualité et Fiabilité, Paris.)

148. The logic of evaluation, being chapter 4 of the book, HANDBOOK OF EVALUATION RESEARCH, by Elmer L. Struening and Marcia Guttentag (Sage Publications, 1975), vol. 1: pp. 53–67

149. On some statistical aids toward economic production, reprinted from INTERFACES, vol. 5, no. 4, Aug. 1975

150. Probability sampling, article in the DICTIONARY OF AMERICAN HISTORY (Scribners, 1973)

151. On trends in the diagnosis of schizophrenia, by Judy Kuriansky, W.

Edwards Deming, and Barry Gurland, Am. J. of Psychiatry, vol. 131: pp. 402–408

152. The role of the statistician, New York Statistician, vol. 18, Feb. 1967: pp. 1–2

153. On the use of judgment-samples, Statistical Applications of Research (Union of Japanese Scientists and Engineers, Tokyo), vol. 23, 1976: pp. 25–31. Delivered at the Institute of Statistical Mathematics, Tokyo, Nov. 1975.

154. My view of quality control in Japan, for the 25th anniversary of the Deming Prize, Reports of Statistical Application Research, Tokyo: vol. 22, June 1975: pp. 73–80

155. Impulsivity and profound early deafness, by Kenneth Z. Altshuler and W. Edwards Deming, American Annals of the Deaf, vol. 121, 1976: pp. 331–345

156. An essay on screening, or on two-phase sampling, applied to surveys of a community, International Statistical Review, vol. 45, 1977: pp. 29–37. Published also in the book by Martin Roth and Valerie Cowie, PSYCHIATRY, GENETICS AND PATHOLOGY, A TRIBUTE TO ELIOT SLATER (Gaskell Press, London 1979), pp. 178–187

157. Mental health and the deaf, a first step toward epidemiology, by W. Edwards Deming, John D. Rainer, M.D., and Kenneth Z. Altshuler, M.D., Mental Health in Deafness (Experimental Issue No. 2, St. Elizabeth's Hospital, Washington, 1978), pp. 14–24

158. On a rational relationship for certain costs of handling motor freight, I. Over the platform, Trans. J., vol. 17, No. 4, 1978: pp. 5–13

159. On a rational relationship for certain costs of handling motor freight, II. Stop-time at pickup and delivery, Transportation Journal, vol. 18, No. 2, 1979: pp. 79–85

160. Some contributions to statistical inference and practice, being a chapter in the book by Eugene I. Burdock entitled QUANTITATIVE TECHNIQUES FOR THE EVALUATION OF THE BEHAVIOR OF PSYCHIATRIC PATIENTS (Marcel Dekker, Inc., New York, 1979)

161. On a problem in standards of auditing from the viewpoint of statistical practice, Journal of Accounting, Auditing, and Finance, vol. 2, No. 3, Spring 1979: pp. 197–208

162. A cross-national comparison of institutionalized elderly in the cities of New York and London, Psychological Medicine, vol. 9, 1979: pp. 781–788, with Barry Gurland, et. al.

163. On the correlation bias in the application of Chandra-Deming method for estimating vital events, by Chandrasekaran and W. Edwards Deming, Cairo Demographic Center, 1981, Working Paper No. 2

164. Tranformation of Western style of management, Interfaces, vol. 15, no. 3, May-June 1985

165. Drastic changes for western management, being an abstract for the meeting of TIMS/ORS at Gold Coast City, Australia, 15–18 July 1986

166. Principles of professional statistical practice, reprinted from Kotz-Johnson, Encyclopedia of Statistical Sciences, 1986, vol. 7

167. On the statistician's contribution to quality, a paper delivered at the meeting of the International Statistical Institute in Tokyo 8–11 September 1987.

168. Changes required in management for quality, a paper delivered at the meeting of the International Conference on Quality Control in Tokyo 20–23 October 1987, to be published in the proceedings.

169. Transformation of Western style of management, in Handbook of Statistics, edited by P.R. Krishnaiah and C.R. Rao (Elsevier Science Publishers, V.V., Amsterdam).

170. Some notes on management in a hospital, Journal of the Society for Health Systems, vol. 2, no. 1, Spring 1990

171. Address to the International Association of Fire Chiefs, Toronto, 22 September 1991

Appendix B
New Deming Prize Information

The author is indebted to the Union of Japanese Scientists and Engineers of Tokyo for granting permission to include this new, updated information about the Deming Prize. This is an exact reproduction of the material from JUSE and contains no deletions or additions.

Appendix B

The History of Quality Control in Japan and the Deming Prize

1.1 A Brief History of Quality Control in Japan

Dr. Shewhart's "Economic Control of the Quality of Manufacturing Products" had already been introduced in Japan in 1931, and the statistical method had been applied to the production of incandescent lamps at that time. After the end of World War II, the U.S. Forces sent a mission headed by Mr. S. A. Rice to Japan in October 1946 to study the Japanese economy in response to requests from the General Headquarters of the Occupation Forces. Dr. W. E. Deming came to Japan in January 1947 and reported that it was necessary to modernize the Japanese organizational structure on statistics.

GHQ issued an order for the Civil Communication Section (CCS) to instruct Japanese communications equipment manufacturers on the improvement of managerial control, since there were many problems concerning the quality and delivery of communication parts and equipments to the occupation forces. A CCS course was held in 1949 and quality control was included in the curriculum.

In 1951 Dr. W. E. Deming visited Japan to lecture on the relation between quality control and statistics to engineers, and in 1954 Dr. J. M. Juran came to lecture on the relation between quality control and management to the Japanese top management. These became the big motive for Japan to introduce quality control.

The Union of Japanese Scientists and Engineers (JUSE) was established in 1946. The Industrial Standardization Law was established in 1949 and JIS was issued. A QC Research Group was set up within JUSE and started to study the theory and practice of quality control. The "quality control basic course" of JUSE started in 1949. The "quality control and standardization seminar" initiated and the Control System Committee (COSCO) was also established by the Japanese Standards Association (JSA). After a while, various groups such as the Central Japan Industries Association, Toyama Prefectural Employers' Association, Industrial Research Institute of Kanagawa Prefecture, The Chemical Society of Japan, and Japan Spinners' Association, etc. organized courses on quality control and the design of experiments, and many people attended them.

The instructors at these courses were college professors and engineers from corporations with backgrounds not only from such fields as mathematical statistics but also from such various fields of intrinsic technology fields as mechanical engineering, metallurgy, chemical engineering, textile engineering, and metrology. These instructors actually solved many problems occurring within companies and became experienced engineers in bridging theory and practice, rather than mere scholars in the field of quality control. These initial leaders were not professional consultants but tried to modernize the basic organizational structure by means of quality control to improve the quality of Japanese products. This seems to be a unique feature of Japan.

The Deming Prize was created in 1951. In 1960 the month of November was designated to be the annual Quality Month, in which many events such as the Deming Prize awarding ceremony, quality control conferences, and lecture meetings became to be held. The first issue of "Hinshitsu Kanri (Quality Control)" was published in 1951. A magazine for shop floor workers was published in 1962 and QC Circle activities started this year among subscribers of the journal. These activities were useful in fostering Japanese corporate quality control to rely not only on specialists but to carry out quality control activities through the involvement of a whole company. The activities also made it not just a managerial problem of an individual corporation but a custom of creating multilateral discussions on the practice of QC among corporations towards mutual enhancement of QC awareness. The Japanese Society for Quality Control (JSQC) was established in 1971.

The quality of Japanese products gradually improved in the 60's, and it reached a level of receiving high appraisal in the world market by the end of the 70's. The Japanese economy faced a tough period in the former half of the 70's due to the oil crisis, environmental problems, and the rapid economic catch-up of neighboring countries. However, large enterprises became able to fully implement companywide quality control under the leadership of top management and with the cooperation of all departments concerned from design, manufacturing, down to sales, and furthermore, middle- and small-sized enterprises and the service industry began to carry out companywide quality control. As a result, Japanese enterprises began to have confidence in their ability to solve the above-mentioned problems. New quality control tools were also developed. The Deming Prize itself also experienced some changes to adapt to the actual situation by revising the check list many times, establishing a Deming Prize for the Implementation of QC to Small Enterprises, Deming Prize for the Implementation of QC to Divisions, and also newly establishing the Japan QC Medal.

The International Conference on Quality Control-Tokyo has been held every 9 years since 1969. We mentioned the following 10 items as the special feature of companywide quality control (quality control or QC) in Japan at the 1987 conference.

1. President-led QC activities in which all departments and all personnels participate
2. Top priority consistently assigned to quality by management
3. Policy dissemination and control by delegation
4. QC audits and their implementation
5. Quality assurance activities ranging from planning & development to sales and servicing
6. QC Circle activities

7. QC education & training
8. Development and implementation of QC techniques
9. Extension of applications from manufacturing to other industries
10. Nationwide QC promotion activities

The responsibility of Japan in the international society has become important in the '80s. Quality control cannot progress without international competition and cooperation. Many quality control seminars involved hierarchies, such as for top management, managers, supervisions, etc., and also according to the type of work, such as office work, sales, and servicing, etc. Seminars for foreigners were also held quite often. Quality control education specific to the daily individual work has been conducted for employees at Japanese overseas factories and branch offices. Many visitors are now coming to see the actual situation of quality control in Japan. The Deming Prize which contributed to improve the level of quality control in Japan has now become globalized since 1984, and the Florida Power and Light Co. of the U.S. won it in 1989 as the first overseas enterprise.

The quality control in Japan has been nurtured with the postwar economic background to secure a long-term profit rather than short-term returns. Cut-throat competitions among corporations in manufacturing industries have helped promote long-term investment to enhance productivity. Top management of corporations have been able to concentrate on intra-corporate problems under the circumstances. The quality control has thus entailed an educational process for employees to develop a common belief in job evaluation in terms of the quality of products and services that meet the customers satisfaction and demand of the society. The quality control is often referred to as a corporate culture in the Japanese expression rather than as a mere management technique. This testifies to the success of the quality control by the Japanese industrial society.

(Ikuro Kusaba)

1.2 The Deming Prize

1.2.1 History of the Deming Prize

It is well known that the widespread adoption of companywide or quality control (CWQC or QC) based on statistical quality control techniques in the Japanese industry has resulted in the major improvement in quality of products and services offered, together with much enhanced productivity and cost reduction.

For a number of years after World War II, the foremost task for Japan was to raise the standard of living through the revitalization of economy. For this, there was no choice because of scarcity of natural resources but to strive toward becoming a vigorous trading nation, and at the same time to improve the image of inferior quality of pre-War Japanese-made products. Nothing could have been more efficient and definite under the circumstances than the adoption and practice of statistical quality control.

In one of the first steps of this approach, the Union of Japanese Scientists and Engineers (JUSE) invited Dr. W. Edwards Deming, an American statistician and proponent of quality control techniques in July 1950 to present a series of lectures at such seminars as an "8-Day Course on Quality Control" organized by JUSE. This provided vital stimulus for our early efforts in the use of industrial quality control.

The Deming Prize was instituted in 1951 by a formal resolution of the JUSE Board of Directors in grateful recognition of Dr. Deming's friendship and his achievements in the cause of industrial quality control, as proposed by the late Mr. Kenichi Koyanagi, a board member and one of the founders of JUSE.

Since that time, the adoption of QC and its techniques has been seen in virtually every sector of the Japanese industry, and there evolved in due time the concept of the companywide quality control (QC or CWQC), which has come to attract much attention abroad.

It has become customary in Japan for corporations wishing to improve their performance in products or services to vie for the *Deming Prize for QC Implementation*, not only for the prestige that goes with this honor but also to benefit from the internal improvements that result from the thoroughgoing implementation of QC or CWQC that is needed in order to qualify at home and abroad.

The funding of the Deming Prize began with the donation of the royalties received by Dr. Deming from the sale of the Japanese edition of his "*Some Theory of Sampling*" and his other works which he used or were published in Japan, supplemented by donations from various other sources. Today, however, the funding is undertaken by the Union of Japanese Scientists and Engineers.

1.2.2 Categories of the Deming Prize

Under the Deming Prize Regulations, there are the **Deming Prize for an Individual Person(s), the Deming Prize for Corporate QC Implementation,** and also **the Factory Quality Control Award,** all judged by the Deming Prize Committee.

The Deming Prize for Individual Person(s)

This Prize is for a person who has shown excellent achievement in the theory or application of the statistical quality control or a person who has made an outstanding contribution to the dissemination of quality control (QC).

The Deming Prizes for Corporate QC Implementation

These Prizes are for enterprises (including public institutions) or their divisions which have achieved a most distinctive improvement in performance through the implementation of companywide quality control based on statistical quality control. Awarded especially to enterprises of medium or small size is **the Deming Prize for Corporate QC Implementation in a Small Enterprise,** while the Prize awarded to corporate divisions is known as **the Deming Prize for Divisional QC Implementation.**

The Japan Quality Control Medal

Celebrating the first International Conference for Quality Control that was held at Tokyo in 1969, the Deming Prize Committee has founded a new prize for an enterprise. The Japan Quality Control Medal is provided for companies already awarded the Deming Prize or the Japan Quality Control Medal more than five years before, aiming to encourage continuous up-grading efforts in quality of these companies. Qualified companies can apply for this prize. And after an examination following almost the same procedure for the Deming Prize but requiring a higher score than the Deming Prize, a qualified company will be awarded this prize.

1.2.3 Organization of and Examination and Selection by the Deming Prize Committee

For the examination, selection and awarding of the Deming Prize, the Deming Prize Regulations stipulate the establishment of the Deming Prize Committee, chaired by the Chairman of the Board of Directors of JUSE or a person recommended by the Board of Directors of JUSE.

The Deming Prize Committee consists of members commissioned by the Chairman from among men of learning and experience and officers of organizations related to quality control. Sub-Committees are formed under the Deming Prize Committee, responsible for the selection of their respective Deming Prizes and other related matters.

The Deming Prize for Corporate QC Implementation Sub-Committee responsible for examining the applicant companies consists of members drawn from among university professors and quality control experts in government and other non-profit institutions. Personnel of profit-making business enterprises are excluded.

The administrative work of the Deming Prize Committee is carried out by JUSE in conformity to the Deming Prize Regulations, with overall responsibility for the office work of the Committee resting with the Secretary General of JUSE.

The Deming Prize for Corporate QC Implementation is awarded each year by the Deming Prize Committee to applicant judged meritorious as a result of a strictly impartial examination and selection conducted by the Committee and the subcommittee in charge.

1.2.4 Deming Prize for Corporate QC Implementation to Non-Japanese Companies

The Deming Prize was restricted to Japanese companies until recently, because its initial purpose was to encourage the development of quality control in Japan. In recent years, however, strong interest in the Deming Prize for Corporate QC Implementation has been shown by non-Japanese companies.

Examination Procedures for the Deming Prizes

2.1 From Application to Winning of the Prize
2.1.1 Eligibility for the Award

There are two categories in the Deming Prizes as mentioned in the first chapter. One is a prize for person and the other, named Deming Prize for Corporate QC Implementation, is for a company. The Deming Prize for Corporate QC Implementation is also divided into two sub-categories, the prize for a whole company and the one for a division in a company.

The Deming Prize for Corporate QC Implementation is an annual award presented to a company or a division which is recognized as having had successful results from the implementation of CWQC based on statistical quality control.

Prior to the explanation on the procedure for examining the Deming Prize for Corporate QC Implementation, the meaning of companywide quality control (CWQC), which is the main object of this prize, should be made clear.

Quality Control is a system of activities to ensure the quality of products and services, in which products and services of a quality required by customers are produced and delivered economically. Quality assurance is carried out not only through in-process or shipping inspection, but through a precise knowledge of the quality required by the customer so that new products may be planned and designed in conformity with the required quality, and manufactured in the production process in conformity with the design quality. Consequently, the responsibilities for acceptable quality, including reliability, are taken not only by those directly in charge of product quality but by all other departments within the company as well as by the management.

In addition to an assured quality of products and services, CWQC demands comprehensive control of cost, productivity, delivery, safety, environmental protection, and any other activities pertaining either directly or indirectly to the quality of performance. For this, from top to bottom in a company, each person in each department including research, development, production, materials, engineering and sales must be quality-minded and aware of the statistical approach for the exercise of control by repetition of plan-do-check-action in order to be able to cooperate systematically in the implementation of quality control for maximal efficiency as an operational whole.

One example of such cooperative contribution to companywide excellent in quality is the QC Circle activities which have won wide and successful acceptance in Japan.

In view of the purpose of the Deming Prize, examinations are conducted in the manner described below to award prizes to those companies which are recognized as having successfully applied CWQC based on statistical quality control and which are likely to keep up with it in the future.

2.1.2 Application Procedure for a Company Outside of Japan

Submission of Application Form

An applying company or division must submit an application form to the Deming Prize Committee. A material describing the outline of the company is requested to be attached to the application form. The closing day is November 20 of the year preceding the year in which the examination will be conducted. Prospective applicants are advised to hold preliminary consultations with the secretariat of the Deming Prize Committee before completing and submitting the application.

Submission of the Description of QC Practices

On receipt of acceptance notification, the applicant is required to submit a Description of QC Practices and a company business prospectus, both written in Japanese, not later than January 20 of the year in which the examination will be conducted. An English version of these documents may be appended if necessary.

The Description of QC Practices should present the actual state of the quality control currently practiced in concise and concrete terms.

Examination Costs

The cost for examination consists of the compensation and traveling expense for the examiners, cost of correspondence and preparation of a written opinion, and cost for an interpreter.

2.1.3 Examination and Selection of Winner

An examination is conducted by the Deming Prize for Corporate QC Implementation Subcommittee, beginning with a review of the contents of the "Description of QC Practices."

If the Description of QC Practices is approved, the applicant is subjected to on-site examination. If the applicant passes this on-site examination, the Deming Prize Committee decides to award a prize to the applicant, and the winner receives the Deming Medal with an accompanying certificate of merit.

A representative of the winner is required to give a briefing and lecture in relation to the prize-winning in a report meeting of awarded companies.

2.2 Examination and Judgement of the Prize

2.2.1 Examination items

The manner in which such activities as investigation, research, development, design, purchase, production, inspection, sales, etc. which are essential for the proper control of product and service quality are conducted by each and every segment of the company is examined and judged. For example, each of the items listed below will be evaluated in regard to the method used to maintain the effective control over costs, profits, appointed dates of deliveries, safety, inventories, manufacturing processes, equipment maintenance, instrumentation, personnel and labor relations, education and training, new product development, research, the relationship with sub-contractors, associates, material suppliers and sales companies, the handling of complaints, the utilization of customers' opinions, the quality assurance and after-sale services to customers, and the relationship with companies to which products are delivered. The term "quality control" as used in this guide denotes companywide quality control (CWQC) based on statistical quality control techniques.

(1)   Company policy and planning
How the policy for management, quality and quality control is determined and transmitted throughout all sectors of the company will be examined together with the results being achieved. Whether the contents of the policy are appropriate and clearly presented will also be examined.

(2)   Organization and its management
Whether the scope of responsibility and authority is clearly defined, how cooperation is promoted among all departments, and how the organization is managed to carry out quality control will be examined.

(3)   QC education and dissemination
How quality control is taught and how employees are trained through training courses and routine work in the company concerned and the related companies will be examined. To what extent the concept of quality control and statistical techniques are understood and utilized, and the activeness of QC circle will be examined.

(4)   Collection, transmission and utilization of information on quality
How the collection and dissemination of information on quality from within and outside the company are conducted by and among the head office, factories, branches, sales offices, and the organizational units will be examined, together with the evaluation of the organization and the systems used, and how fast information is transmitted, sorted, analyzed and utilized.

(5)   Analysis
Whether or not critical problems regarding quality are properly grasped and analyzed with respect to overall quality and the existing production process, and whether the results are being interpreted in the frame of available technology will be subject to scrutiny, while a check will be made on whether proper statistical methods are being used.

(6)   Standardization
The establishment, revision, and abolishment of standards and the manner of

their control and systematization will be examined, together with the use of standards for the enhancement of company technology.

(7)   Control ("Kanri")

How the procedures used for the maintenance and improvement of quality are reviewed from time to time when necessary will be examined. Also scrutinized will be how the responsibility for and the authority over these matters are defined, while a check will be made on the use of control charts and other related statistical techniques.

(8)   Quality Assurance

New product development, quality analysis, design, production, inspection, equipment maintenance, purchasing, sales, services and other activities at each stage of the operation, which are essential for quality assurance, including reliability, will be closely examined, together with the overall quality assurance management system.

(9)   Effects

What effects were produced or are being produced on the quality of products and services through the implementation of quality control will be examined. Whether products of sufficiently good quality are being manufactured and sold will be examined. Whether products have been improved from the viewpoint of quality, quantity and cost, and whether the whole company has been improved not only in the quantitative effect of quality and profit, but also in the scientific way of thinking of the employers and employees and their heightened will to work will be examined.

(10)   Future plans

Whether the strong and weak points in the present situation are properly recognized and whether the promotion of quality control is planned and likely to continue in the future will be examined.

2.2.2 Description of QC Practices

It is suggested that the description as a rule is subdivided into the following divisions. The company as a whole; head office; divisions; branches; factories; research facilities; sales offices.

No description is needed to be submitted for divisions employing less than 10 workers. On-site examination does not necessarily follow the above dividing of the Description of QC Practices.

The actual conditions under which quality control is being implemented should be concisely described in line with the items to be examined in accordance with the instructions below. Particularly, the relationship between cross-functions and their respective departments should be clarified with an explanation as to how responsibilities are organizationally allocated and collaborative coordination is maintained for such activities as new product development, quality assurance, production planning & product delivery control, and cost control.

In the case of entries for the Deming Prize for Corporate QC Implementation for Corporate Divisions, the relationship between the division concerned and the head office in regard to such functions as quality planning and quality assurance should be clearly explained. In this case the description of the division concerned should be submitted instead of that of the company as a whole and its head office.

The Description of QC Practices should not be too formal when describing about the examination items, but should give a concise explanation of the company's priorities, features, weak points, and future plans with regard to quality control so that it may be useful for the on-site examination.

2.2.3 Examination Objectives and Procedure
Examination Objectives

The main objective of the examination is to ascertain that good results are being comprehensively achieved through the implementation of companywide quality control (CWQC), particularly in regard to the potential for the future advancement of the company's CWQC. Especially, emphasis will be laid on whether the quality control being practiced is of the type most suitable for the business, its size, and other conditions of the company.

The practice of companywide quality control in this case is defined as the designing, production and supply of products or services of a quality level demanded by the customer at an economically acceptable cost, the basic approach being that of obtaining customer satisfaction together with a wide attention to public welfare. Also implied is better understanding and application of statistical concepts and methods by all members of the company in the train of activities involving studies, research, development, designing, purchasing, manufacture, inspection, and sales as well as other related activities inside and outside the company, together with a rational reiteration of planning, implementation, evaluation and improvement, all for the attainment of beneficial business goals.

New product development, administration of research and development, control of materials and supplies, management of physical facilities, instrumentation control, management of subcontracted work, personnel education and training, and various other activities will also be subject to examination from the viewpoint of quality assurance. See the attached check list regarding the foregoing.

Examination Procedure

The investigation work relating to the examination will be undertaken by the Deming Prize for Corporate QC Implementation Subcommittee and the results will be reported to the chairperson of the Deming Prize Committee.

The investigation work consists of examining of documents and on-site examination.

Pre-examination by Documents

The Description of QC Practices submitted by the applicant will be examined and judged to ascertain whether quality control is being practiced systematically and effectively throughout the company. Upon passing this test, the applicant is duly notified, and on-site examination will be performed in the manner set forth below, on the basis of the information contained in the Description of QC Practices.

If the applicant is disqualified after the examination of documents, a written opinion giving the reasons for non-acceptance will be provided.

On-site Examination

(1)   Examination Units

Examination units are the chief executive officers (CEO), the head and regional offices, corporate divisions, branches, works and factories, laboratories, and sales and local offices. (Work places with less than 10 employees are not counted as units.)

Not all the units cited by the applicant will be inspected. Only the units selected by the committee will be visited, in some cases only a single location being designated depending on the actual conditions. The above matters will be subject to consultations between the applicant and the Committee.

(2)   On-site Examination

a)   On-site examination will be performed at the units selected by the Committee. However, as mentioned above, examination by sampling may be conducted if deemed necessary.

Also, the examination units need not necessarily be the same as the division set forth in the Description of QC Practices.

b)   The examiners will, as a rule, consist of more than two persons per examination unit (normally, two to six persons), one of whom is designated as the team leader, in charge of liaison and consultation with the applicant.

[sic]   e)   The days to be spent at the examination units are generally as listed below.

Examination unit	Days required
Head Office, regional offices	2 to 3 days
Factories	2 to 3 days
Branches, sales offices	1 to 2 days
Laboratories	1 to 2 days

f) On-site examination consists of three parts:
Schedule A, Schedule B, and interviews with the CEO.

f-1) Schedule A is to be prepared by the applicant and decided after consultations with the examination team leader concerned. Schedule A is made up of two parts: the presentation of important points and the presentation of operation sites.

In case of business locations, the time allocation to these presentations should be roughly 2:1.

Presentation of important points:

i) Explanation of the points considered to be particularly important in the Description of QC Practices.

ii) Explanation of the situation after submission of the Description of QC Practices.

iii) Discussion of the contents of the above reports.

Materials in support of the presentation of the important points may be submitted at the time of presentation or distributed to the Examination and Appraisal Committee members, who will not be under the obligation to read through all such materials.

Presentation of Operations Sites:

In the case of a production factory, a general explanation of the processes and the methods of management of manufacturing, inspection, testing, packaging, storage, etc. should be given. The presentation for other sites should be structured generally in the same way.

f-2) Schedule B consists of on-site investigation and general interrogation. After the examination by the Examination Committee under Schedule A, the Committee with the due respect for the applicant's opinions prepares draft for the implementation of Schedule B, which becomes final upon approval by the applicant.

The on-site investigation as prescribed by Schedule B is performed as directed by the Examination Committee, the methods and procedures all being as determined by the committee. For instance, it may be that on-site examination will entail only simple questioning.

If, at the time of on-site examination, confusion or embarrassment is caused on the part of the applicant, the examination team leader should be promptly informed and consulted.

f-3) For the interview with the CEO, it may be that the examination team leader concerned will consult with the applicant beforehand as to who will participate on the applicant's side.

2.2.4 Evaluation of Examination Results
Scoring Method

The Examination Committee evaluates the results reported by the on-site examination teams comprehensively. Each team member's score is treated equally, on the basis of one hundred points. The passing points are:

1) the CEO	70 points or more
2) whole company average, excluding the CEO	70 points or more
3) minimum for any inspected unit	50 points or more

Totalization:
1) The score for each inspected unit is the median value of the points awarded by each of the members of the Examination Committee.
2) For the head office as an examination unit, the scoring for the CEO and other organizational departments are done separately.
3) The score for the whole company is in terms of the weighted average of the scores won by each inspected unit, apart from the CEO.
4) There will be no disclosure of the above-mentioned scores.

Judgement:

The judgement of the Deming Prize Committee is based on the report to it from the Deming Prize for Corporate QC Implementation Subcommittee.
1) The Deming Prize for Corporate QC Implementation is awarded by the Deming Prize Committee to the applicant considered to have qualified on the basis of the above-mentioned report.
2) Judgement is reserved in the event that the passing point score has not been attained by the applicant, and the examination process is not terminated unless withdrawal is expressed by the applicant. Extension is limited to two times and to a period of three years. In the case of extended examination, emphasis is laid on the controversial points raised at the time of the preceding examination. The applicant is selected as an awardee when it is considered to attain the passing standard after the points of issue are improved.

2.2.5 Notification and Publication of the Result
Notification

A successful applicant is informed of the examination result as promptly as possible, followed by a formal written notice. In the case of extension of the examination process, a formal written notice only is provided.

Written opinions

A written opinion on the examination of the applicant's company and its respective work sites will be delivered to the successful applicant on the day of the Deming

Prize Awards ceremony. A similar document will be furnished at a later date to unsuccessful applicants on extended examination.

Reports by the Prize Winner

The prize winner will be asked to make a report at a Reporting and Lecture Meeting on the actions and events leading to the receiving of the award, and may be requested to make further reports on subsequent developments in the following years.

2.2.6 Schedule of Examination

Preceding year

November 20:	closing date for the filing of applications for the Deming Prize for Corporate QC Implementation or Deming Prize for Divisional QC Implementation.
December 20:	final date for the decision of acceptance

Examination and Awarding Year

January 20:	closing date for the submission of the Description of QC Practices
January 21~30:	decision of the examination schedule; appointment of examiner; notification to the applicant of the examination schedule
February 18~28:	decision on results of documentary examination
March 20~September 30:	on-site examinations
October 10~20:	selection of prize awardees; notifications, public announcement
November:	Deming Prize awarding ceremony and reporting sessions

2.2.7 Other Matters

Comments on the Examination

Any comments on the announced results of the examination and appraisal should be submitted in writing to the Deming Prize Committee not later than September 30.

The Deming Prize Consultation Meeting

1) For companies which intend to apply to the examination of the Deming Prize for Corporate QC Implementation, the Deming Prize Committee provides a consulting meeting to give advice and/or answer inquires concerning the examination procedures.

2) Members of the Deming Prize for Corporate QC Implementation Subcommittee will be ready for consultation at a meeting which takes place in the Union of Japanese Scientists and Engineers.

3) The cost for consultation will be charged to the company.

4) Consultation will be conducted in Japanese. Arrangements for an interpreter should be made if necessary.

5) Application for this consulting meeting should be sent to the Secretariat of the Deming Prize Committee in the form that is defined by the Committee.

The Deming Prize for Divisional QC Implementation to a Division

1) The divisional headquarters or a division of a company will be considered eligible for entry provided that the conditions given below are fulfilled.

   i) The applicant must possess enough authority to administer personnel, funds, equipment, and material with the freedom necessary for autonomous operation.

   ii) The applicant must have the authority and responsibility to undertake quality assurance with consistency and integrity.

   iii) The applicant must have proper responsibility as well as accountability for future betterment of performance and advancement of management.

2) The details listed below must accompany the application as evidence of being an independent division because only duly qualified corporate divisions will be subjected to examination upon acceptance of application for entry:

   size of the division; organization; relationship to the company as a whole; authority to exercise independent management and such other functional matters as funding, costing, personnel affairs, purchasing, production, sales, etc.

3) Examination procedures are the same as for the Deming Prize for Divisional QC Implementation contestants, the top management group in this case being the management team at the divisional headquarters.

   Examination will be conducted also of the company top management group and the head office departments considered necessary to be checked. As in the case of the Deming Prize for Corporate QC Implementation, supplementary examinations will be conducted on related companies (affiliated companies, subcontractors, consignees, distributors, etc.)

Quality Control Diagnosis

When implementing companywide quality control, objective analysis and advice by a third party is meaningful for ascertaining how matters stand and for aiming at the effective progress in quality control.

From this standpoint, the Deming Prize Committee will undertake on request the diagnoses of quality control programs instituted by companies for the purpose of assisting their advancement. This practice began in 1971, and the diagnoses have been carried out by the members of the Deming Prize for Corporate QC Implementation Subcommittee. A detailed written report on the findings is delivered upon completion of the examination.

Request for quality diagnosis may be made at any time. But such examination is in no way a preliminary investigation for Deming Prize eligibility. It is furthermore stipulated that no company undergoing diagnosis by members of the Deming Prize for Corporate QC Implementation Subcommittee can apply for the Deming Prize for Corporate QC Implementation in the same year (January through December).

There is no relation between whether the diagnosis is done or not and the evaluation of the Deming Prize for Corporate QC Implementation examination.

CHECKLIST FOR THE DEMING PRIZE FOR CORPORATE QC IMPLEMENTATION

ITEM	PARTICULARS

1. Policy

(1) Policies pursued for management, quality, and quality control
(2) Method of establishing policies
(3) Justifibility and consistency of policies
(4) Utilization of statistical methods
(5) Transmission and diffusion of policies
(6) Review of policies and the results achieved
(7) Relationship between policies and long- and short-term planning

2. Organization and its Management

(1) Explicitness of the scopes of authority and responsibility
(2) Appropriateness of delegations of authority
(3) Interdivisional cooperation
(4) Committees and their activities
(5) Utilization of staff
(6) Utilization of QC Circle activities
(7) Quality control diagnosis

3. Education and Dissemination

(1) Education programs and results
(2) Quality- and control-consciousness, degree of understanding quality control
(3) Teaching statistical concepts and methods, and the extent of their dissemination
(4) Grasping the effectiveness of quality control
(5) Education of related companies (particularly those in the same group, subcontractors, consignees, and distributors)
(6) QC Circle activities
(7) System for suggesting ways of improvements and its actual conditions

4. Collection, Dissemination and Use of Information on Quality

(1) Collection of external information
(2) Transmission of information between divisions
(3) Speed of information transmission (use of computers)
(4) Data processing, statistical analysis of information, and utilization of the results

5. Analysis

(1) Selection of key problems and themes
(2) Propriety of the analytical approach
(3) Utilization of statistical methods
(4) Linkage with proper technology
(5) Quality analysis, process analysis
(6) Utilization of analytical results
(7) Assertiveness of improvement suggestions

CHECKLIST FOR THE DEMING PRIZE FOR CORPORATE QC IMPLEMENTATION

ITEM	PARTICULARS

6. Standardization

   (1) Systematization of standards
   (2) Method of establishing, revising, and abolishing standards
   (3) Outcome of the establishment, revision, or abolition of standards
   (4) Contents of the standards
   (5) Utilization of statistical methods
   (6) Accumulation of technology
   (7) Utilization of standards

7. Control

   (1) Systems for the control of quality and such related matters as cost and quantity
   (2) Control items and control points
   (3) Utilization of such statistical control methods as control charts and other statistical concepts
   (4) Contribution to performance of QC Circle activities
   (5) Actual conditions of control activities
   (6) State of matters under control

8. Quality Assurance

   (1) Procedure for the development of new products and services (analysis and upgrading of quality, checking of design, reliability, and other properties)
   (2) Safety and immunity from product liability
   (3) Process design, process analysis, and process control and improvement
   (4) Process capability
   (5) Instrumentation, gauging, testing, and inspecting
   (6) Equipment maintenance, and control of subcontracting, purchasing, and services
   (7) Quality assurance system and its audit
   (8) Utilization of statistical methods
   (9) Evaluation and audit of quality
  (10) Actual state of quality assurance

9. Results

   (1) Measurement of results
   (2) Substantive results in quality, services, delivery time, cost, profits, safety, environment, etc.
   (3) Intangible results
   (4) Measures for overcoming defects

10. Planning for the Future

   (1) Grasping the present state of affairs and the concreteness of the plan
   (2) Measures for overcoming defects
   (3) Plans for further advances
   (4) Linkage with long-term plans

Index of Photographs and Illustrations

Index of Figures

Index